Garfield chickens out

BY JIM DAVIS

Ballantine Books • New York

A Ballantine Books Trade Paperback Original

Published in the United States by Ballantine Books, an imprint of Random House,
a division of Penguin Random House LLC, New York.

BALLANTINE and the HOUSE colophon are registered trademarks of Penguin Random House LLC.

ISBN 978-0-425-28515-2
ebook ISBN 978-0-425-28550-3

Printed in the United States of America on acid-free paper

randomhousebooks.com

9 8 7 6 5 4 3 2

The TRUTH about cats

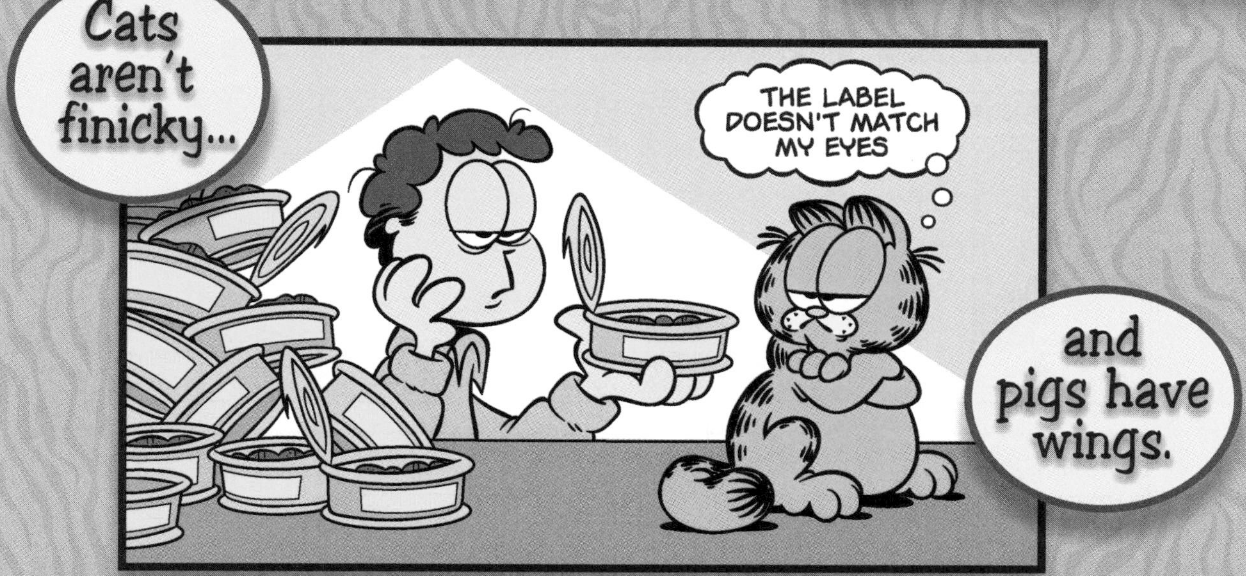
Cats aren't finicky...
THE LABEL DOESN'T MATCH MY EYES
and pigs have wings.

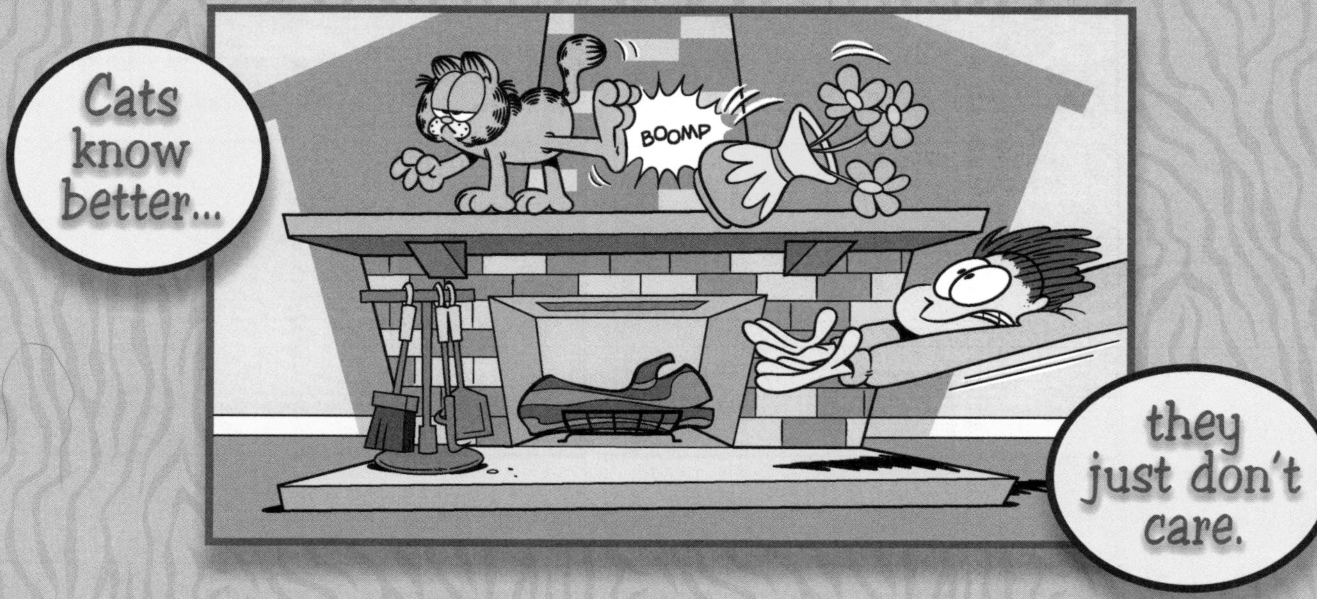
Cats know better...
BOOMP
they just don't care.

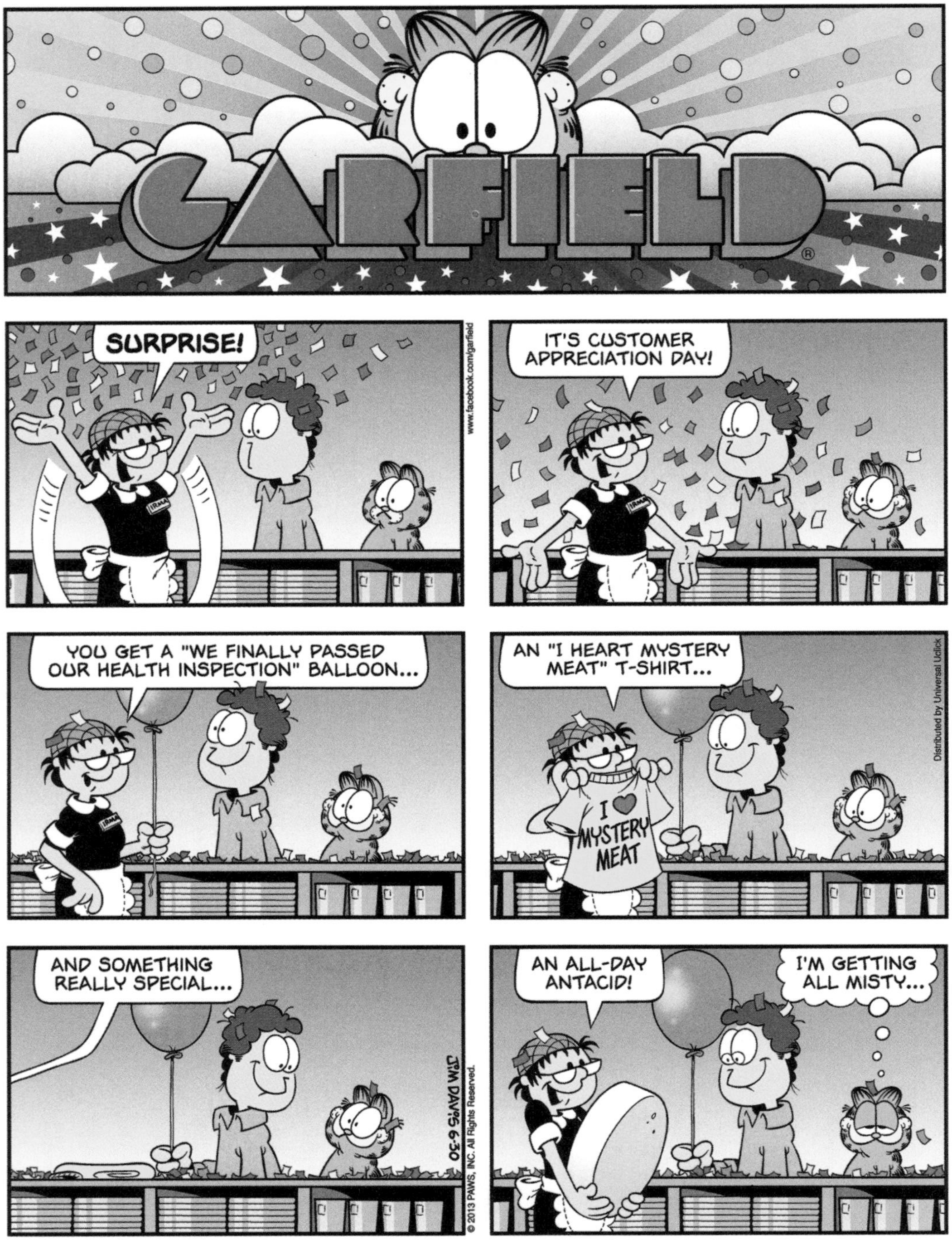
GARFIELD®
SURPRISE!
www.facebook.com/garfield
IT'S CUSTOMER APPRECIATION DAY!
YOU GET A "WE FINALLY PASSED OUR HEALTH INSPECTION" BALLOON...
AN "I HEART MYSTERY MEAT" T-SHIRT...
I ♥ MYSTERY MEAT
Distributed by Universal Uclick
AND SOMETHING REALLY SPECIAL...
JIM DAVIS 6-30
© 2013 PAWS, INC. All Rights Reserved.
AN ALL-DAY ANTACID!
I'M GETTING ALL MISTY...

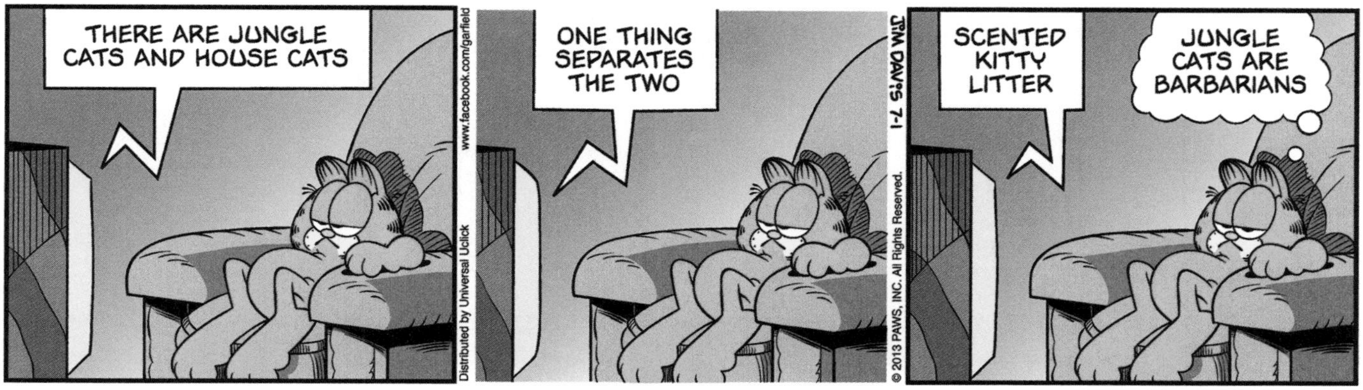
THERE ARE JUNGLE CATS AND HOUSE CATS
www.facebook.com/garfield
Distributed by Universal Uclick
ONE THING SEPARATES THE TWO
JIM DAVIS 7-1
© 2013 PAWS, INC. All Rights Reserved.
SCENTED KITTY LITTER
JUNGLE CATS ARE BARBARIANS

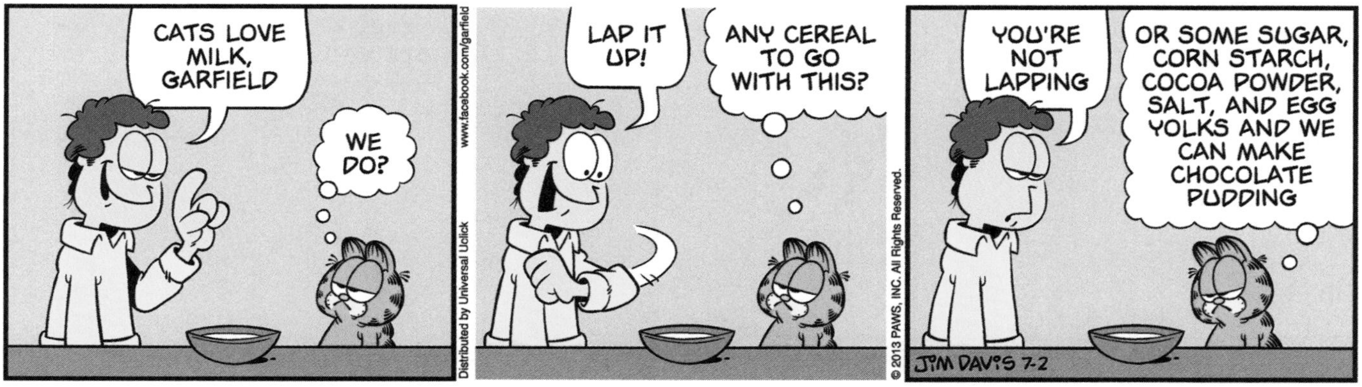
CATS LOVE MILK, GARFIELD
WE DO?
www.facebook.com/garfield
Distributed by Universal Uclick
LAP IT UP!
ANY CEREAL TO GO WITH THIS?
© 2013 PAWS, INC. All Rights Reserved.
YOU'RE NOT LAPPING
OR SOME SUGAR, CORN STARCH, COCOA POWDER, SALT, AND EGG YOLKS AND WE CAN MAKE CHOCOLATE PUDDING
JIM DAVIS 7-2

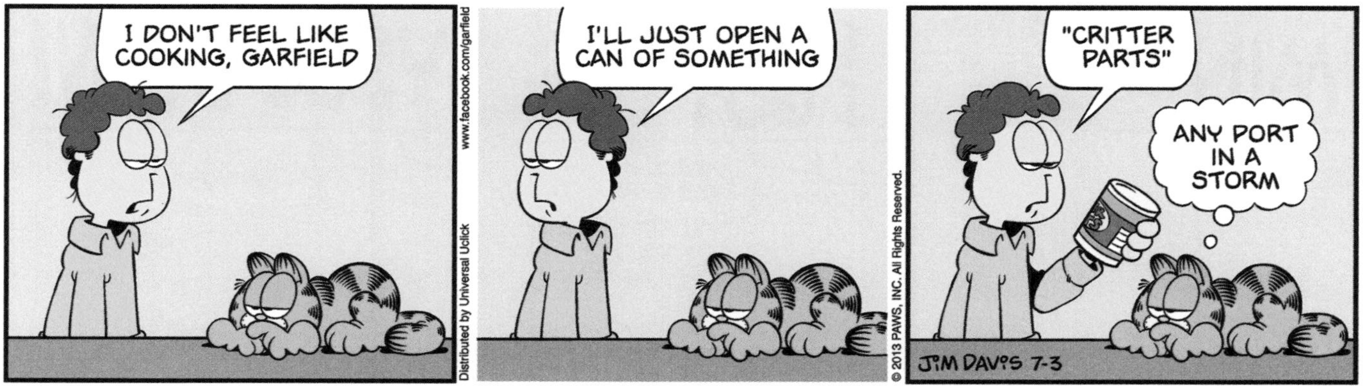
I DON'T FEEL LIKE COOKING, GARFIELD
www.facebook.com/garfield
Distributed by Universal Uclick
I'LL JUST OPEN A CAN OF SOMETHING
© 2013 PAWS, INC. All Rights Reserved.
"CRITTER PARTS"
ANY PORT IN A STORM
JIM DAVIS 7-3

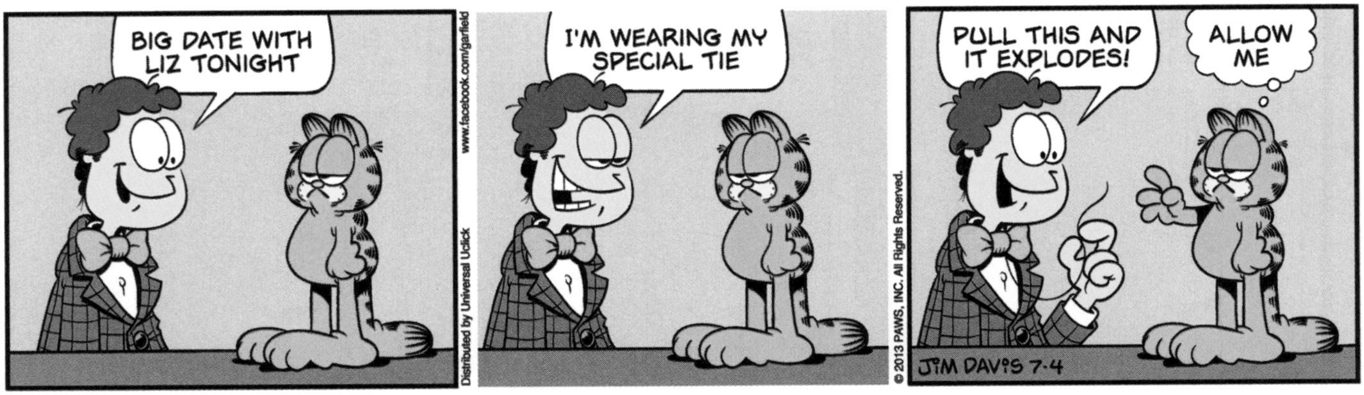
BIG DATE WITH LIZ TONIGHT
I'M WEARING MY SPECIAL TIE
PULL THIS AND IT EXPLODES!
ALLOW ME
JIM DAVIS 7-4
Distributed by Universal Uclick
www.facebook.com/garfield
© 2013 PAWS, INC. All Rights Reserved.

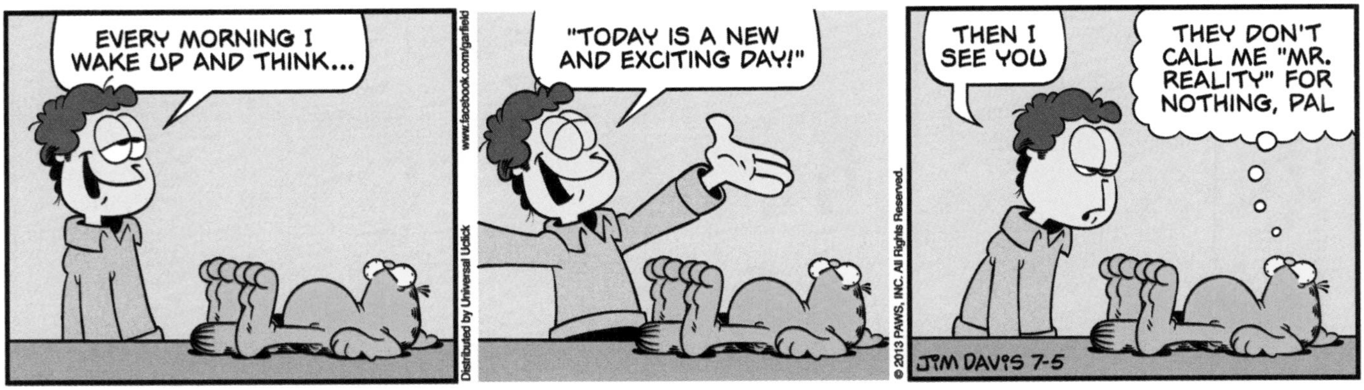
EVERY MORNING I WAKE UP AND THINK...
"TODAY IS A NEW AND EXCITING DAY!"
THEN I SEE YOU
THEY DON'T CALL ME "MR. REALITY" FOR NOTHING, PAL
JIM DAVIS 7-5
Distributed by Universal Uclick
www.facebook.com/garfield
© 2013 PAWS, INC. All Rights Reserved.

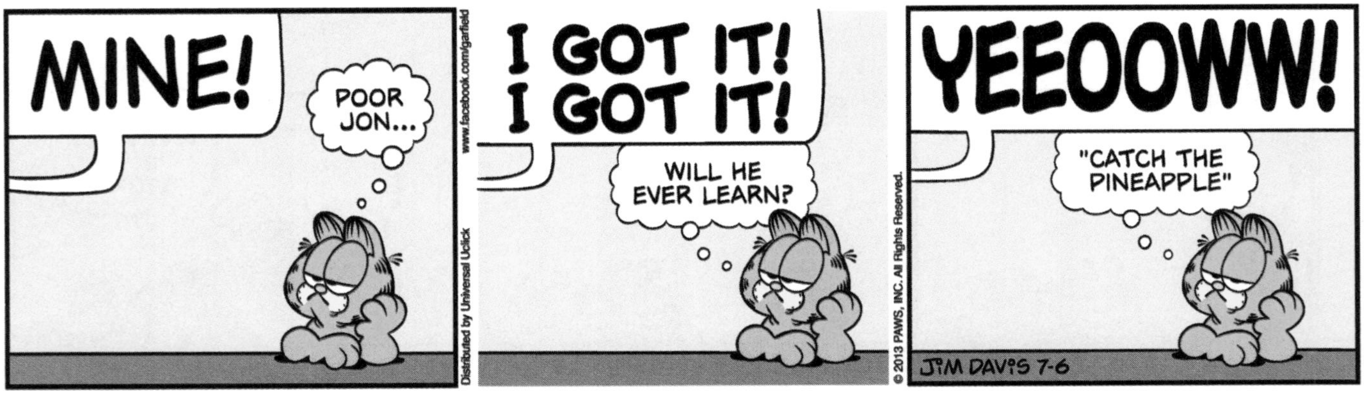
MINE!
POOR JON...
I GOT IT! I GOT IT!
WILL HE EVER LEARN?
YEEOOWW!
"CATCH THE PINEAPPLE"
JIM DAVIS 7-6
Distributed by Universal Uclick
www.facebook.com/garfield
© 2013 PAWS, INC. All Rights Reserved.

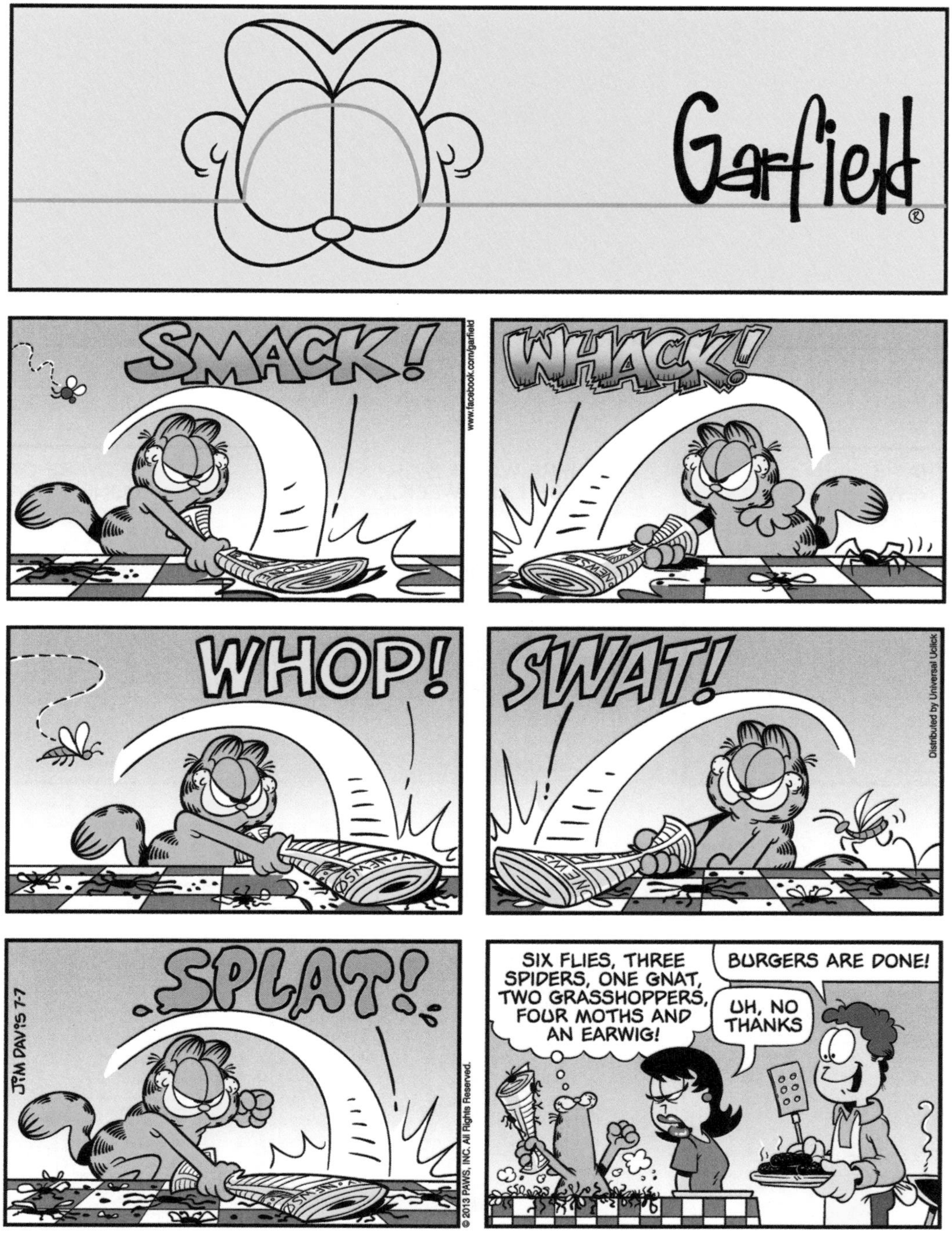
Garfield®
SMACK!
www.facebook.com/garfield
WHACK!
WHOP!
SWAT!
Distributed by Universal Uclick
SPLAT!
JIM DAVIS 7-7
© 2013 PAWS, INC. All Rights Reserved.
SIX FLIES, THREE SPIDERS, ONE GNAT, TWO GRASSHOPPERS, FOUR MOTHS AND AN EARWIG!
BURGERS ARE DONE!
UH, NO THANKS

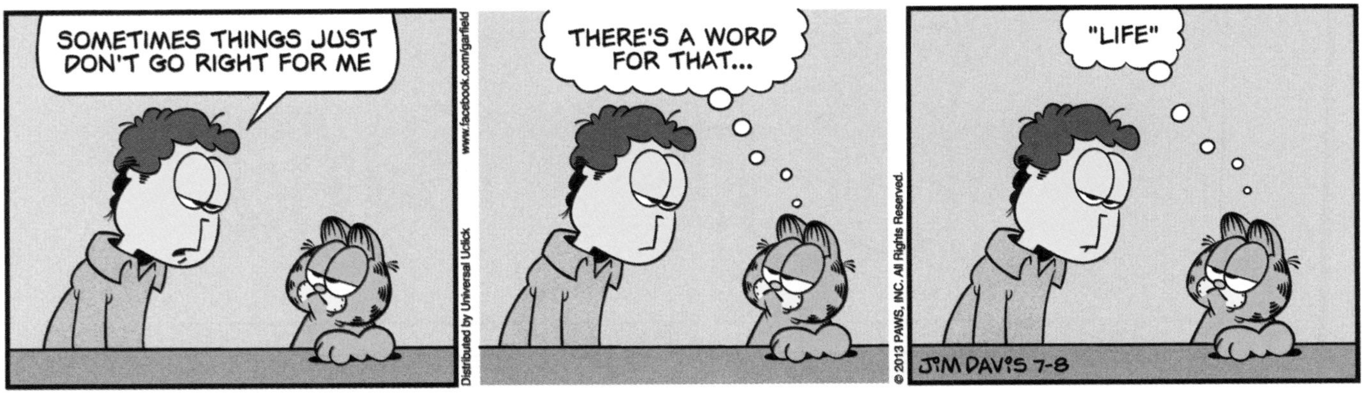
SOMETIMES THINGS JUST DON'T GO RIGHT FOR ME
THERE'S A WORD FOR THAT...
"LIFE"
Distributed by Universal Uclick www.facebook.com/garfield
© 2013 PAWS, INC. All Rights Reserved.
JIM DAVIS 7-8

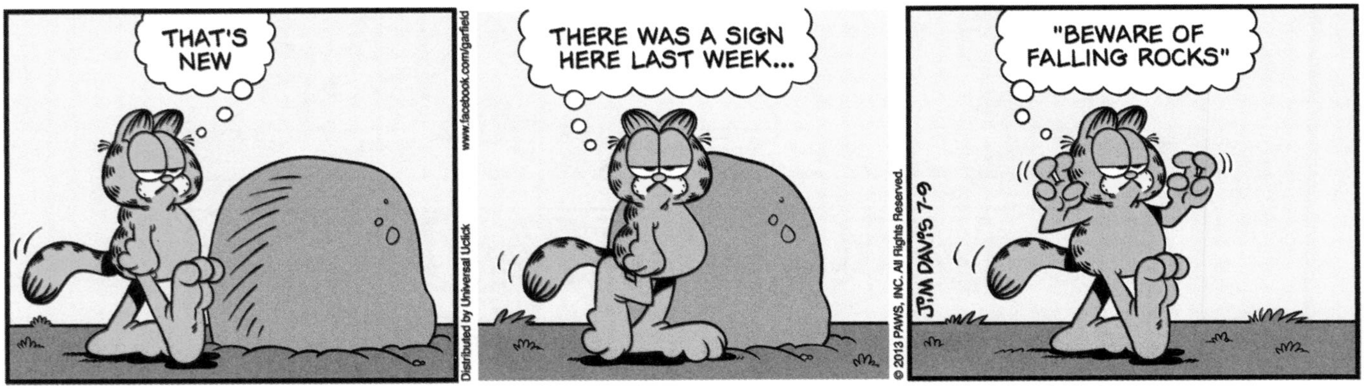
THAT'S NEW
THERE WAS A SIGN HERE LAST WEEK...
"BEWARE OF FALLING ROCKS"
Distributed by Universal Uclick www.facebook.com/garfield
© 2013 PAWS, INC. All Rights Reserved.
JIM DAVIS 7-9

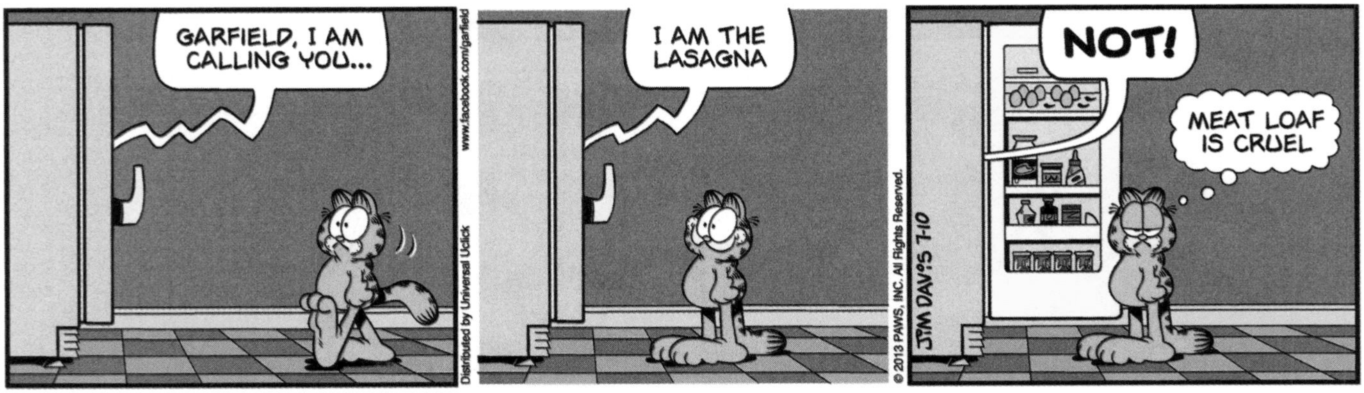
GARFIELD, I AM CALLING YOU...
I AM THE LASAGNA
NOT!
MEAT LOAF IS CRUEL
Distributed by Universal Uclick www.facebook.com/garfield
© 2013 PAWS, INC. All Rights Reserved.
JIM DAVIS 7-10

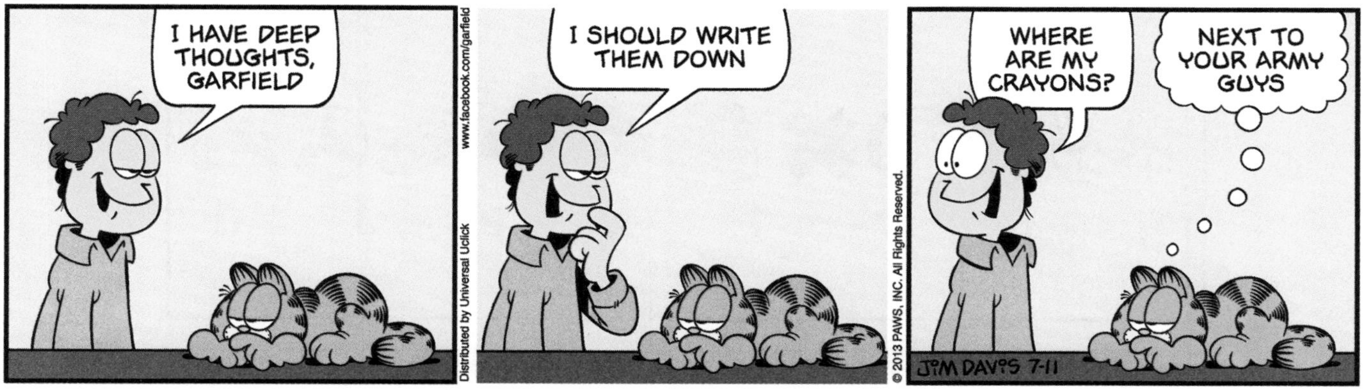
I HAVE DEEP THOUGHTS, GARFIELD
I SHOULD WRITE THEM DOWN
WHERE ARE MY CRAYONS?
NEXT TO YOUR ARMY GUYS
JIM DAVIS 7-11
Distributed by Universal Uclick www.facebook.com/garfield
© 2013 PAWS, INC. All Rights Reserved.

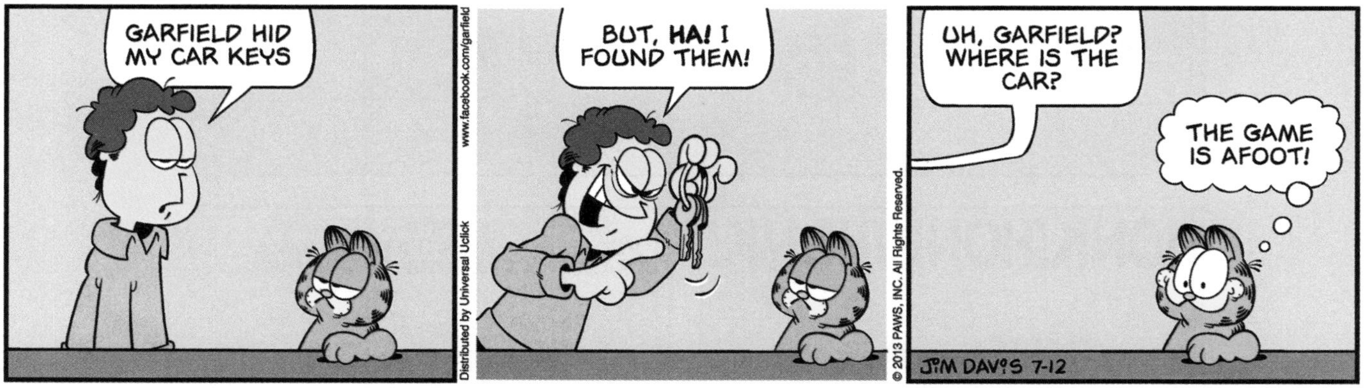
GARFIELD HID MY CAR KEYS
BUT, HA! I FOUND THEM!
UH, GARFIELD? WHERE IS THE CAR?
THE GAME IS AFOOT!
JIM DAVIS 7-12
Distributed by Universal Uclick www.facebook.com/garfield
© 2013 PAWS, INC. All Rights Reserved.

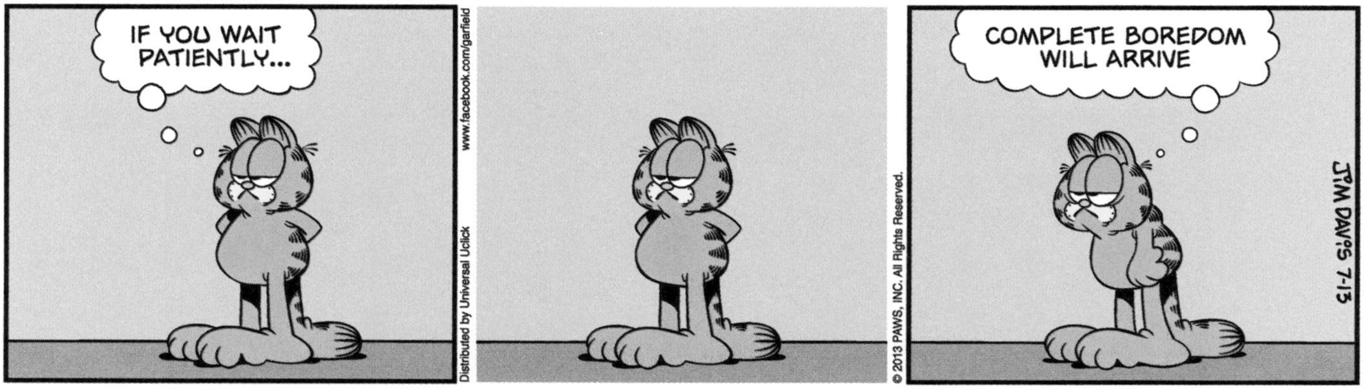
IF YOU WAIT PATIENTLY...
COMPLETE BOREDOM WILL ARRIVE
JIM DAVIS 7-13
Distributed by Universal Uclick www.facebook.com/garfield
© 2013 PAWS, INC. All Rights Reserved.

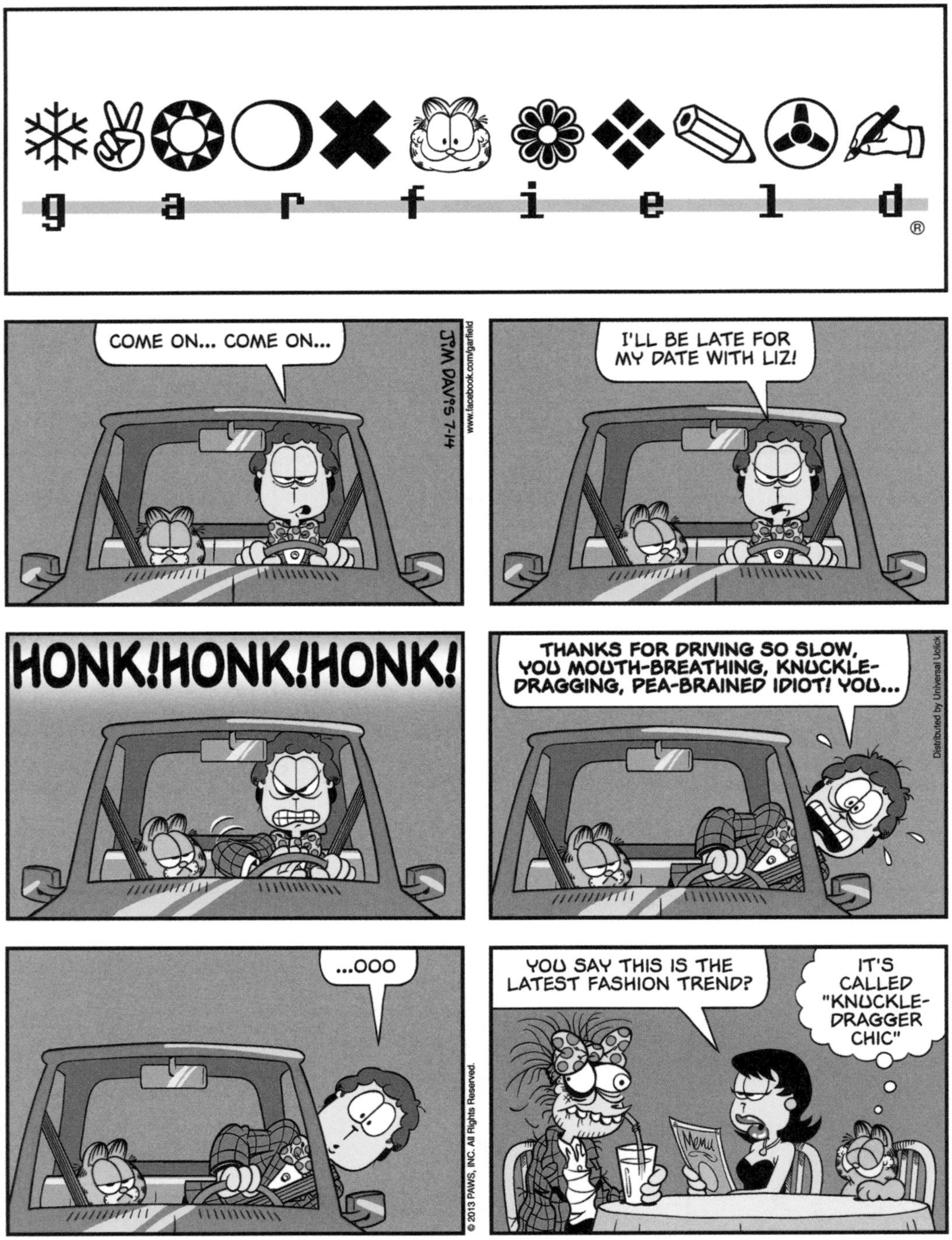
garfield®
JIM DAVIS 7-14
www.facebook.com/garfield
COME ON... COME ON...
I'LL BE LATE FOR MY DATE WITH LIZ!
HONK!HONK!HONK!
THANKS FOR DRIVING SO SLOW, YOU MOUTH-BREATHING, KNUCKLE-DRAGGING, PEA-BRAINED IDIOT! YOU...
Distributed by Universal Uclick
...OOO
© 2013 PAWS, INC. All Rights Reserved.
YOU SAY THIS IS THE LATEST FASHION TREND?
IT'S CALLED "KNUCKLE-DRAGGER CHIC"
Menu

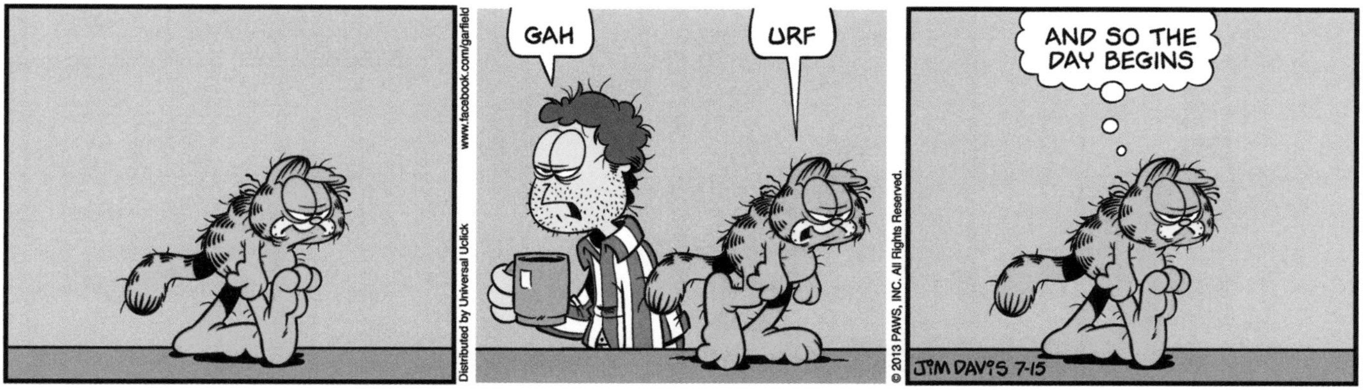
GAH
URF
AND SO THE DAY BEGINS
JIM DAVIS 7-15
Distributed by Universal Uclick www.facebook.com/garfield
© 2013 PAWS, INC. All Rights Reserved.

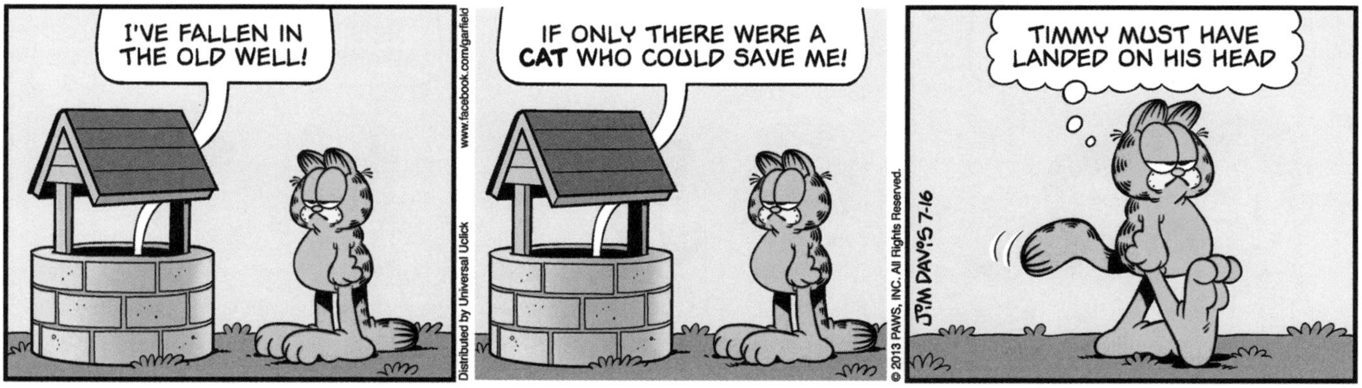
I'VE FALLEN IN THE OLD WELL!
IF ONLY THERE WERE A **CAT** WHO COULD SAVE ME!
TIMMY MUST HAVE LANDED ON HIS HEAD
JIM DAVIS 7-16
Distributed by Universal Uclick www.facebook.com/garfield
© 2013 PAWS, INC. All Rights Reserved.

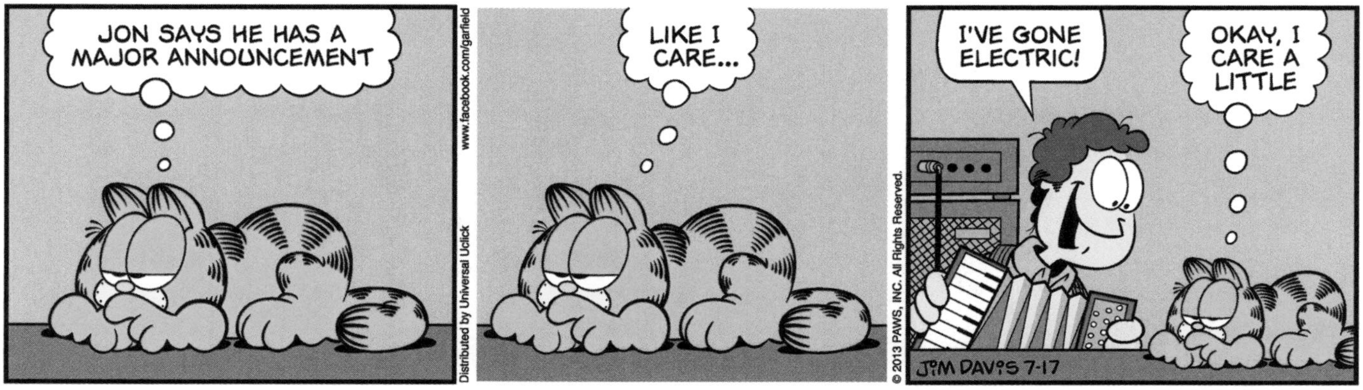
JON SAYS HE HAS A MAJOR ANNOUNCEMENT
LIKE I CARE...
I'VE GONE ELECTRIC!
OKAY, I CARE A LITTLE
JIM DAVIS 7-17
Distributed by Universal Uclick www.facebook.com/garfield
© 2013 PAWS, INC. All Rights Reserved.

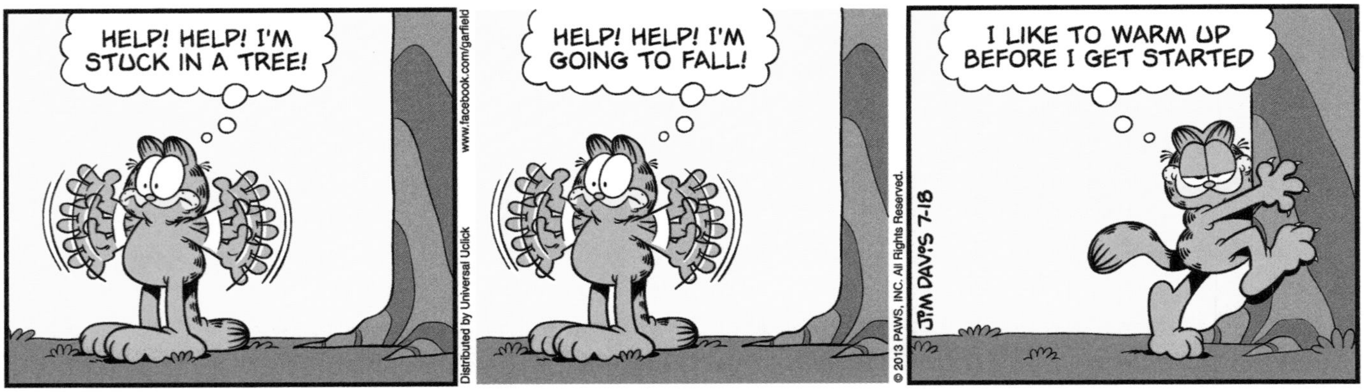
HELP! HELP! I'M STUCK IN A TREE!
HELP! HELP! I'M GOING TO FALL!
I LIKE TO WARM UP BEFORE I GET STARTED
JIM DAVIS 7-18
Distributed by Universal Uclick
www.facebook.com/garfield
© 2013 PAWS, INC. All Rights Reserved.

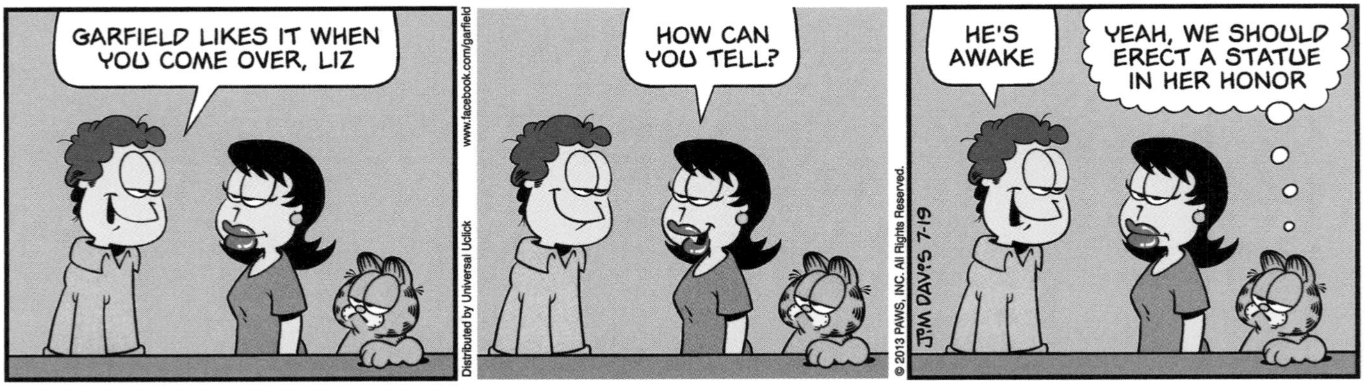
GARFIELD LIKES IT WHEN YOU COME OVER, LIZ
HOW CAN YOU TELL?
HE'S AWAKE
YEAH, WE SHOULD ERECT A STATUE IN HER HONOR
JIM DAVIS 7-19
Distributed by Universal Uclick
www.facebook.com/garfield
© 2013 PAWS, INC. All Rights Reserved.

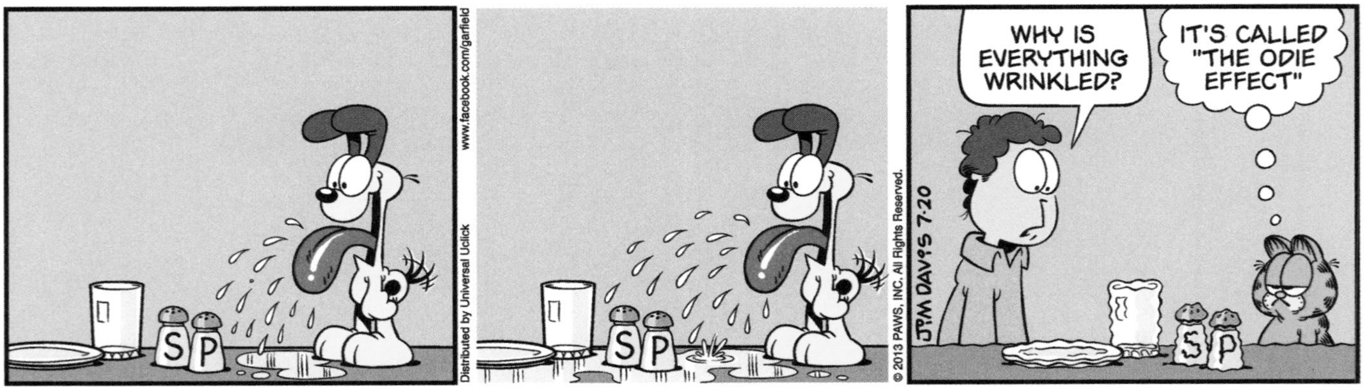
S
P
S
P
WHY IS EVERYTHING WRINKLED?
IT'S CALLED "THE ODIE EFFECT"
S
P
JIM DAVIS 7-20
Distributed by Universal Uclick
www.facebook.com/garfield
© 2013 PAWS, INC. All Rights Reserved.

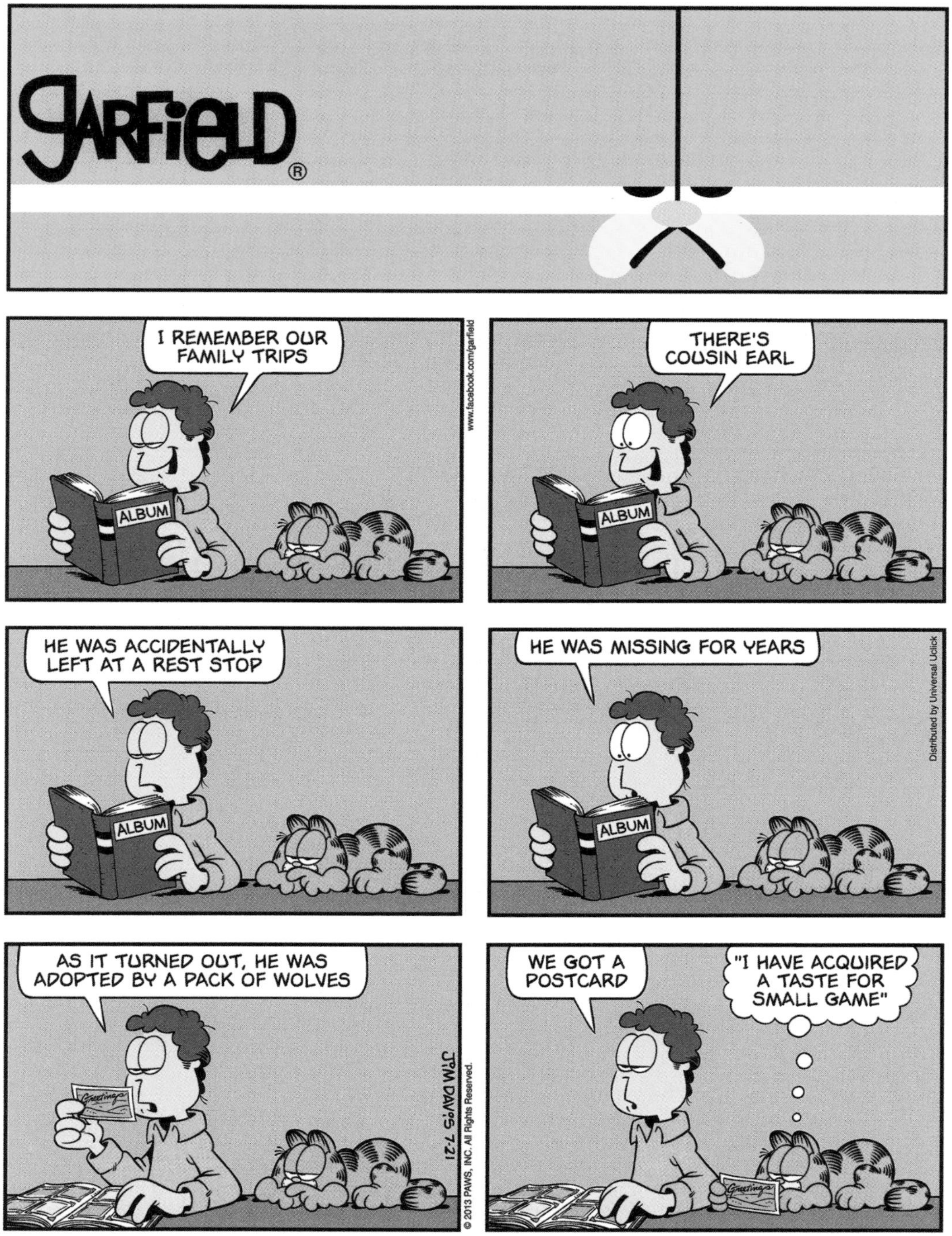
GARFIELD®
I REMEMBER OUR FAMILY TRIPS
www.facebook.com/garfield
THERE'S COUSIN EARL
HE WAS ACCIDENTALLY LEFT AT A REST STOP
HE WAS MISSING FOR YEARS
Distributed by Universal Uclick
AS IT TURNED OUT, HE WAS ADOPTED BY A PACK OF WOLVES
JIM DAVIS 7-21
© 2013 PAWS, INC. All Rights Reserved.
WE GOT A POSTCARD
"I HAVE ACQUIRED A TASTE FOR SMALL GAME"

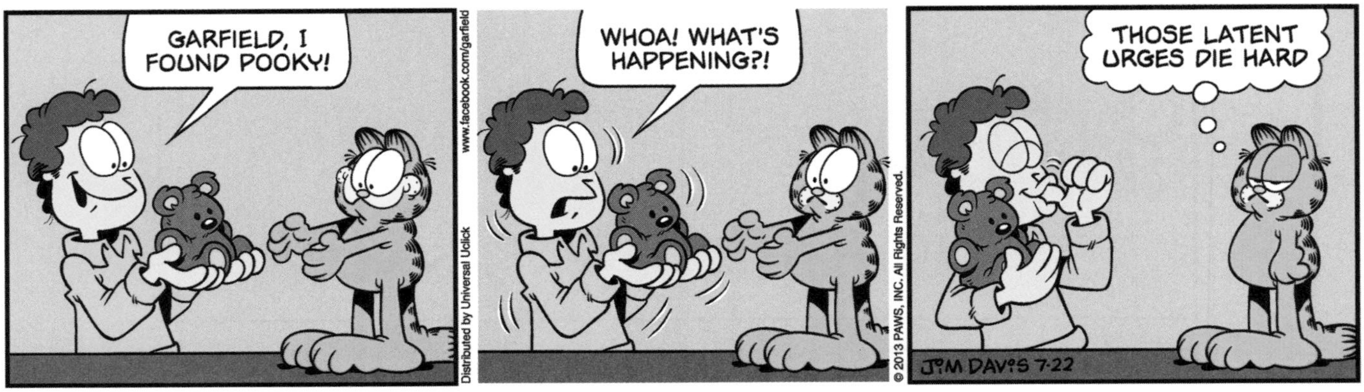
GARFIELD, I FOUND POOKY!
WHOA! WHAT'S HAPPENING?!
THOSE LATENT URGES DIE HARD
JIM DAVIS 7-22
Distributed by Universal Uclick www.facebook.com/garfield
© 2013 PAWS, INC. All Rights Reserved.

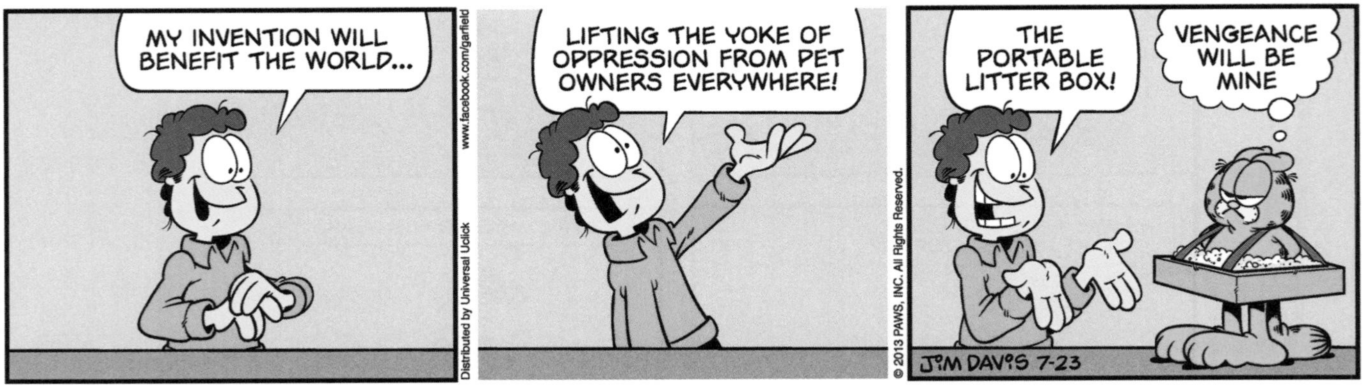
MY INVENTION WILL BENEFIT THE WORLD...
LIFTING THE YOKE OF OPPRESSION FROM PET OWNERS EVERYWHERE!
THE PORTABLE LITTER BOX!
VENGEANCE WILL BE MINE
JIM DAVIS 7-23
Distributed by Universal Uclick www.facebook.com/garfield
© 2013 PAWS, INC. All Rights Reserved.

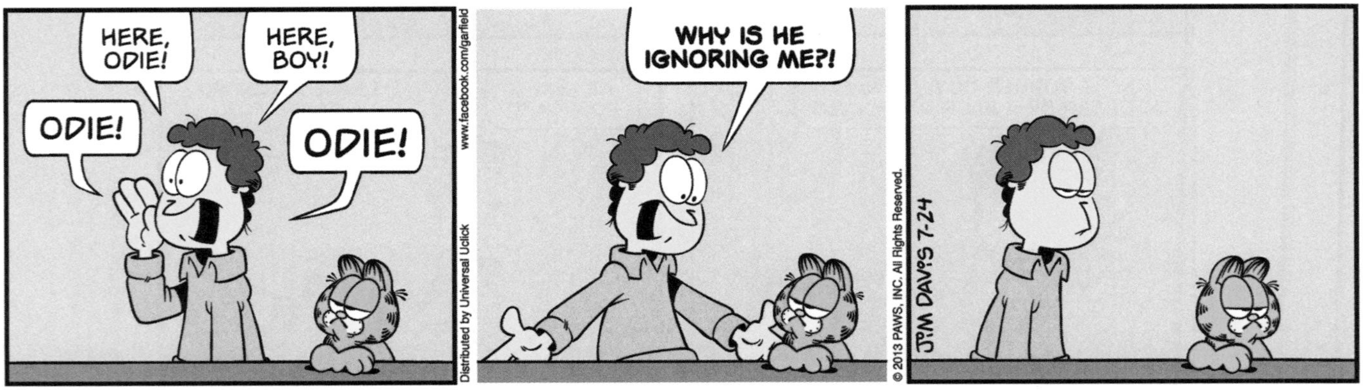
ODIE!
HERE, ODIE!
HERE, BOY!
ODIE!
WHY IS HE IGNORING ME?!
JIM DAVIS 7-24
Distributed by Universal Uclick www.facebook.com/garfield
© 2013 PAWS, INC. All Rights Reserved.

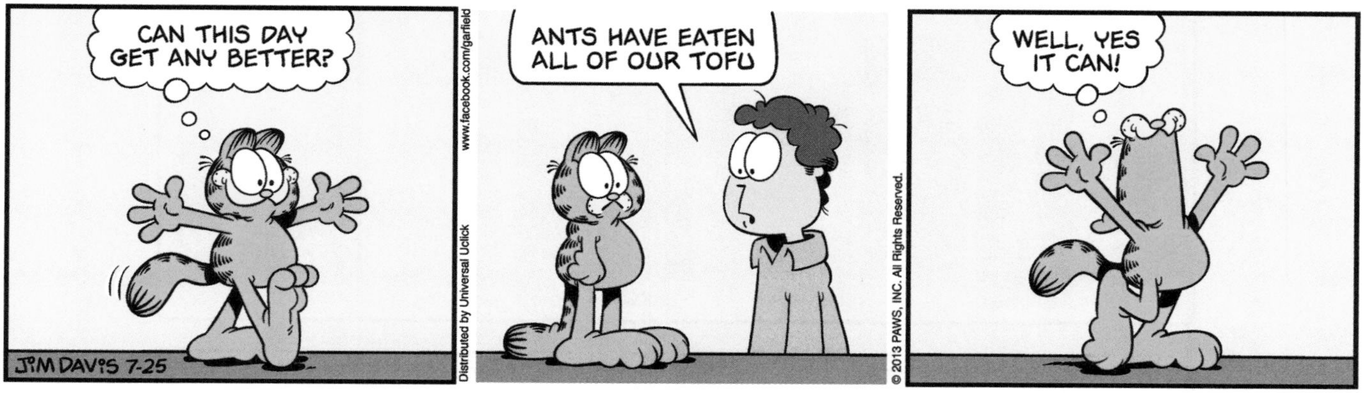
CAN THIS DAY GET ANY BETTER?
JIM DAVIS 7-25
Distributed by Universal Uclick
www.facebook.com/garfield
ANTS HAVE EATEN ALL OF OUR TOFU
© 2013 PAWS, INC. All Rights Reserved.
WELL, YES IT CAN!

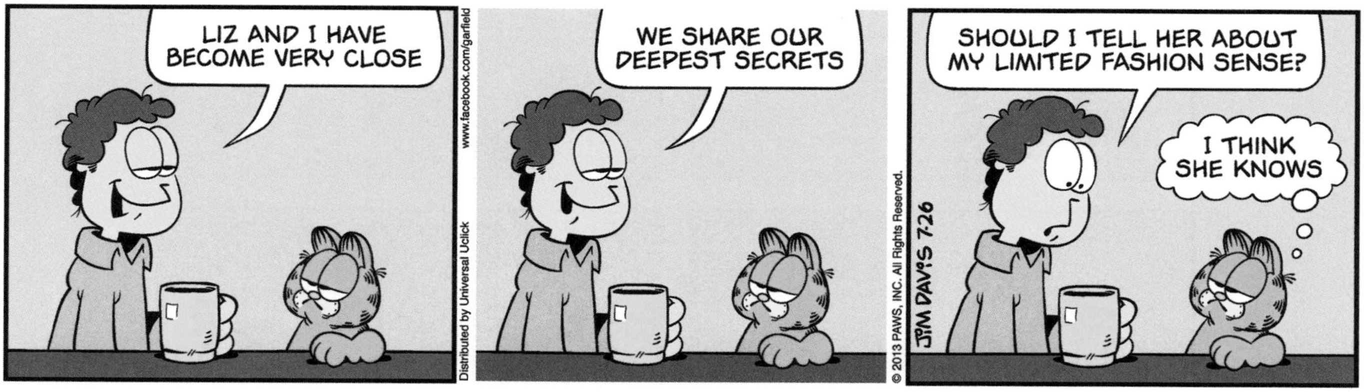
LIZ AND I HAVE BECOME VERY CLOSE
Distributed by Universal Uclick
www.facebook.com/garfield
WE SHARE OUR DEEPEST SECRETS
© 2013 PAWS, INC. All Rights Reserved.
JIM DAVIS 7-26
SHOULD I TELL HER ABOUT MY LIMITED FASHION SENSE?
I THINK SHE KNOWS

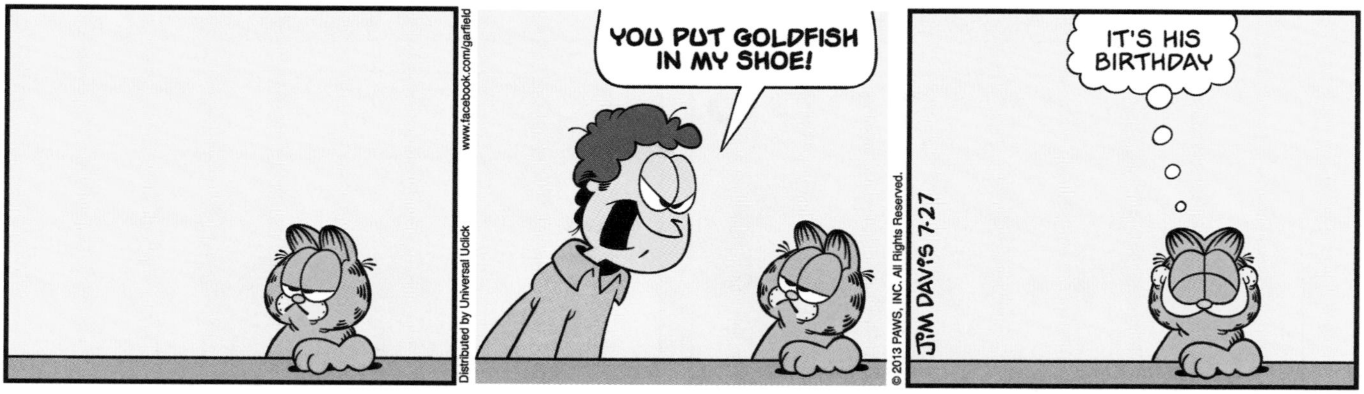
Distributed by Universal Uclick
www.facebook.com/garfield
YOU PUT GOLDFISH IN MY SHOE!
© 2013 PAWS, INC. All Rights Reserved.
JIM DAVIS 7-27
IT'S HIS BIRTHDAY

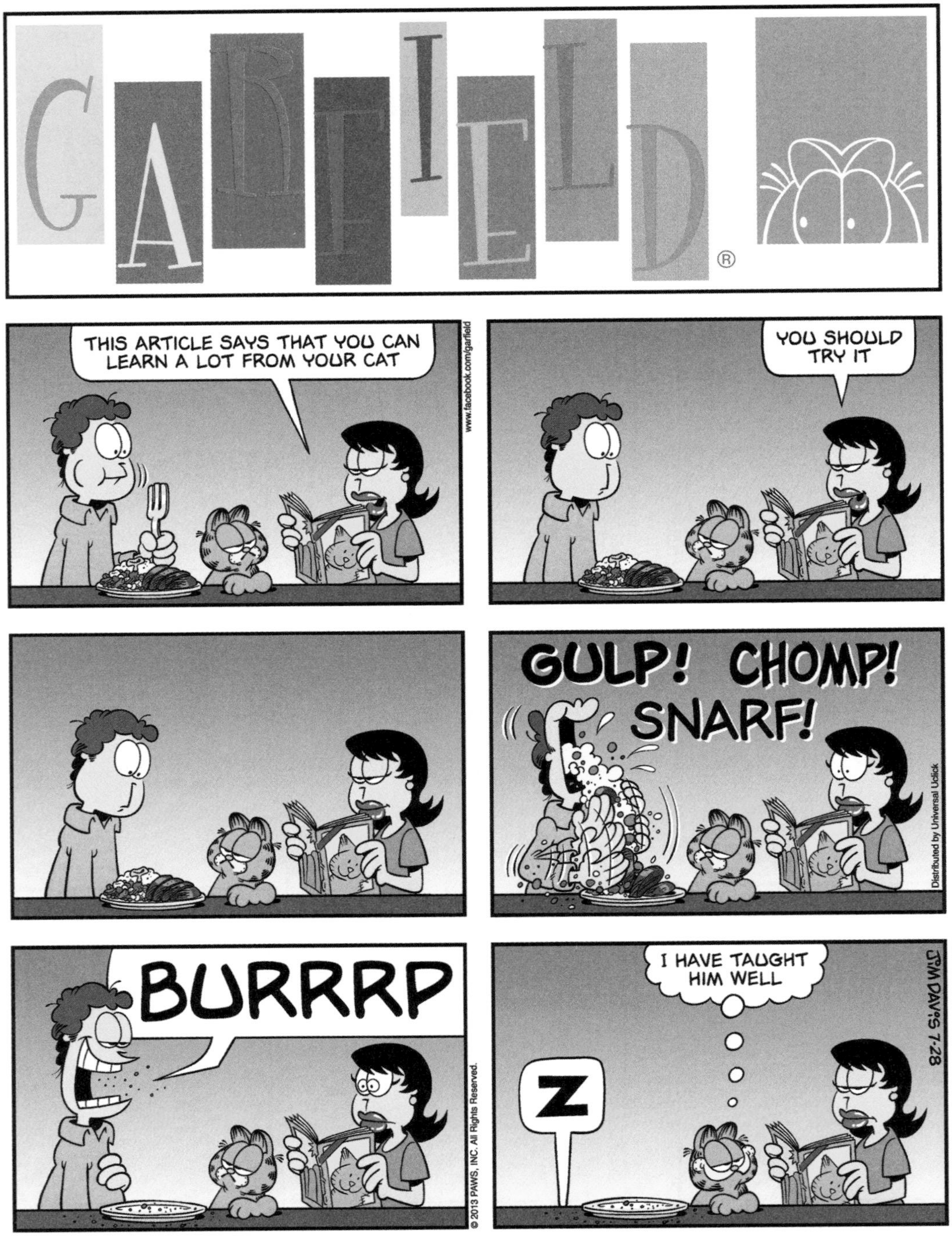
GARFIELD®
THIS ARTICLE SAYS THAT YOU CAN LEARN A LOT FROM YOUR CAT
www.facebook.com/garfield
YOU SHOULD TRY IT
GULP! CHOMP!
SNARF!
Distributed by Universal Uclick
BURRRP
© 2013 PAWS, INC. All Rights Reserved.
Z
I HAVE TAUGHT HIM WELL
JIM DAVIS 7-28

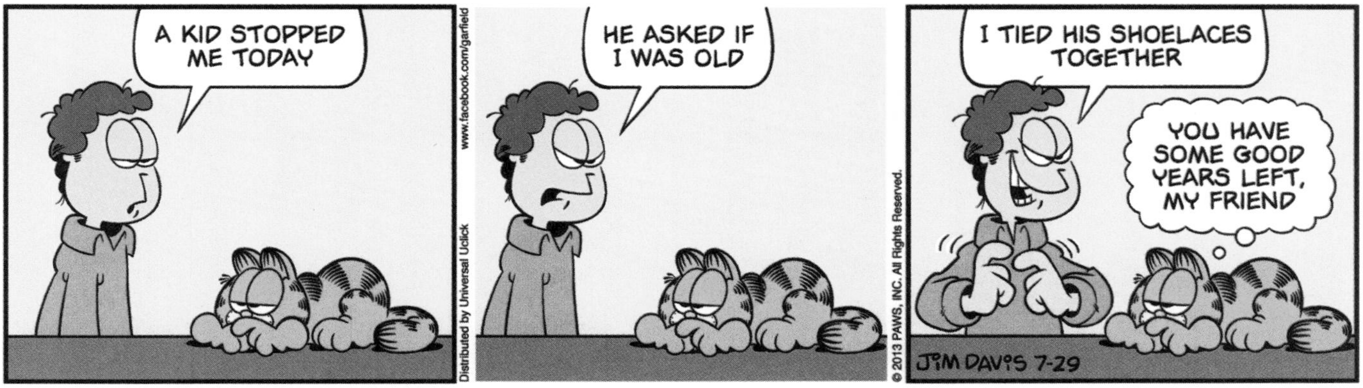
A KID STOPPED ME TODAY
HE ASKED IF I WAS OLD
I TIED HIS SHOELACES TOGETHER
YOU HAVE SOME GOOD YEARS LEFT, MY FRIEND
Distributed by Universal Uclick www.facebook.com/garfield
© 2013 PAWS, INC. All Rights Reserved.
JIM DAVIS 7-29

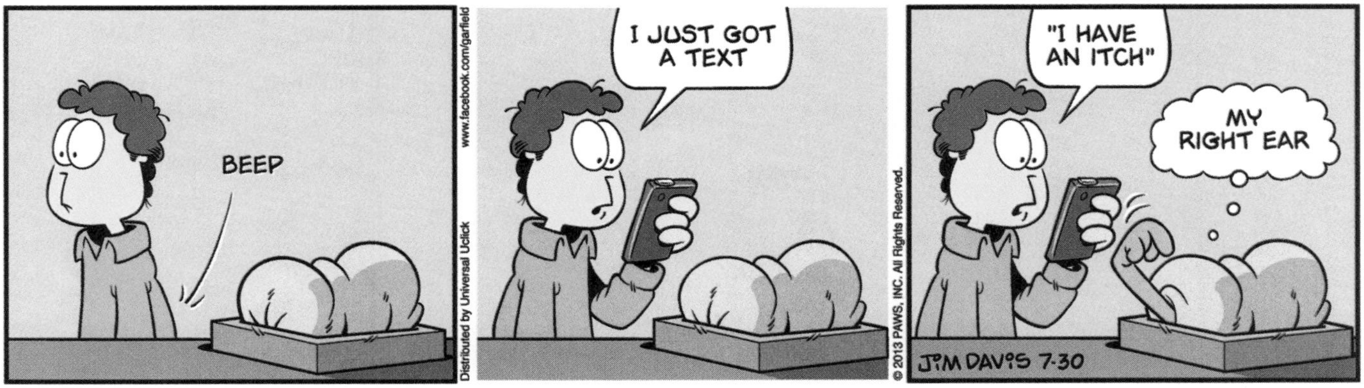
BEEP
I JUST GOT A TEXT
"I HAVE AN ITCH"
MY RIGHT EAR
Distributed by Universal Uclick www.facebook.com/garfield
© 2013 PAWS, INC. All Rights Reserved.
JIM DAVIS 7-30

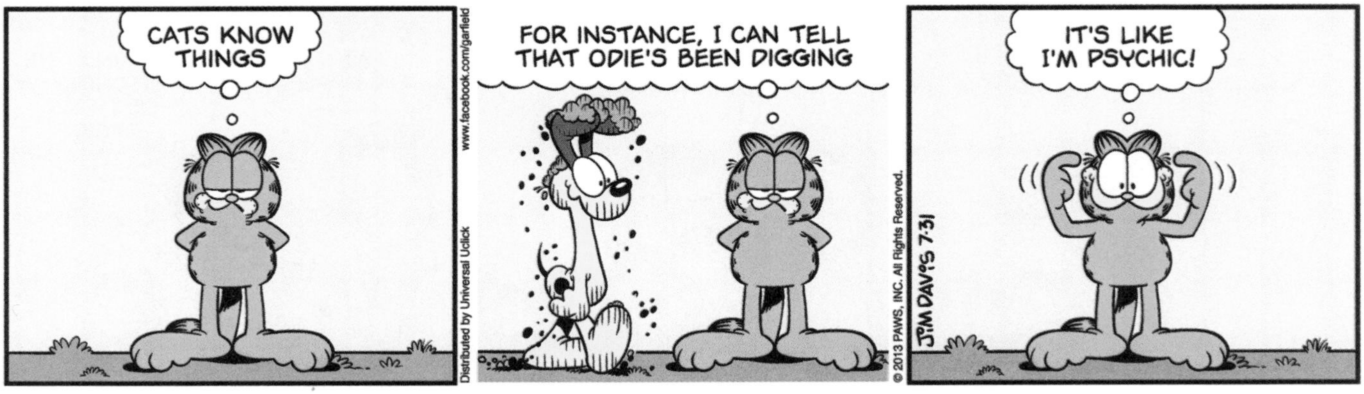
CATS KNOW THINGS
FOR INSTANCE, I CAN TELL THAT ODIE'S BEEN DIGGING
IT'S LIKE I'M PSYCHIC!
Distributed by Universal Uclick www.facebook.com/garfield
© 2013 PAWS, INC. All Rights Reserved.
JIM DAVIS 7-31

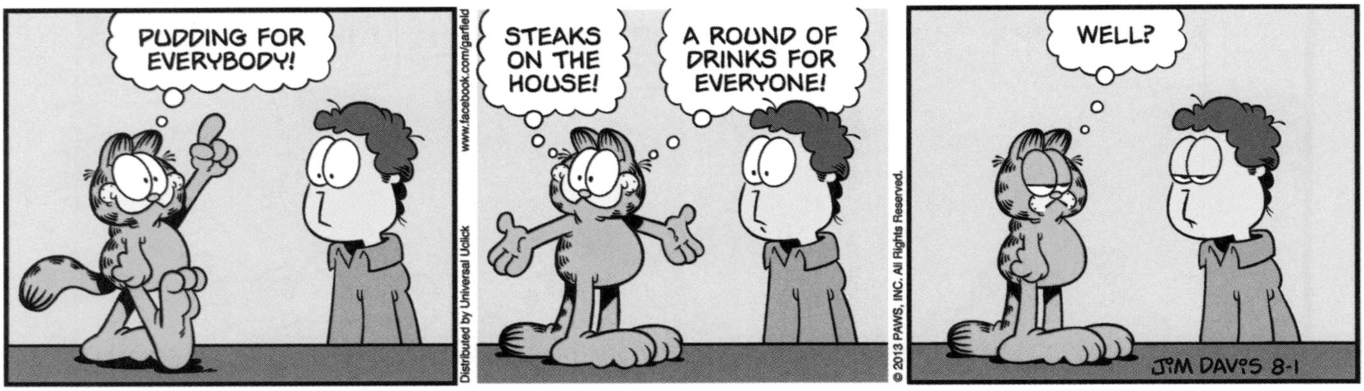
PUDDING FOR EVERYBODY!
Distributed by Universal Uclick www.facebook.com/garfield
STEAKS ON THE HOUSE!
A ROUND OF DRINKS FOR EVERYONE!
© 2013 PAWS, INC. All Rights Reserved.
WELL?
JIM DAVIS 8-1

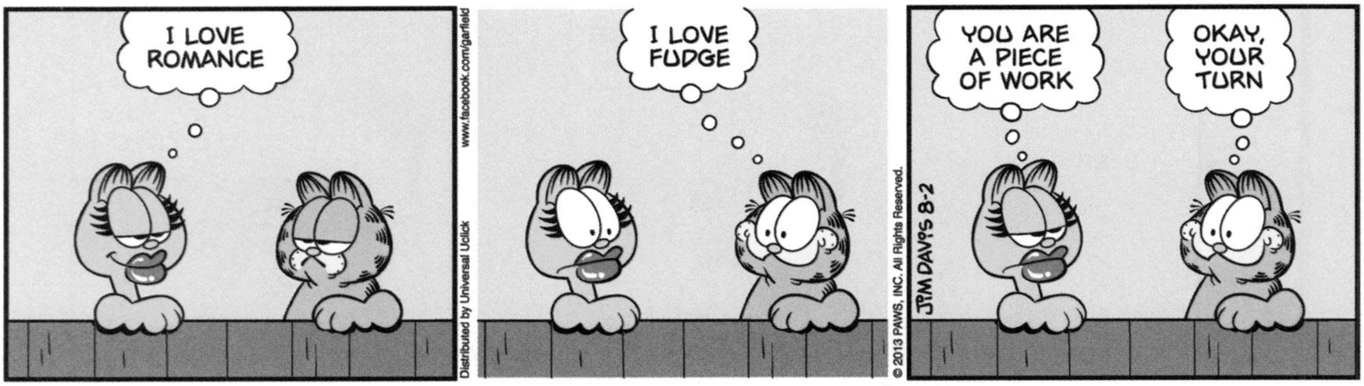
I LOVE ROMANCE
Distributed by Universal Uclick www.facebook.com/garfield
I LOVE FUDGE
© 2013 PAWS, INC. All Rights Reserved.
JIM DAVIS 8-2
YOU ARE A PIECE OF WORK
OKAY, YOUR TURN

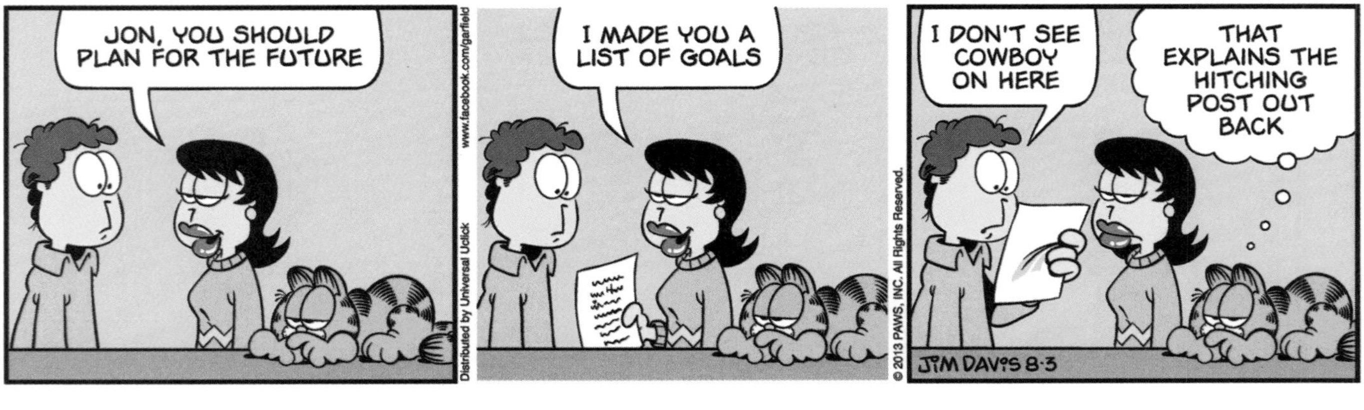
JON, YOU SHOULD PLAN FOR THE FUTURE
Distributed by Universal Uclick www.facebook.com/garfield
I MADE YOU A LIST OF GOALS
© 2013 PAWS, INC. All Rights Reserved.
I DON'T SEE COWBOY ON HERE
THAT EXPLAINS THE HITCHING POST OUT BACK
JIM DAVIS 8-3

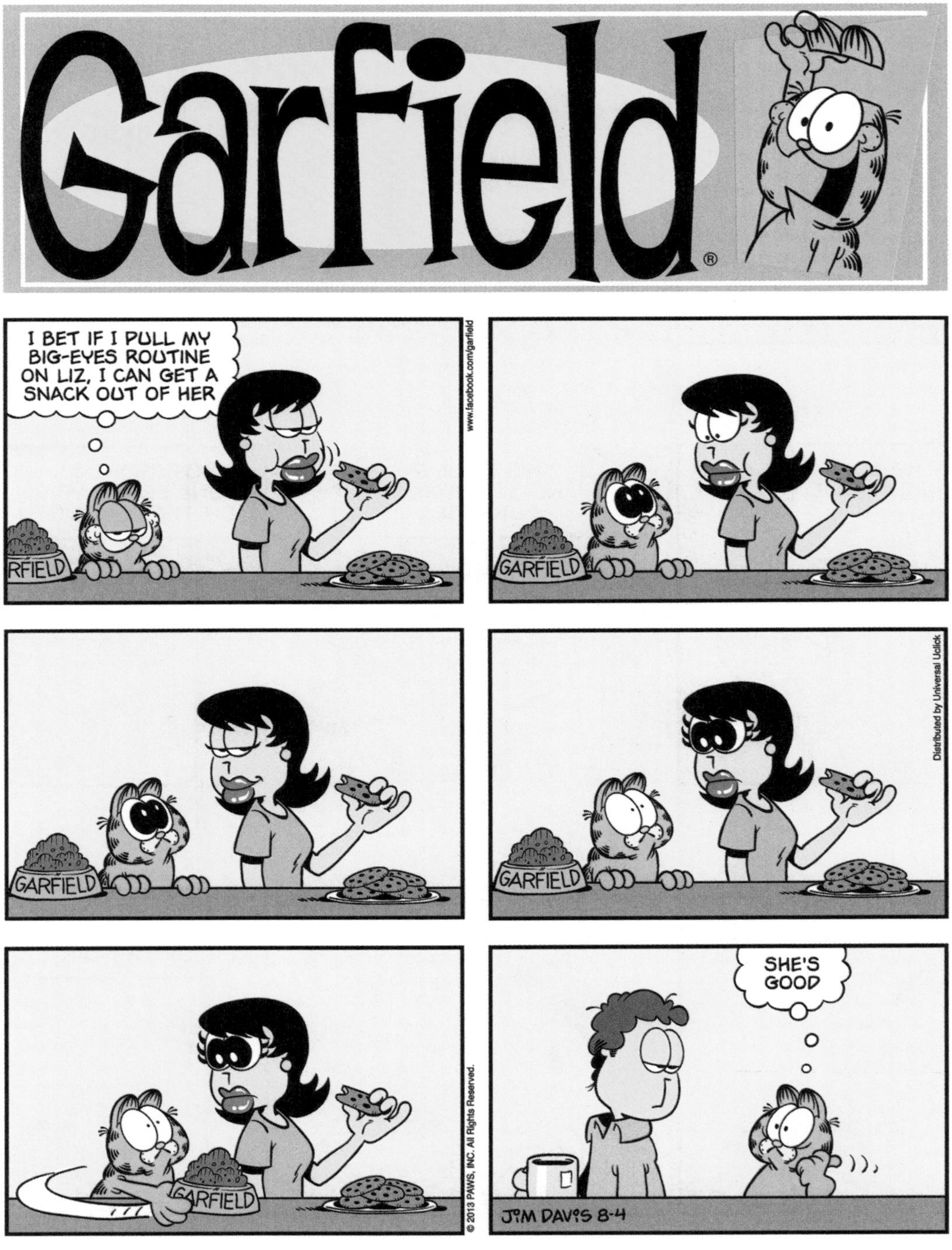
Garfield®
www.facebook.com/garfield
I BET IF I PULL MY BIG-EYES ROUTINE ON LIZ, I CAN GET A SNACK OUT OF HER
RFIELD
GARFIELD
GARFIELD
GARFIELD
Distributed by Universal Uclick
GARFIELD
© 2013 PAWS, INC. All Rights Reserved.
SHE'S GOOD
JIM DAVIS 8-4

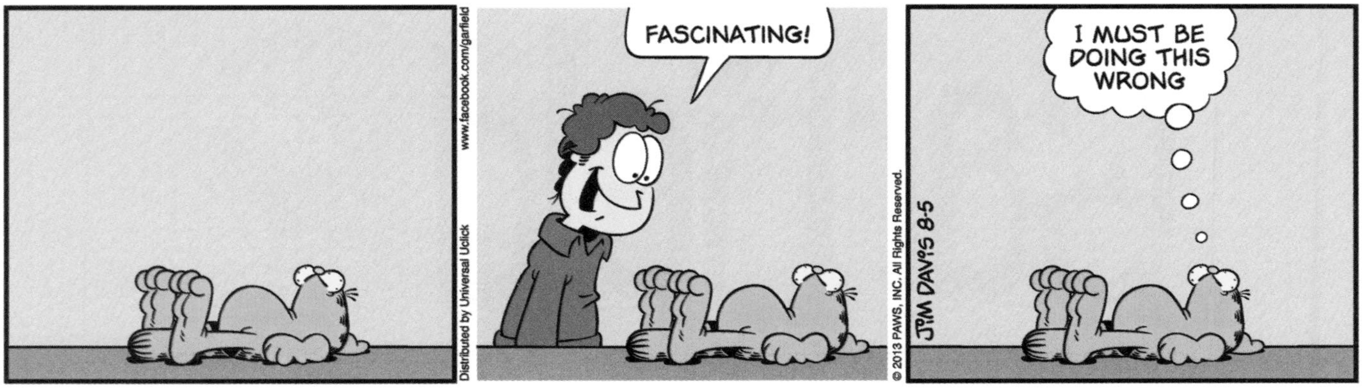
FASCINATING!
I MUST BE DOING THIS WRONG
JIM DAVIS 8-5
Distributed by Universal Uclick www.facebook.com/garfield
© 2013 PAWS, INC. All Rights Reserved.

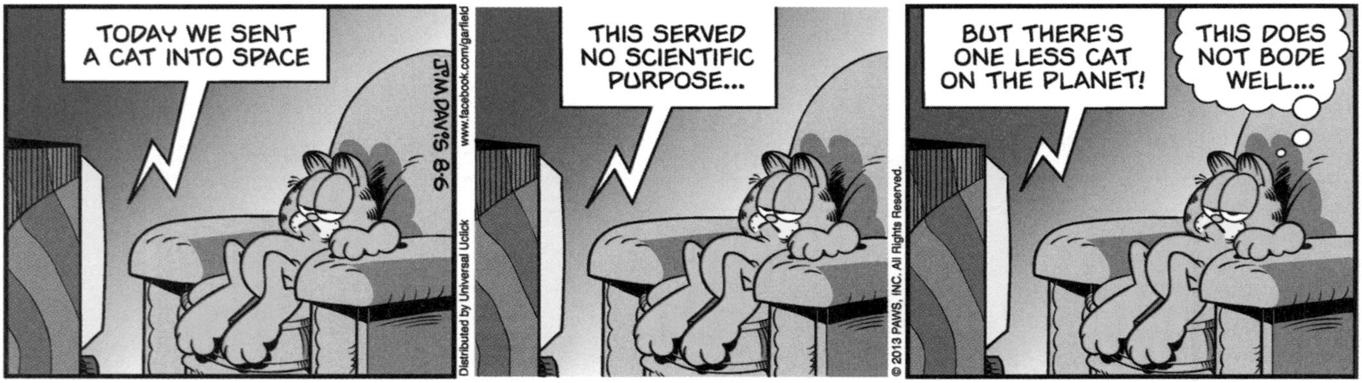
TODAY WE SENT A CAT INTO SPACE
JIM DAVIS 8-6
THIS SERVED NO SCIENTIFIC PURPOSE...
BUT THERE'S ONE LESS CAT ON THE PLANET!
THIS DOES NOT BODE WELL...
Distributed by Universal Uclick www.facebook.com/garfield
© 2013 PAWS, INC. All Rights Reserved.

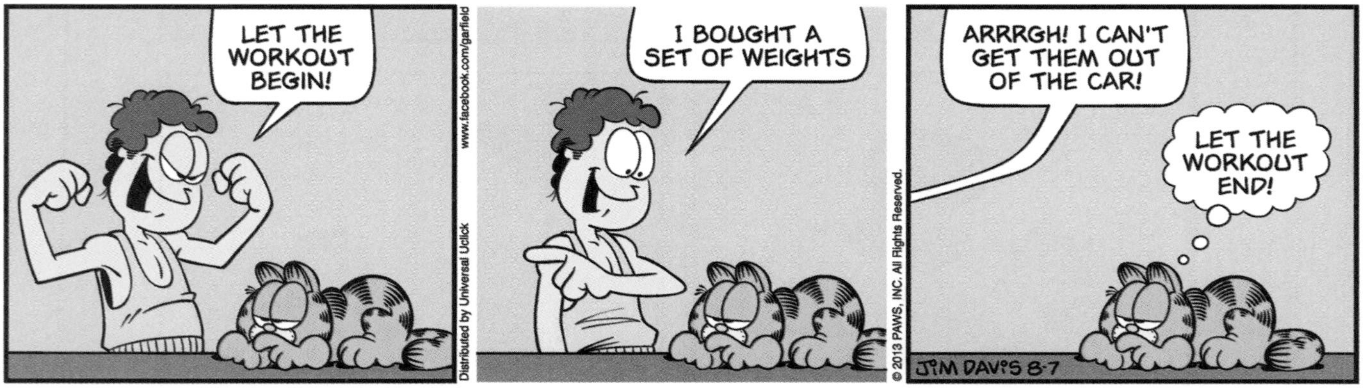
LET THE WORKOUT BEGIN!
I BOUGHT A SET OF WEIGHTS
ARRRGH! I CAN'T GET THEM OUT OF THE CAR!
LET THE WORKOUT END!
JIM DAVIS 8-7
Distributed by Universal Uclick www.facebook.com/garfield
© 2013 PAWS, INC. All Rights Reserved.

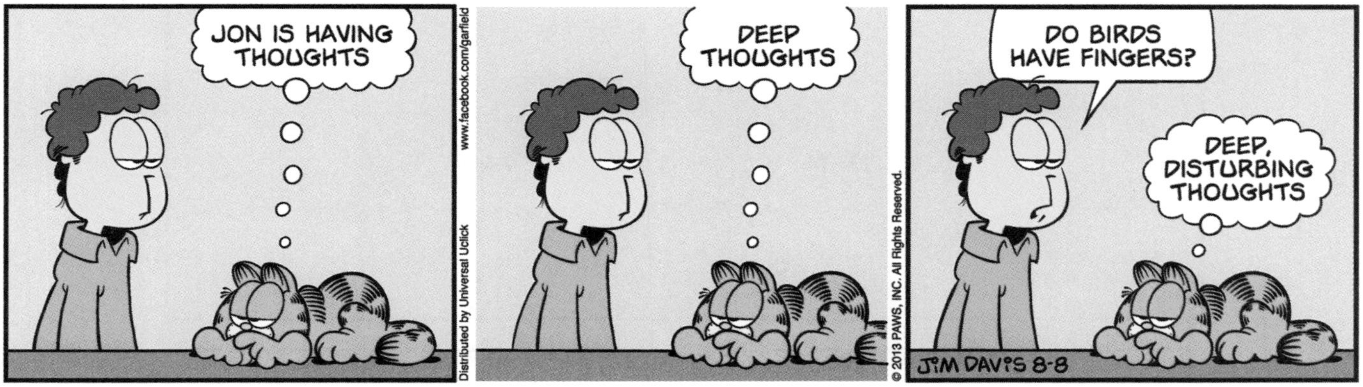
JON IS HAVING THOUGHTS
DEEP THOUGHTS
DO BIRDS HAVE FINGERS?
DEEP, DISTURBING THOUGHTS
JIM DAVIS 8-8
www.facebook.com/garfield
Distributed by Universal Uclick
© 2013 PAWS, INC. All Rights Reserved.

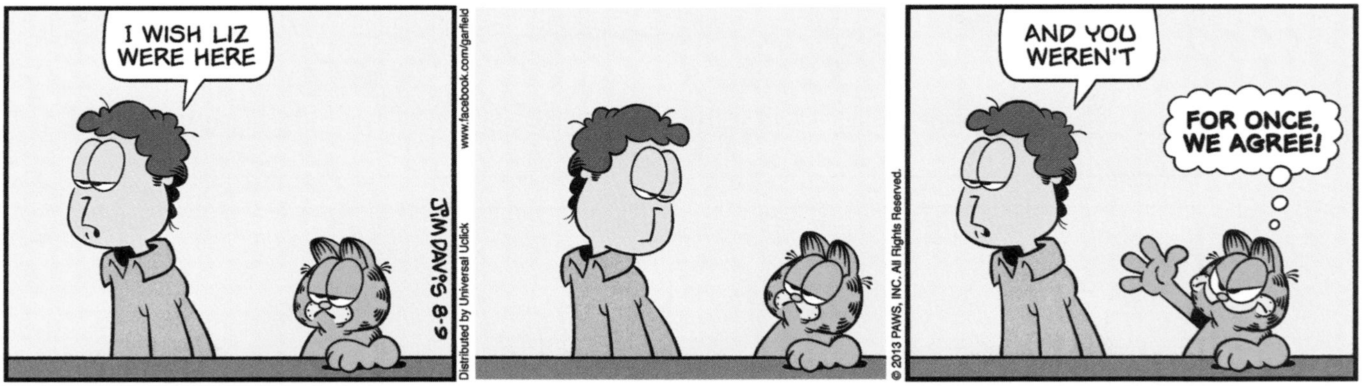
I WISH LIZ WERE HERE
JIM DAVIS 8-9
AND YOU WEREN'T
FOR ONCE, WE AGREE!
www.facebook.com/garfield
Distributed by Universal Uclick
© 2013 PAWS, INC. All Rights Reserved.

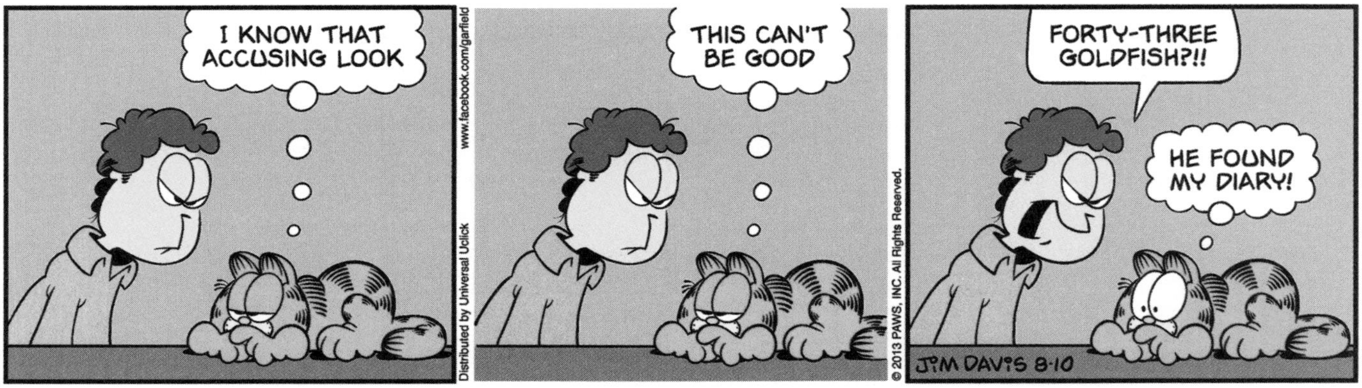
I KNOW THAT ACCUSING LOOK
THIS CAN'T BE GOOD
FORTY-THREE GOLDFISH?!!
HE FOUND MY DIARY!
JIM DAVIS 8-10
www.facebook.com/garfield
Distributed by Universal Uclick
© 2013 PAWS, INC. All Rights Reserved.

Garfield
www.facebook.com/garfield
Distributed by Universal Uclick
GARFIEEELD...
OH, SURE. BLAME THE COACH...UH, I MEAN CAT
JIM DAVIS 8-11
© 2013 PAWS, INC. All Rights Reserved.

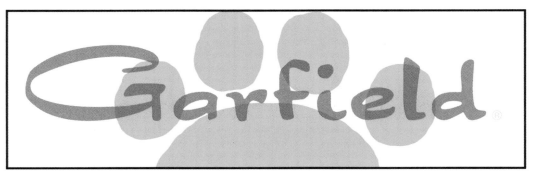

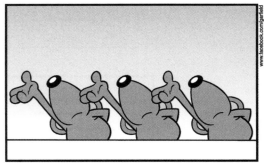

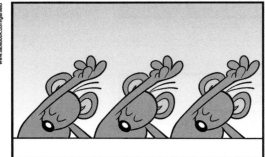

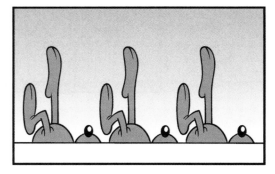

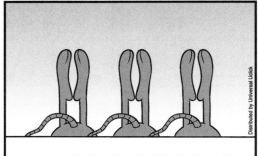

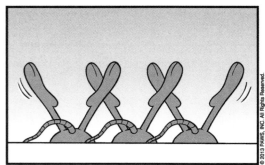

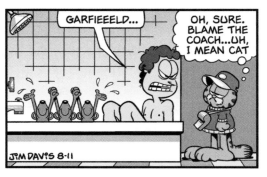

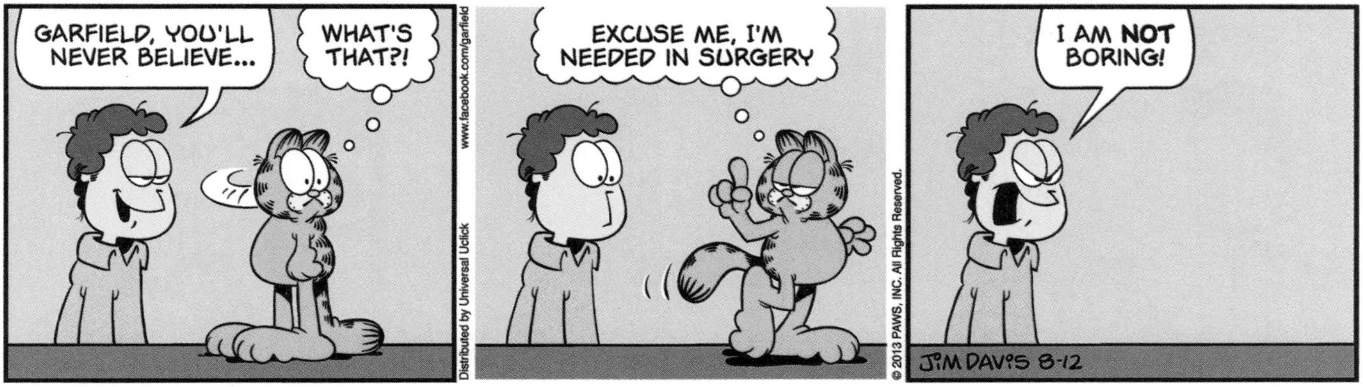
GARFIELD, YOU'LL NEVER BELIEVE...
WHAT'S THAT?!
EXCUSE ME, I'M NEEDED IN SURGERY
I AM **NOT** BORING!
JIM DAVIS 8-12

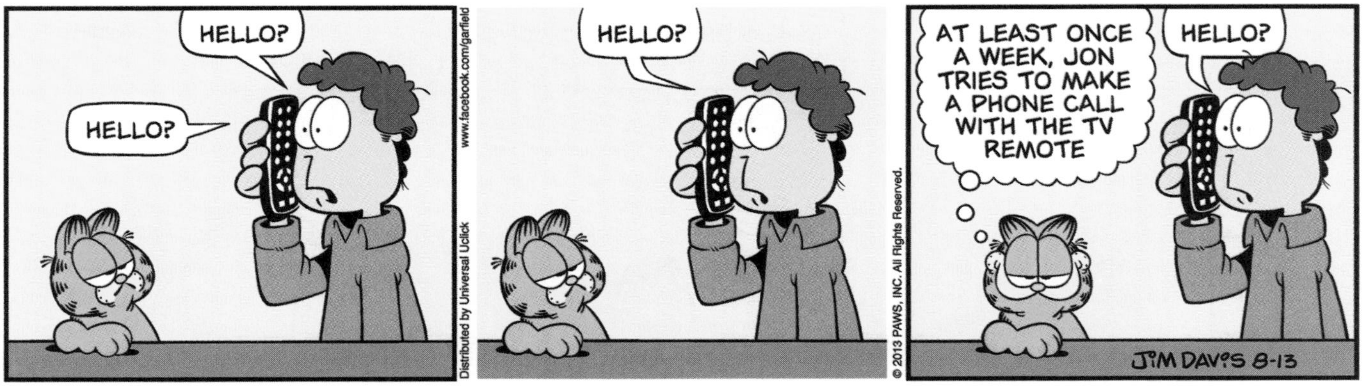
HELLO?
HELLO?
HELLO?
AT LEAST ONCE A WEEK, JON TRIES TO MAKE A PHONE CALL WITH THE TV REMOTE
HELLO?
JIM DAVIS 8-13

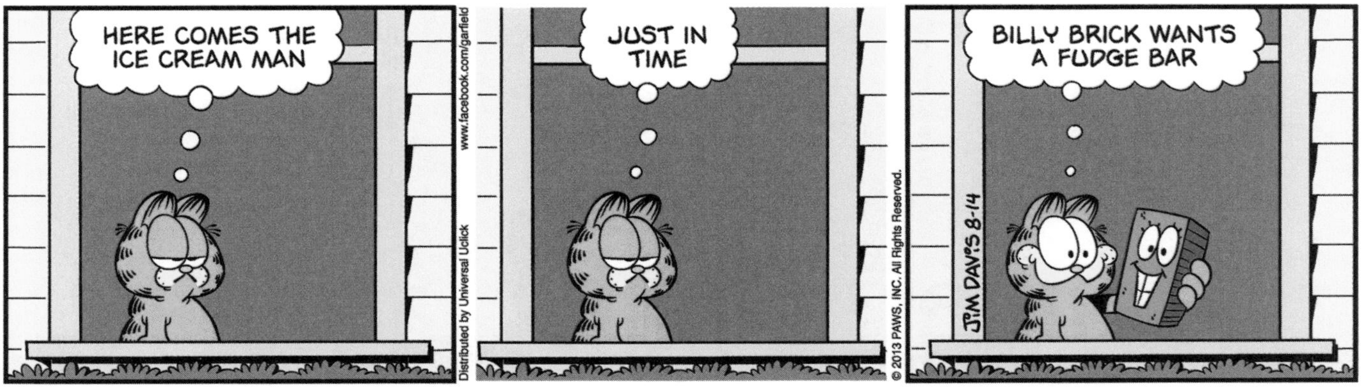
HERE COMES THE ICE CREAM MAN
JUST IN TIME
BILLY BRICK WANTS A FUDGE BAR
JIM DAVIS 8-14

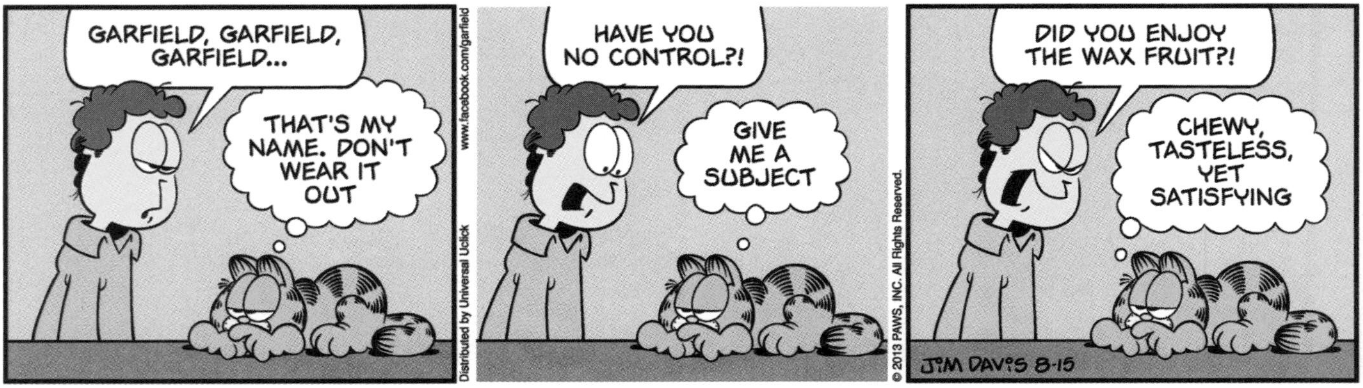
GARFIELD, GARFIELD, GARFIELD...
THAT'S MY NAME. DON'T WEAR IT OUT
Distributed by Universal Uclick www.facebook.com/garfield
HAVE YOU NO CONTROL?!
GIVE ME A SUBJECT
© 2013 PAWS, INC. All Rights Reserved.
DID YOU ENJOY THE WAX FRUIT?!
CHEWY, TASTELESS, YET SATISFYING
JIM DAVIS 8-15

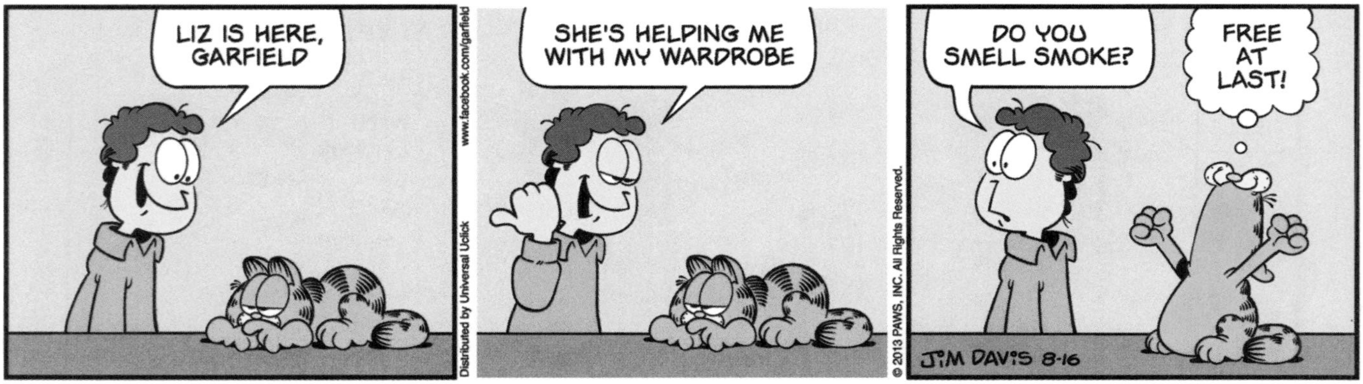
LIZ IS HERE, GARFIELD
Distributed by Universal Uclick www.facebook.com/garfield
SHE'S HELPING ME WITH MY WARDROBE
© 2013 PAWS, INC. All Rights Reserved.
DO YOU SMELL SMOKE?
FREE AT LAST!
JIM DAVIS 8-16

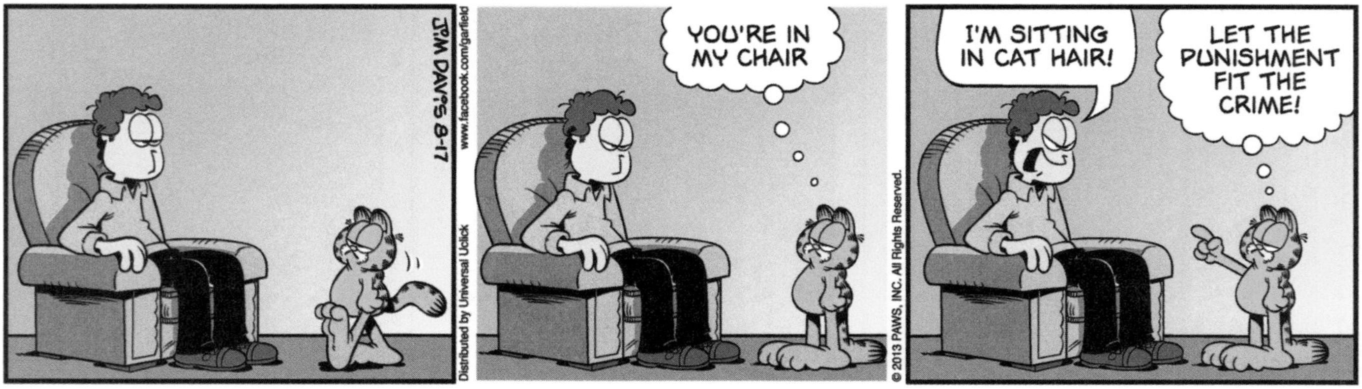
JIM DAVIS 8-17
Distributed by Universal Uclick www.facebook.com/garfield
YOU'RE IN MY CHAIR
© 2013 PAWS, INC. All Rights Reserved.
I'M SITTING IN CAT HAIR!
LET THE PUNISHMENT FIT THE CRIME!

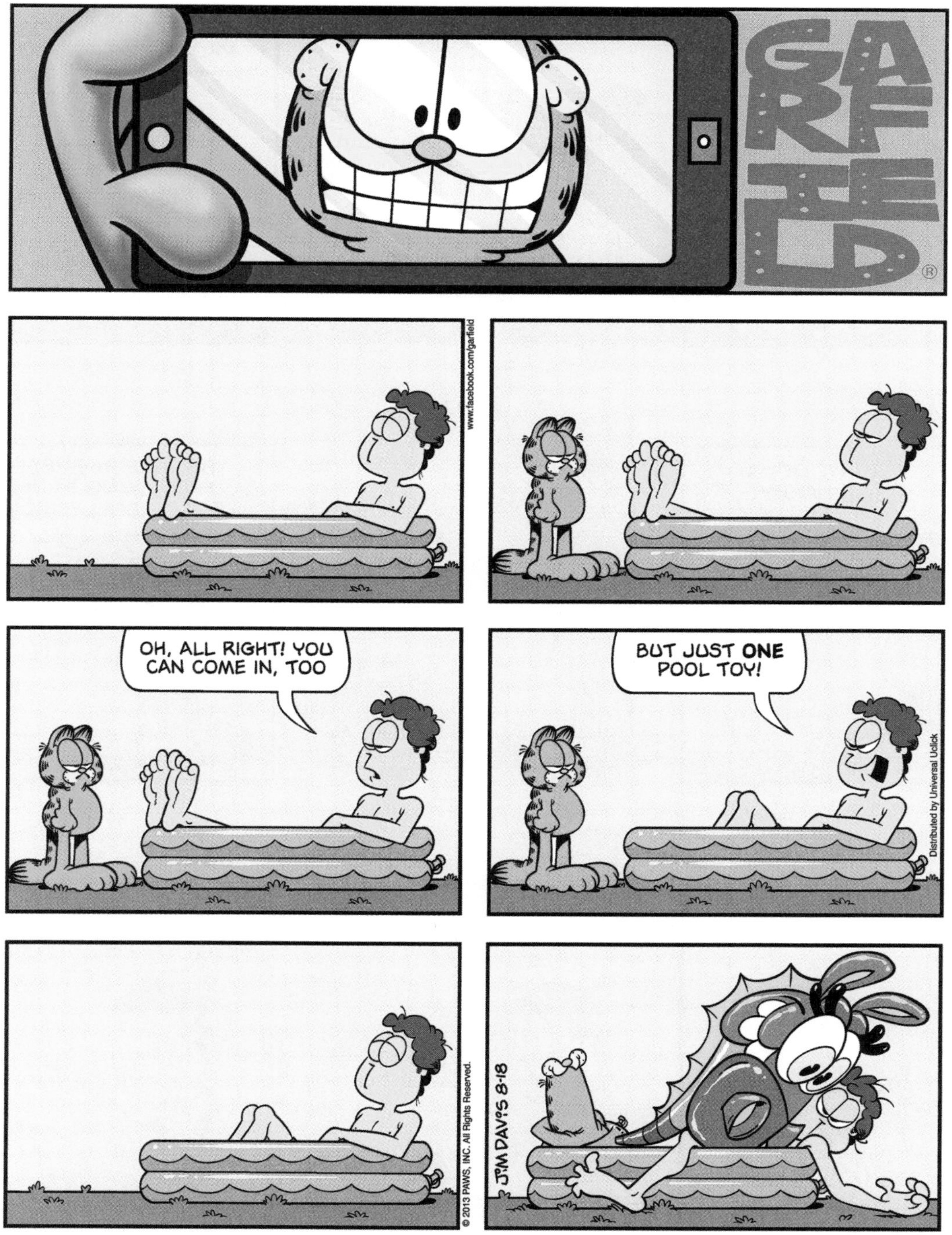
GARFIELD®
www.facebook.com/garfield
OH, ALL RIGHT! YOU CAN COME IN, TOO
BUT JUST **ONE** POOL TOY!
Distributed by Universal Uclick
© 2013 PAWS, INC. All Rights Reserved.
JIM DAVIS 8-18

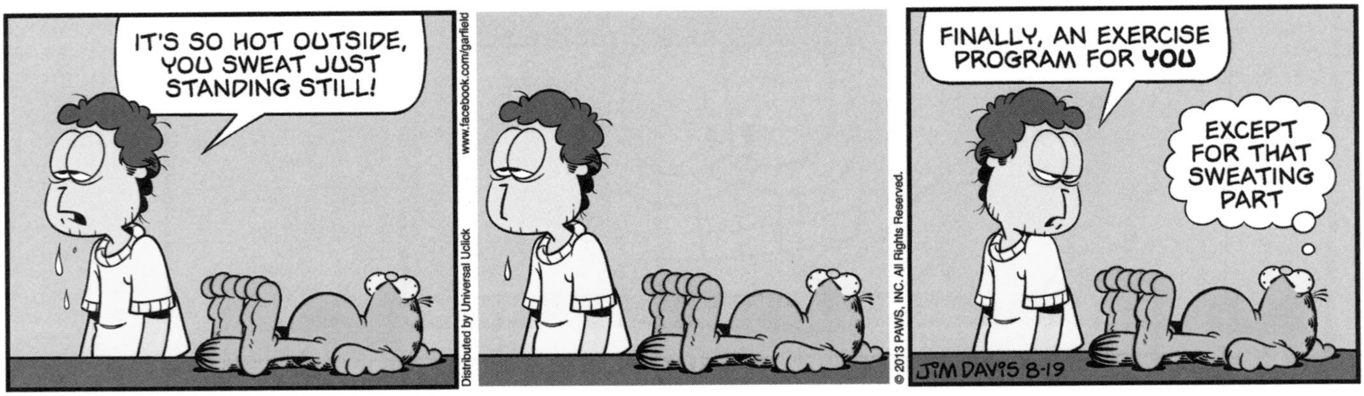
IT'S SO HOT OUTSIDE, YOU SWEAT JUST STANDING STILL!
Distributed by Universal Uclick www.facebook.com/garfield
FINALLY, AN EXERCISE PROGRAM FOR **YOU**
EXCEPT FOR THAT SWEATING PART
© 2013 PAWS, INC. All Rights Reserved.
JIM DAVIS 8-19

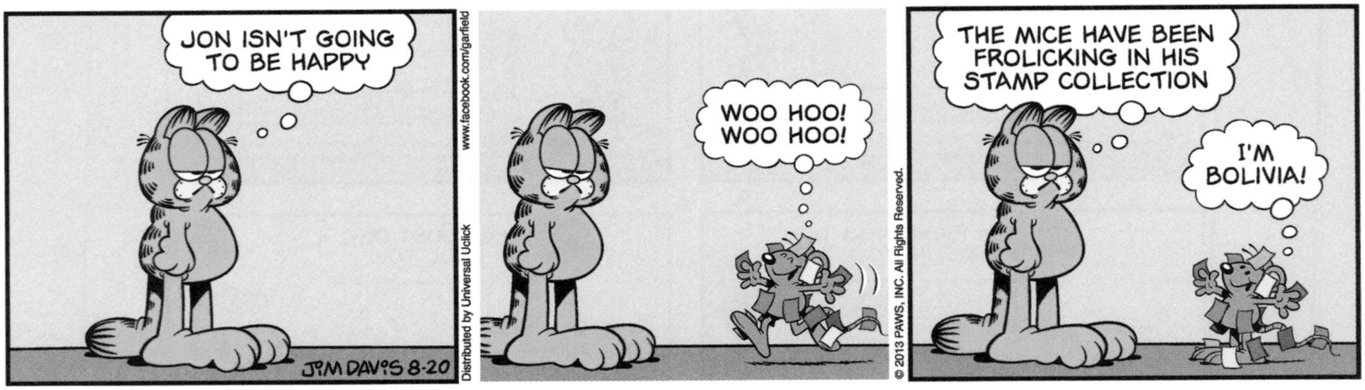
JON ISN'T GOING TO BE HAPPY
JIM DAVIS 8-20
Distributed by Universal Uclick www.facebook.com/garfield
WOO HOO! WOO HOO!
© 2013 PAWS, INC. All Rights Reserved.
THE MICE HAVE BEEN FROLICKING IN HIS STAMP COLLECTION
I'M BOLIVIA!

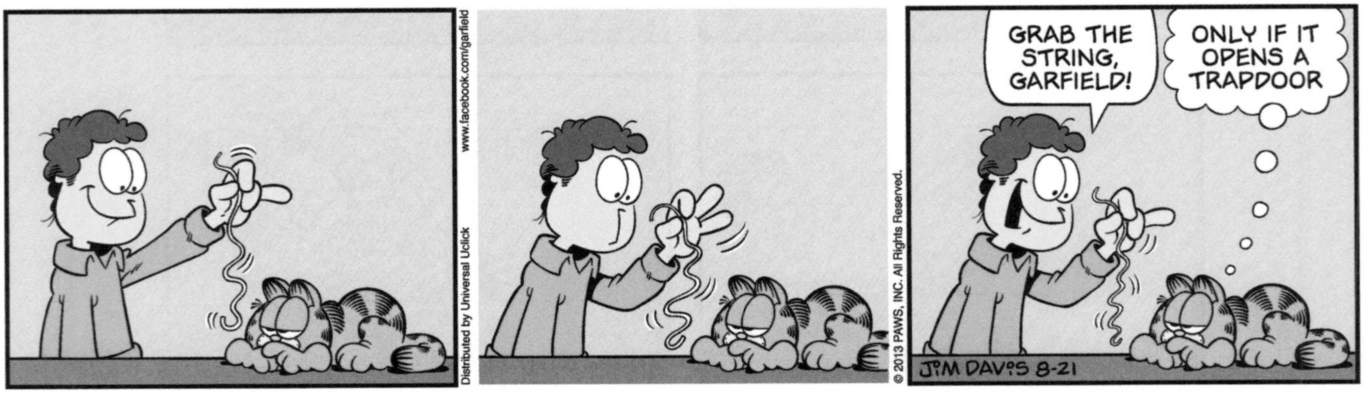
Distributed by Universal Uclick www.facebook.com/garfield
© 2013 PAWS, INC. All Rights Reserved.
GRAB THE STRING, GARFIELD!
ONLY IF IT OPENS A TRAPDOOR
JIM DAVIS 8-21

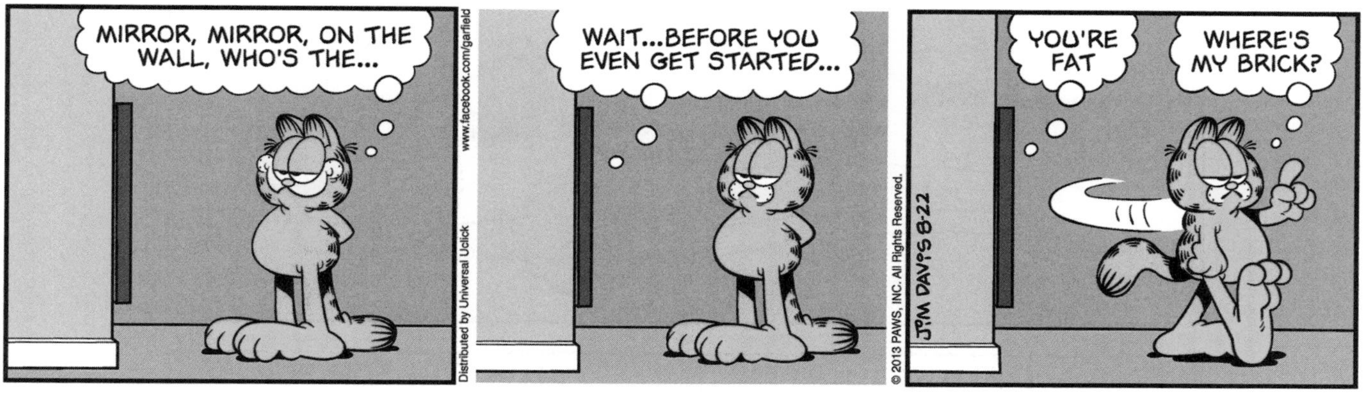
MIRROR, MIRROR, ON THE WALL, WHO'S THE...
Distributed by Universal Uclick www.facebook.com/garfield
WAIT...BEFORE YOU EVEN GET STARTED...
© 2013 PAWS, INC. All Rights Reserved.
JIM DAVIS 8-22
YOU'RE FAT
WHERE'S MY BRICK?

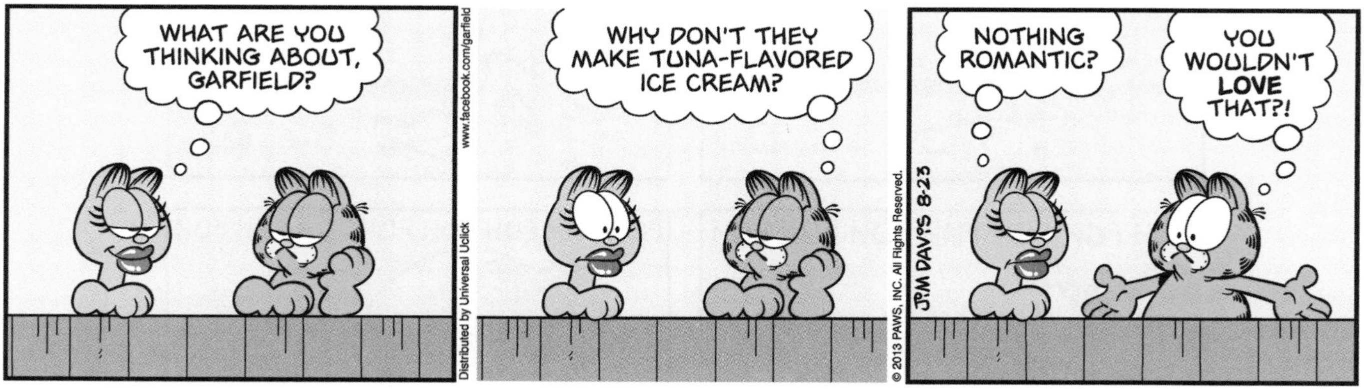
WHAT ARE YOU THINKING ABOUT, GARFIELD?
Distributed by Universal Uclick www.facebook.com/garfield
WHY DON'T THEY MAKE TUNA-FLAVORED ICE CREAM?
© 2013 PAWS, INC. All Rights Reserved.
JIM DAVIS 8-23
NOTHING ROMANTIC?
YOU WOULDN'T **LOVE** THAT?!

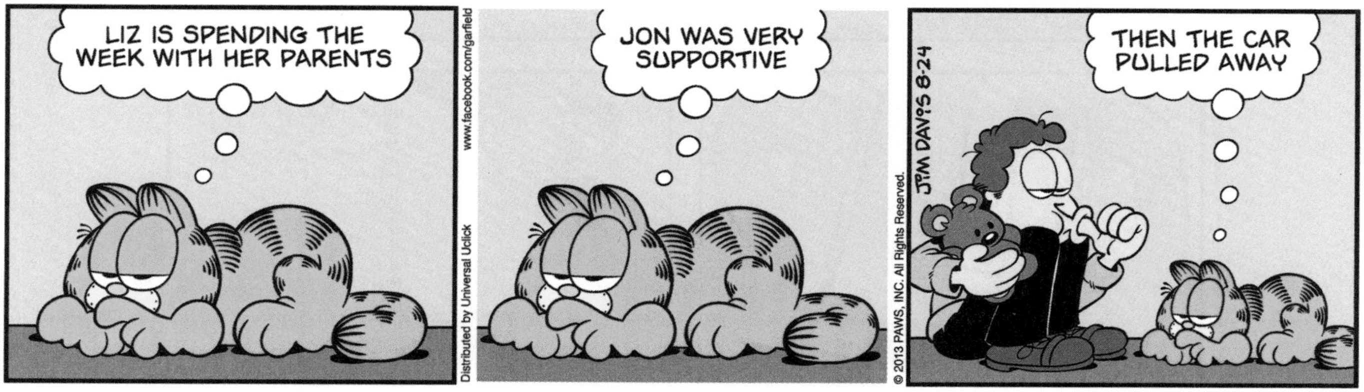
LIZ IS SPENDING THE WEEK WITH HER PARENTS
Distributed by Universal Uclick www.facebook.com/garfield
JON WAS VERY SUPPORTIVE
© 2013 PAWS, INC. All Rights Reserved.
JIM DAVIS 8-24
THEN THE CAR PULLED AWAY

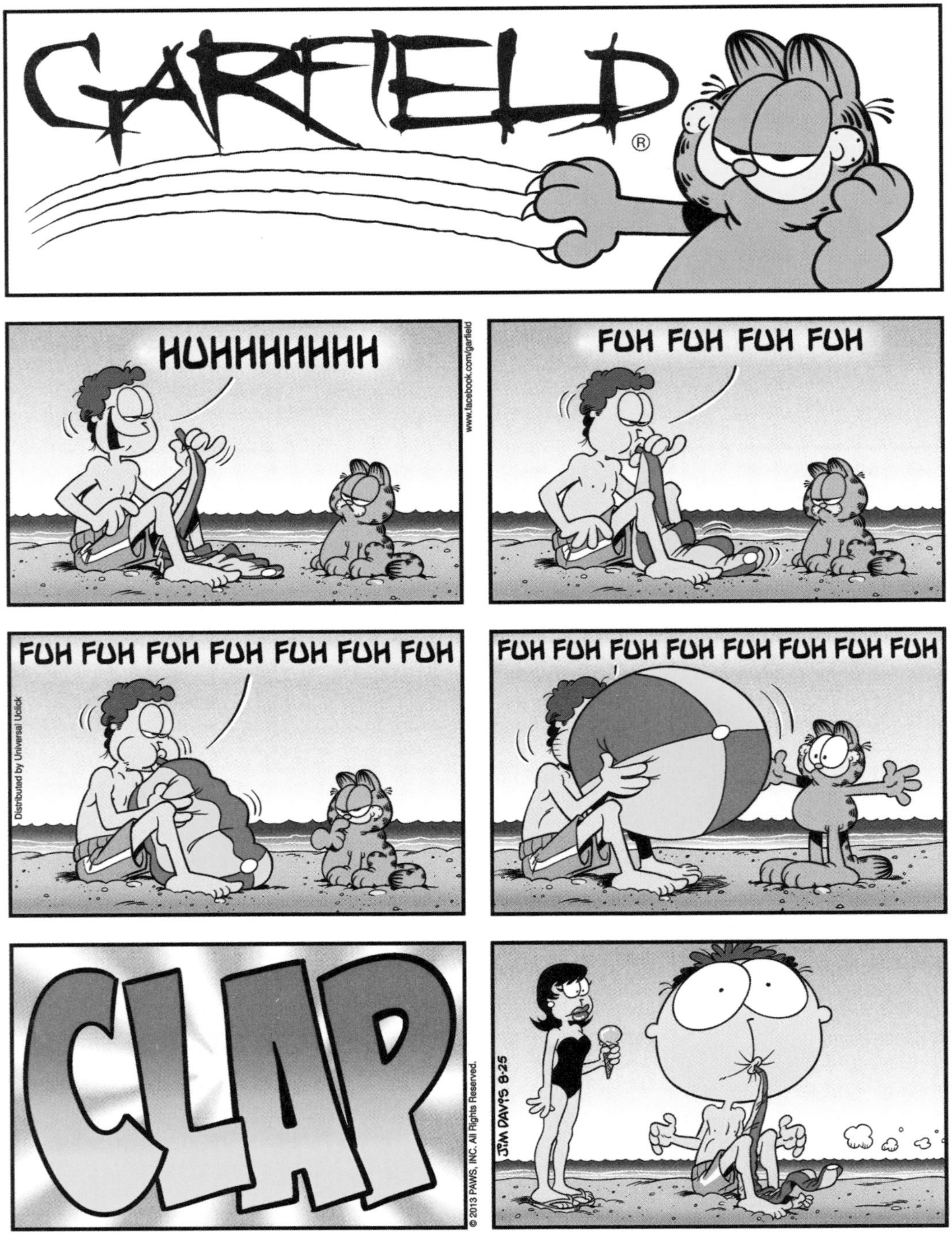
GARFIELD®
HUHHHHHHH
www.facebook.com/garfield
FUH FUH FUH FUH
FUH FUH FUH FUH FUH FUH FUH
Distributed by Universal Uclick
FUH FUH FUH FUH FUH FUH FUH FUH
CLAP
© 2013 PAWS, INC. All Rights Reserved.
JIM DAVIS 8-25

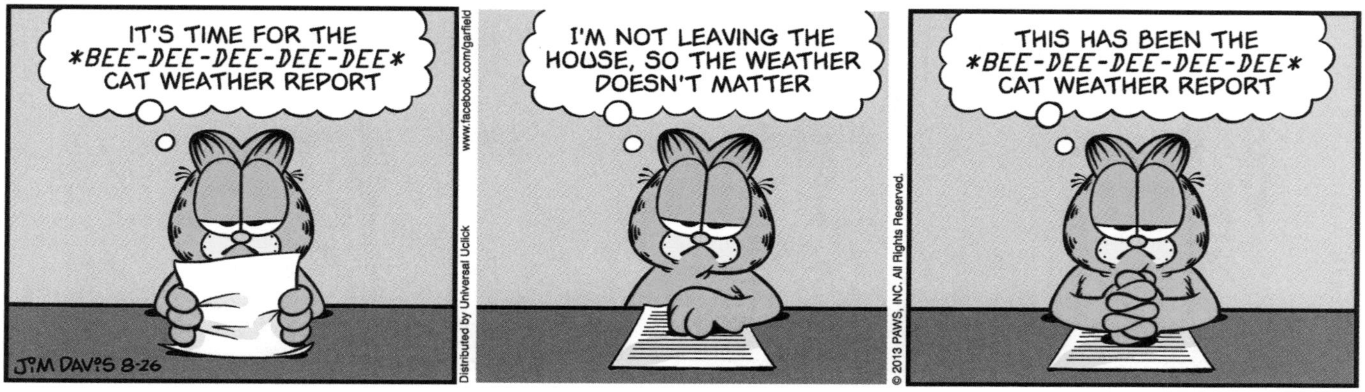
IT'S TIME FOR THE *BEE-DEE-DEE-DEE-DEE* CAT WEATHER REPORT
JIM DAVIS 8-26
Distributed by Universal Uclick www.facebook.com/garfield
I'M NOT LEAVING THE HOUSE, SO THE WEATHER DOESN'T MATTER
© 2013 PAWS, INC. All Rights Reserved.
THIS HAS BEEN THE *BEE-DEE-DEE-DEE-DEE* CAT WEATHER REPORT

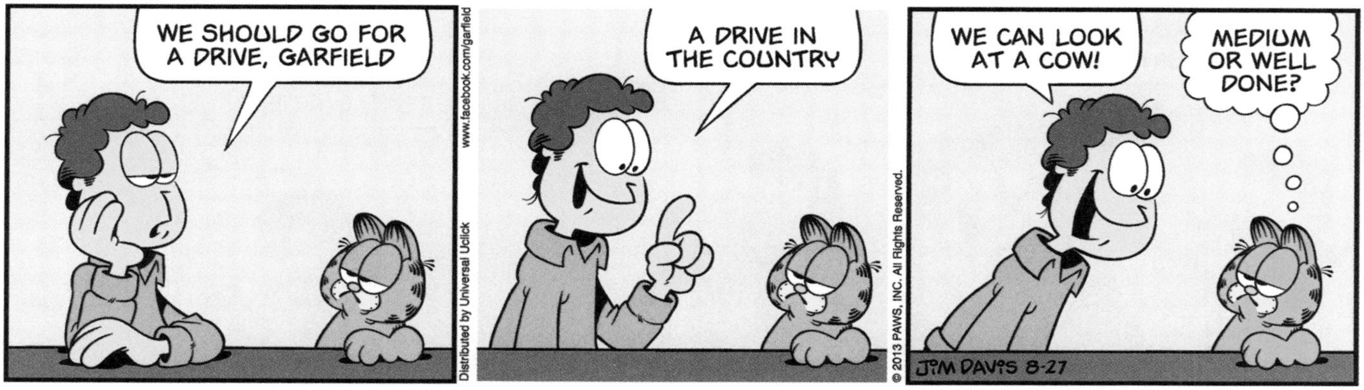
WE SHOULD GO FOR A DRIVE, GARFIELD
Distributed by Universal Uclick www.facebook.com/garfield
A DRIVE IN THE COUNTRY
© 2013 PAWS, INC. All Rights Reserved.
WE CAN LOOK AT A COW!
MEDIUM OR WELL DONE?
JIM DAVIS 8-27

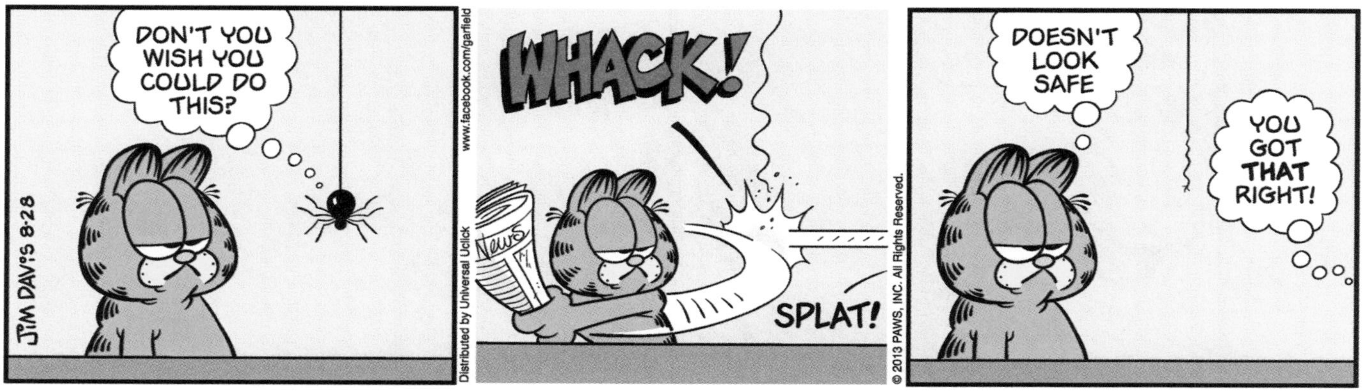
JIM DAVIS 8-28
DON'T YOU WISH YOU COULD DO THIS?
Distributed by Universal Uclick www.facebook.com/garfield
WHACK!
NEWS
SPLAT!
© 2013 PAWS, INC. All Rights Reserved.
DOESN'T LOOK SAFE
YOU GOT THAT RIGHT!

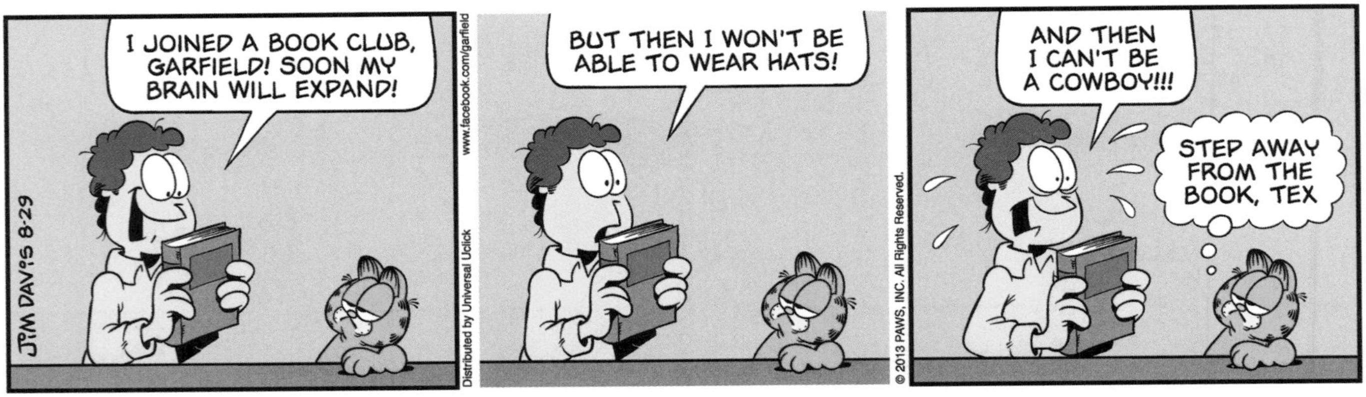
JIM DAVIS 8-29
I JOINED A BOOK CLUB, GARFIELD! SOON MY BRAIN WILL EXPAND!
Distributed by Universal Uclick www.facebook.com/garfield
BUT THEN I WON'T BE ABLE TO WEAR HATS!
© 2013 PAWS, INC. All Rights Reserved.
AND THEN I CAN'T BE A COWBOY!!!
STEP AWAY FROM THE BOOK, TEX

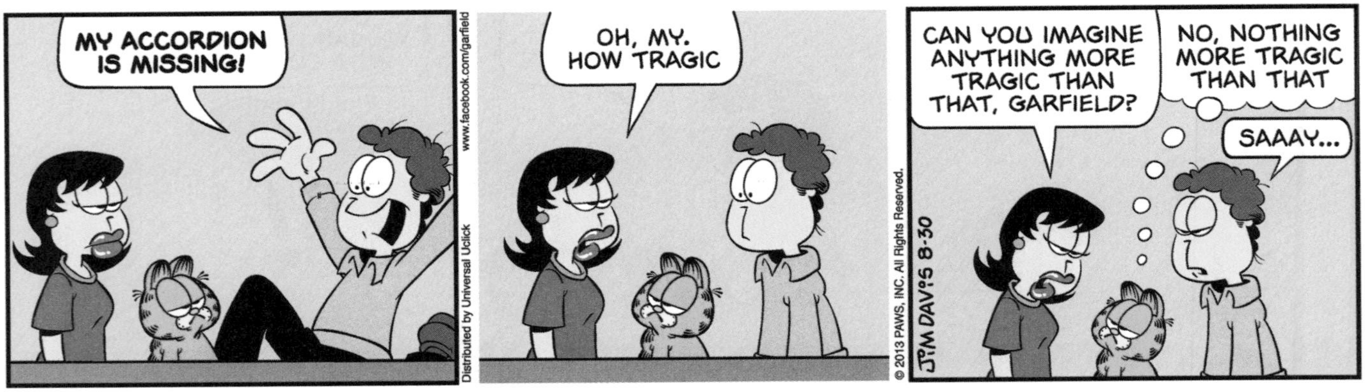
MY ACCORDION IS MISSING!
Distributed by Universal Uclick www.facebook.com/garfield
OH, MY. HOW TRAGIC
© 2013 PAWS, INC. All Rights Reserved.
JIM DAVIS 8-30
CAN YOU IMAGINE ANYTHING MORE TRAGIC THAN THAT, GARFIELD?
NO, NOTHING MORE TRAGIC THAN THAT
SAAAY...

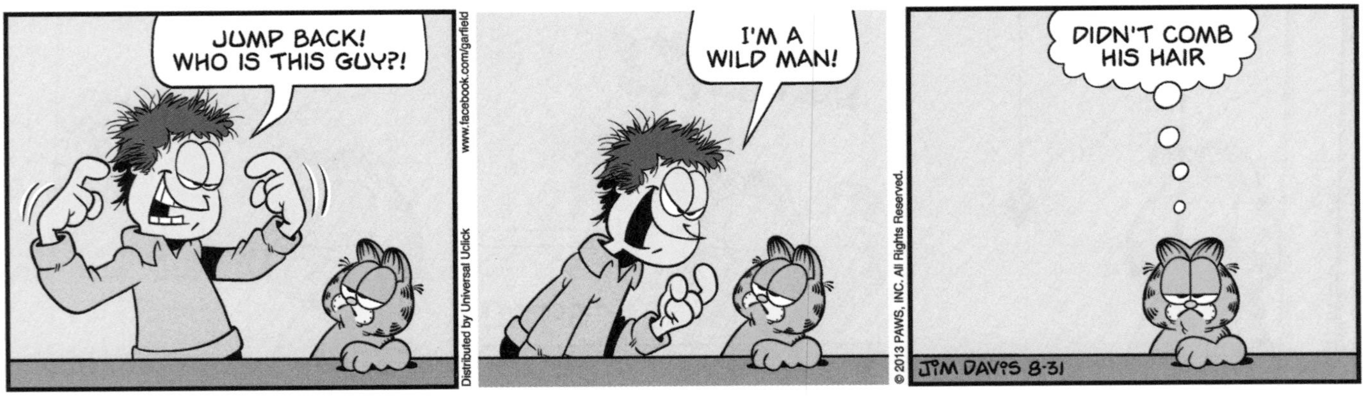
JUMP BACK! WHO IS THIS GUY?!
Distributed by Universal Uclick www.facebook.com/garfield
I'M A WILD MAN!
© 2013 PAWS, INC. All Rights Reserved.
DIDN'T COMB HIS HAIR
JIM DAVIS 8-31

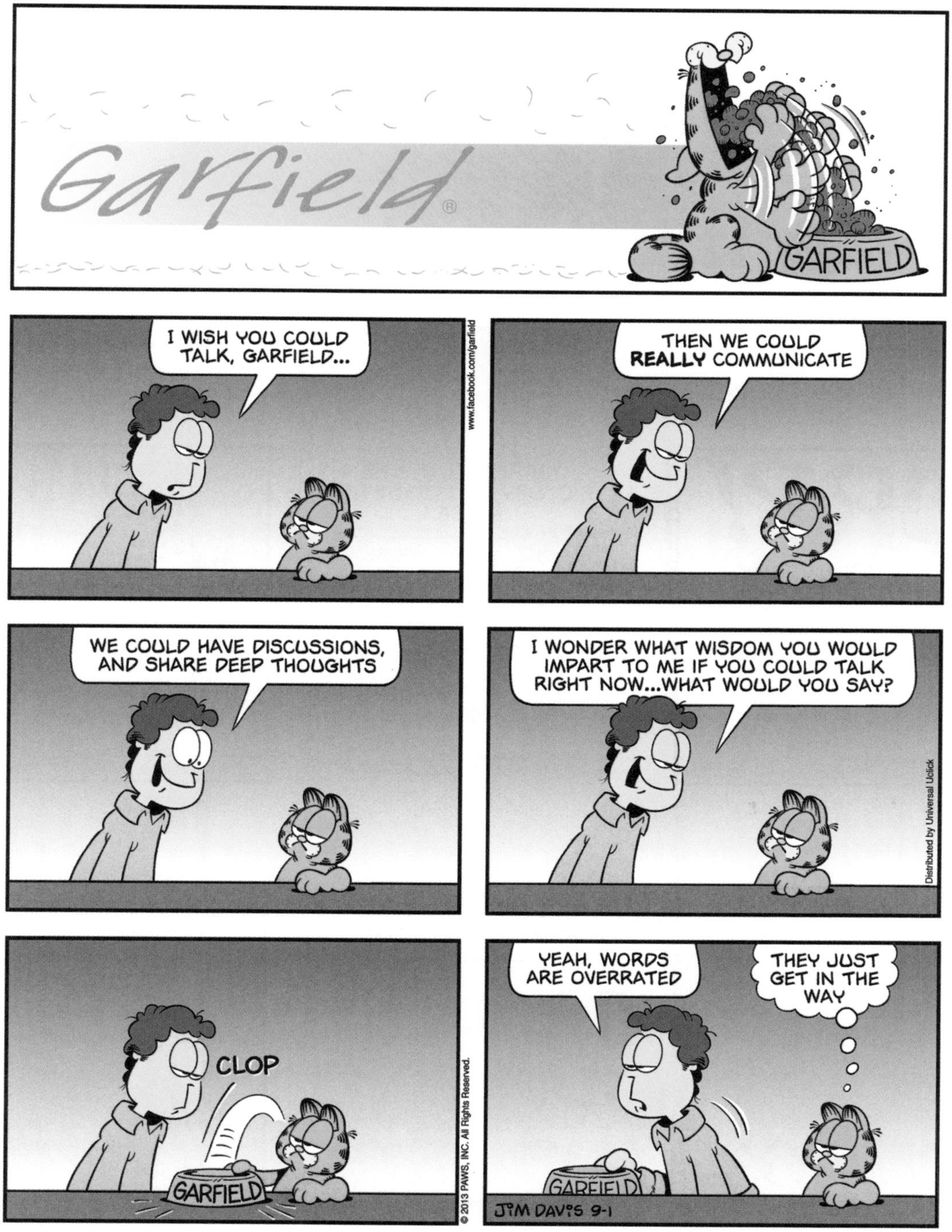
Garfield®
GARFIELD
I WISH YOU COULD TALK, GARFIELD...
www.facebook.com/garfield
THEN WE COULD **REALLY** COMMUNICATE
WE COULD HAVE DISCUSSIONS, AND SHARE DEEP THOUGHTS
I WONDER WHAT WISDOM YOU WOULD IMPART TO ME IF YOU COULD TALK RIGHT NOW...WHAT WOULD YOU SAY?
Distributed by Universal Uclick
CLOP
GARFIELD
© 2013 PAWS, INC. All Rights Reserved.
YEAH, WORDS ARE OVERRATED
THEY JUST GET IN THE WAY
GARFIELD
JIM DAVIS 9-1

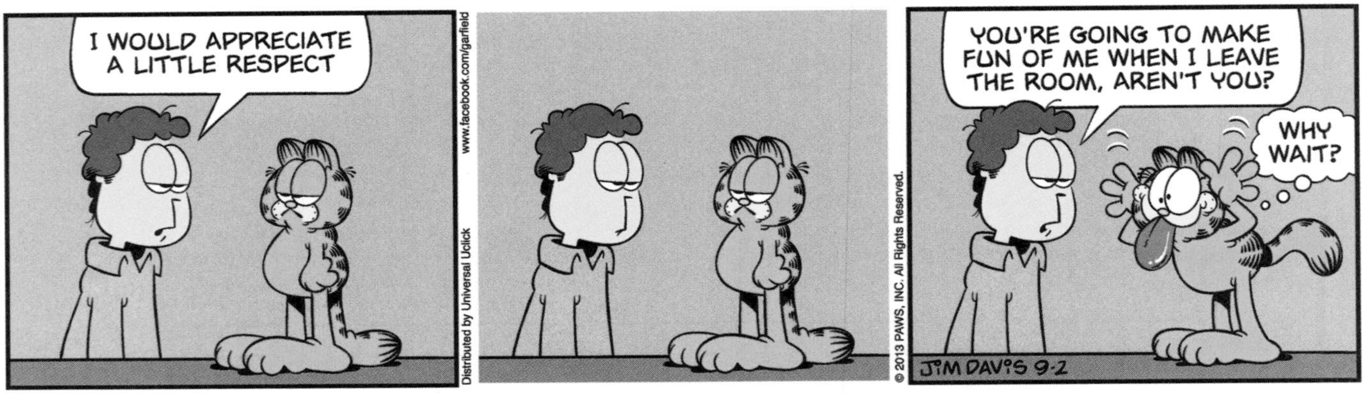
I WOULD APPRECIATE A LITTLE RESPECT
Distributed by Universal Uclick www.facebook.com/garfield
YOU'RE GOING TO MAKE FUN OF ME WHEN I LEAVE THE ROOM, AREN'T YOU?
WHY WAIT?
© 2013 PAWS, INC. All Rights Reserved.
JIM DAVIS 9-2

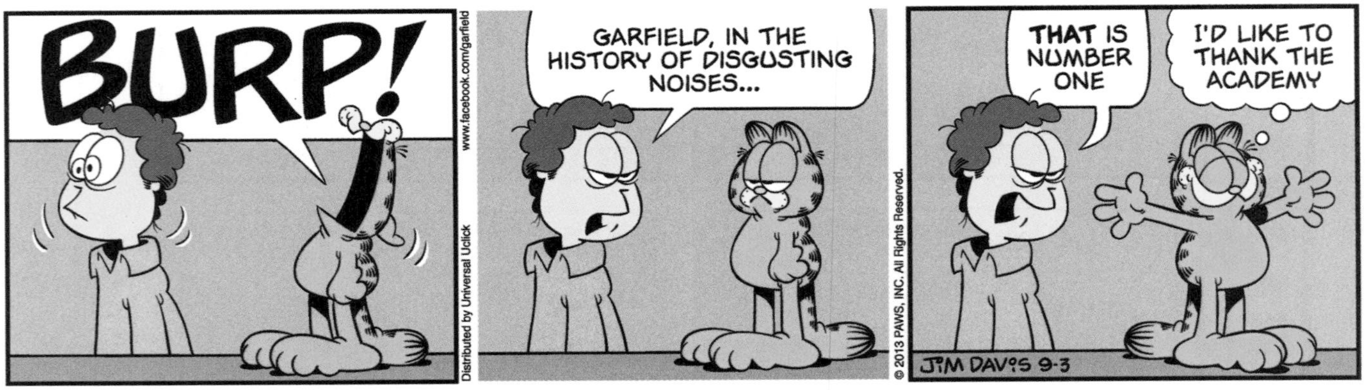
BURP!
Distributed by Universal Uclick www.facebook.com/garfield
GARFIELD, IN THE HISTORY OF DISGUSTING NOISES...
THAT IS NUMBER ONE
I'D LIKE TO THANK THE ACADEMY
© 2013 PAWS, INC. All Rights Reserved.
JIM DAVIS 9-3

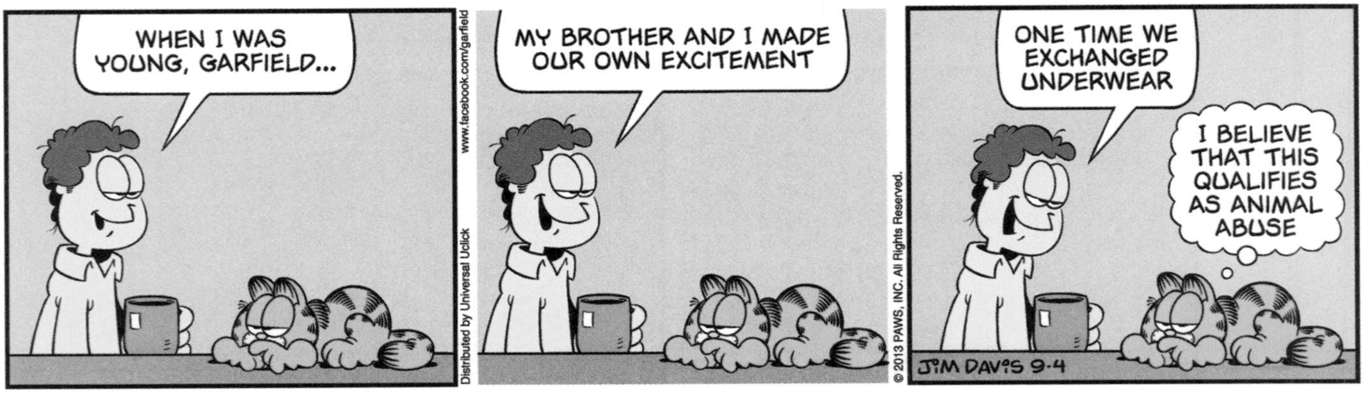
WHEN I WAS YOUNG, GARFIELD...
Distributed by Universal Uclick www.facebook.com/garfield
MY BROTHER AND I MADE OUR OWN EXCITEMENT
ONE TIME WE EXCHANGED UNDERWEAR
I BELIEVE THAT THIS QUALIFIES AS ANIMAL ABUSE
© 2013 PAWS, INC. All Rights Reserved.
JIM DAVIS 9-4

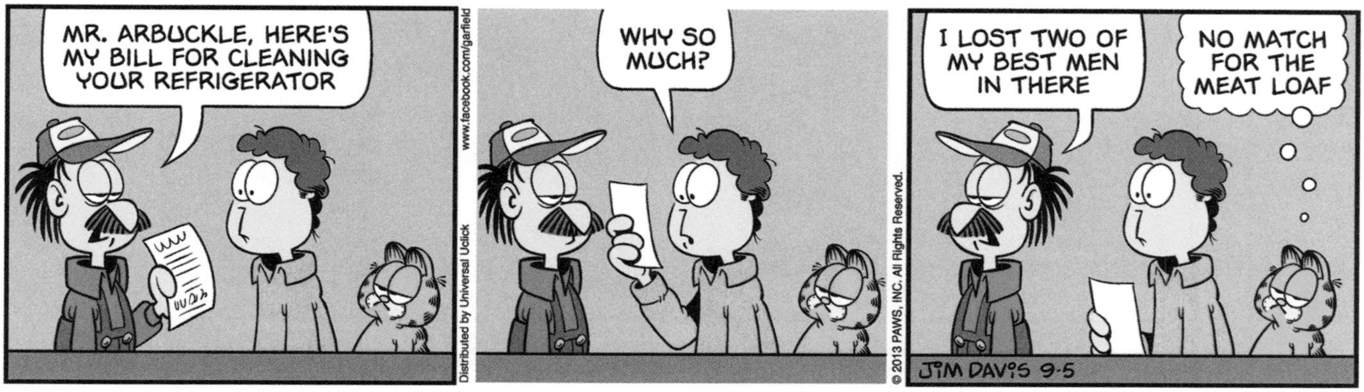
MR. ARBUCKLE, HERE'S MY BILL FOR CLEANING YOUR REFRIGERATOR
WHY SO MUCH?
I LOST TWO OF MY BEST MEN IN THERE
NO MATCH FOR THE MEAT LOAF
JIM DAVIS 9-5
Distributed by Universal Uclick
www.facebook.com/garfield
© 2013 PAWS, INC. All Rights Reserved.

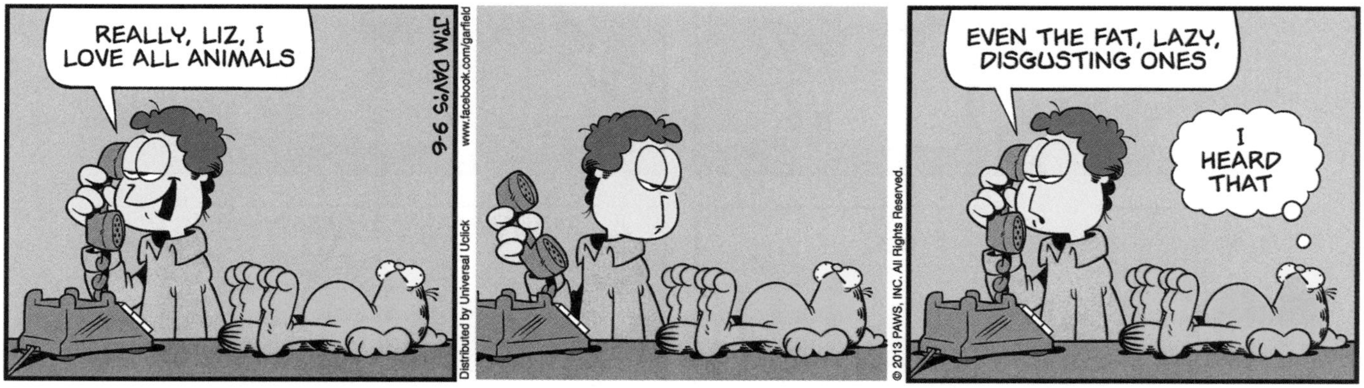
REALLY, LIZ, I LOVE ALL ANIMALS
EVEN THE FAT, LAZY, DISGUSTING ONES
I HEARD THAT
JIM DAVIS 9-6
Distributed by Universal Uclick
www.facebook.com/garfield
© 2013 PAWS, INC. All Rights Reserved.

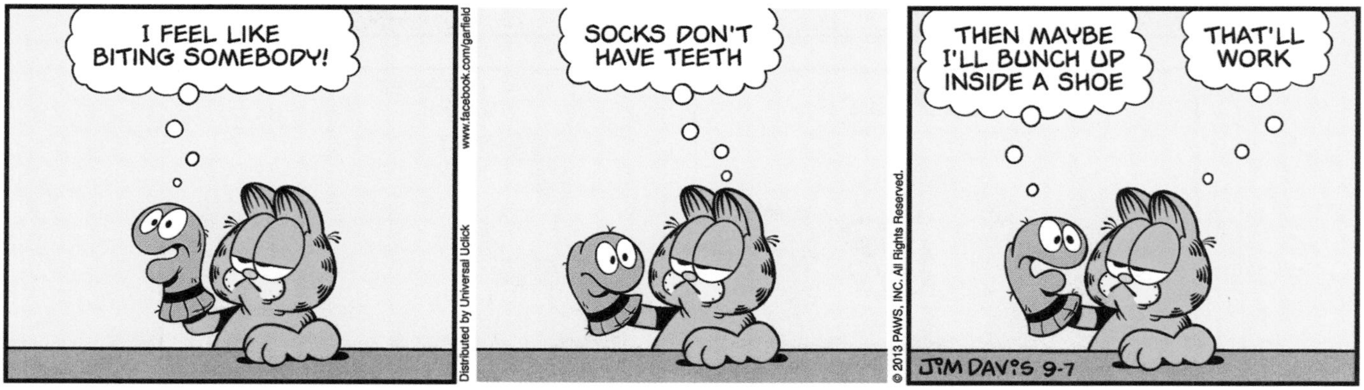
I FEEL LIKE BITING SOMEBODY!
SOCKS DON'T HAVE TEETH
THEN MAYBE I'LL BUNCH UP INSIDE A SHOE
THAT'LL WORK
JIM DAVIS 9-7
Distributed by Universal Uclick
www.facebook.com/garfield
© 2013 PAWS, INC. All Rights Reserved.

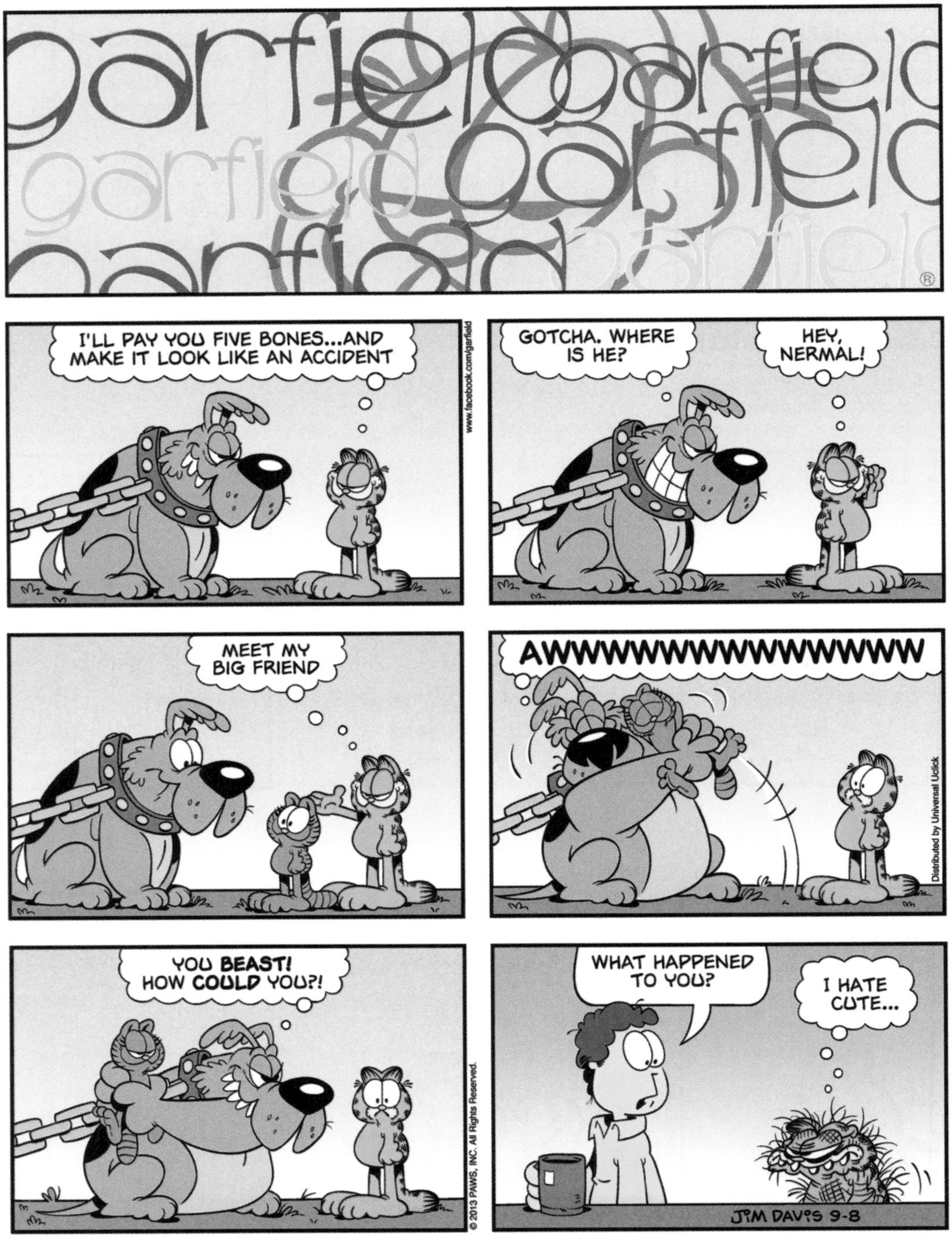
garfield
I'LL PAY YOU FIVE BONES...AND MAKE IT LOOK LIKE AN ACCIDENT
www.facebook.com/garfield
GOTCHA. WHERE IS HE?
HEY, NERMAL!
MEET MY BIG FRIEND
AWWWWWWWWWWWWWW
Distributed by Universal Uclick
YOU **BEAST!** HOW **COULD** YOU?!
© 2013 PAWS, INC. All Rights Reserved.
WHAT HAPPENED TO YOU?
I HATE CUTE...
JIM DAVIS 9-8

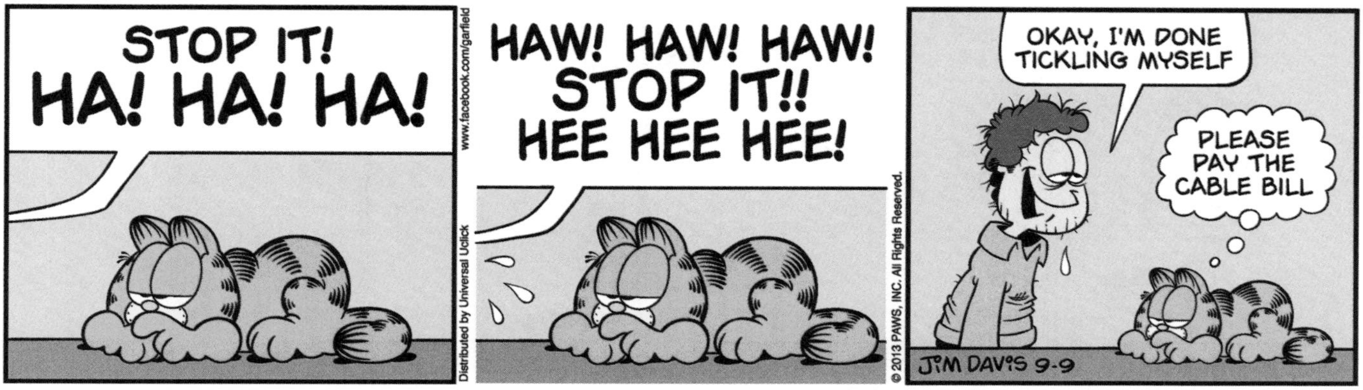
STOP IT!
HA! HA! HA!
HAW! HAW! HAW! STOP IT!! HEE HEE HEE!
OKAY, I'M DONE TICKLING MYSELF
PLEASE PAY THE CABLE BILL
JIM DAVIS 9-9
www.facebook.com/garfield
Distributed by Universal Uclick
© 2013 PAWS, INC. All Rights Reserved.

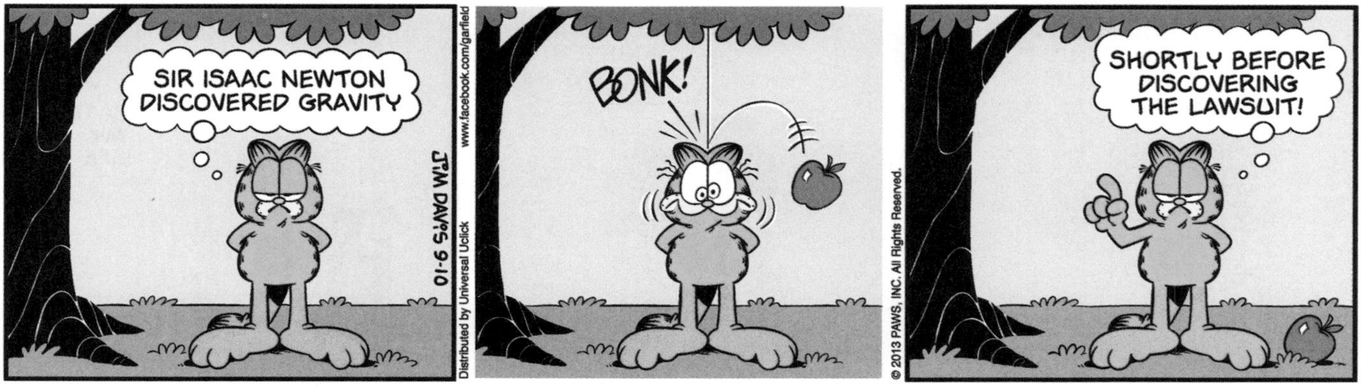
SIR ISAAC NEWTON DISCOVERED GRAVITY
JIM DAVIS 9-10
BONK!
SHORTLY BEFORE DISCOVERING THE LAWSUIT!
www.facebook.com/garfield
Distributed by Universal Uclick
© 2013 PAWS, INC. All Rights Reserved.

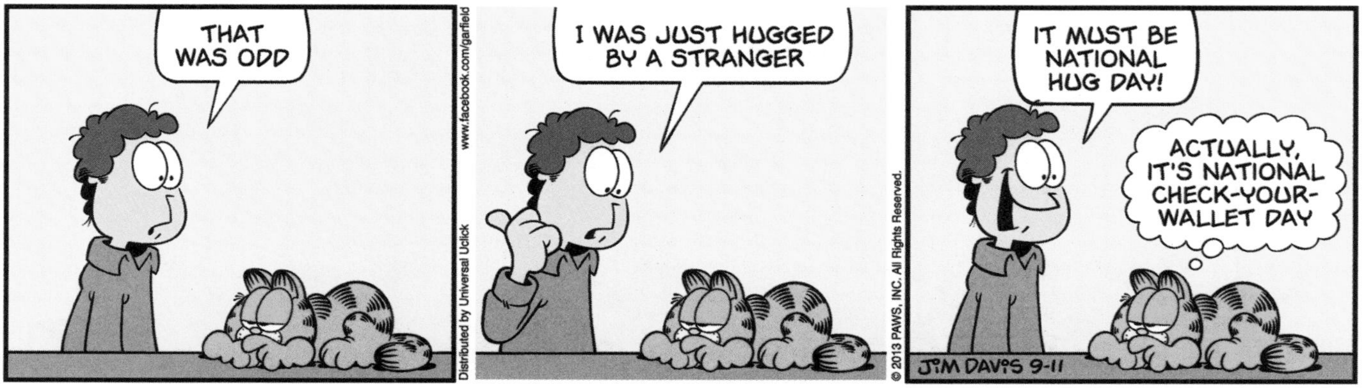
THAT WAS ODD
I WAS JUST HUGGED BY A STRANGER
IT MUST BE NATIONAL HUG DAY!
ACTUALLY, IT'S NATIONAL CHECK-YOUR-WALLET DAY
JIM DAVIS 9-11
www.facebook.com/garfield
Distributed by Universal Uclick
© 2013 PAWS, INC. All Rights Reserved.

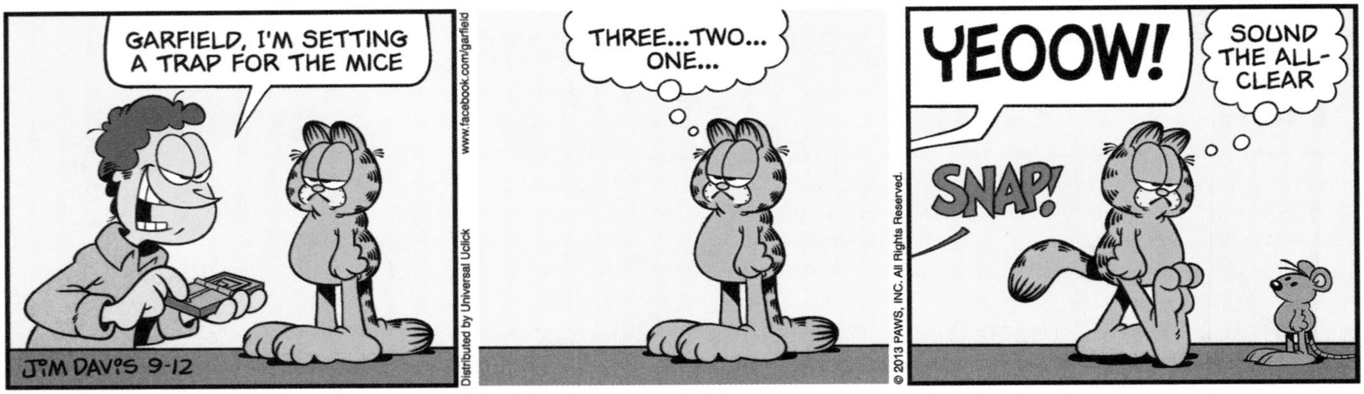
GARFIELD, I'M SETTING A TRAP FOR THE MICE
JIM DAVIS 9-12
Distributed by Universal Uclick www.facebook.com/garfield
THREE...TWO... ONE...
YEOOW!
SNAP!
SOUND THE ALL-CLEAR
© 2013 PAWS, INC. All Rights Reserved.

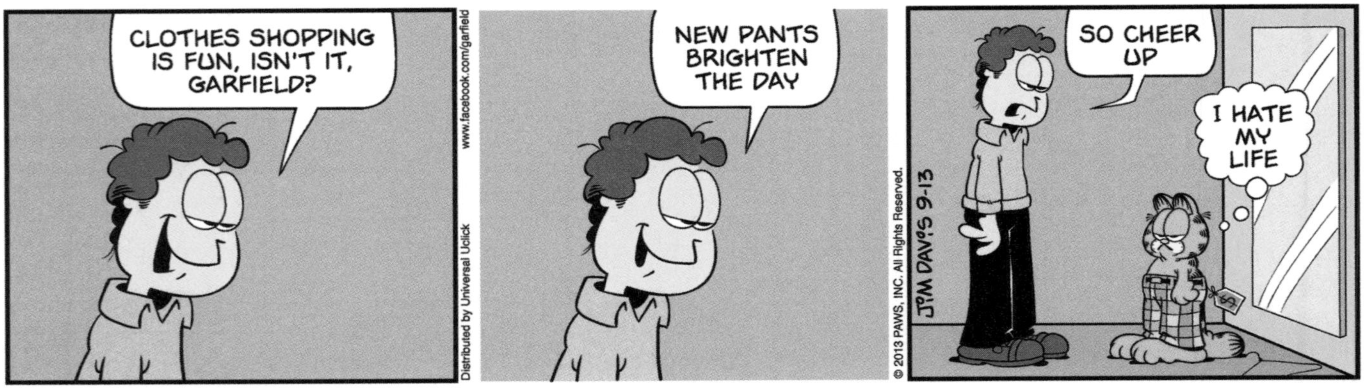
CLOTHES SHOPPING IS FUN, ISN'T IT, GARFIELD?
Distributed by Universal Uclick www.facebook.com/garfield
NEW PANTS BRIGHTEN THE DAY
SO CHEER UP
I HATE MY LIFE
JIM DAVIS 9-13
© 2013 PAWS, INC. All Rights Reserved.

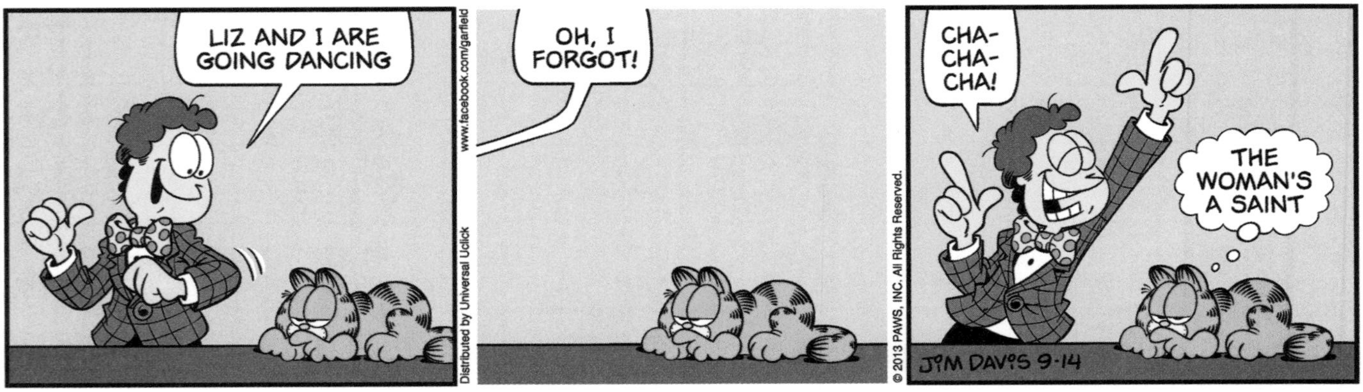
LIZ AND I ARE GOING DANCING
Distributed by Universal Uclick www.facebook.com/garfield
OH, I FORGOT!
CHA-CHA-CHA!
THE WOMAN'S A SAINT
JIM DAVIS 9-14
© 2013 PAWS, INC. All Rights Reserved.

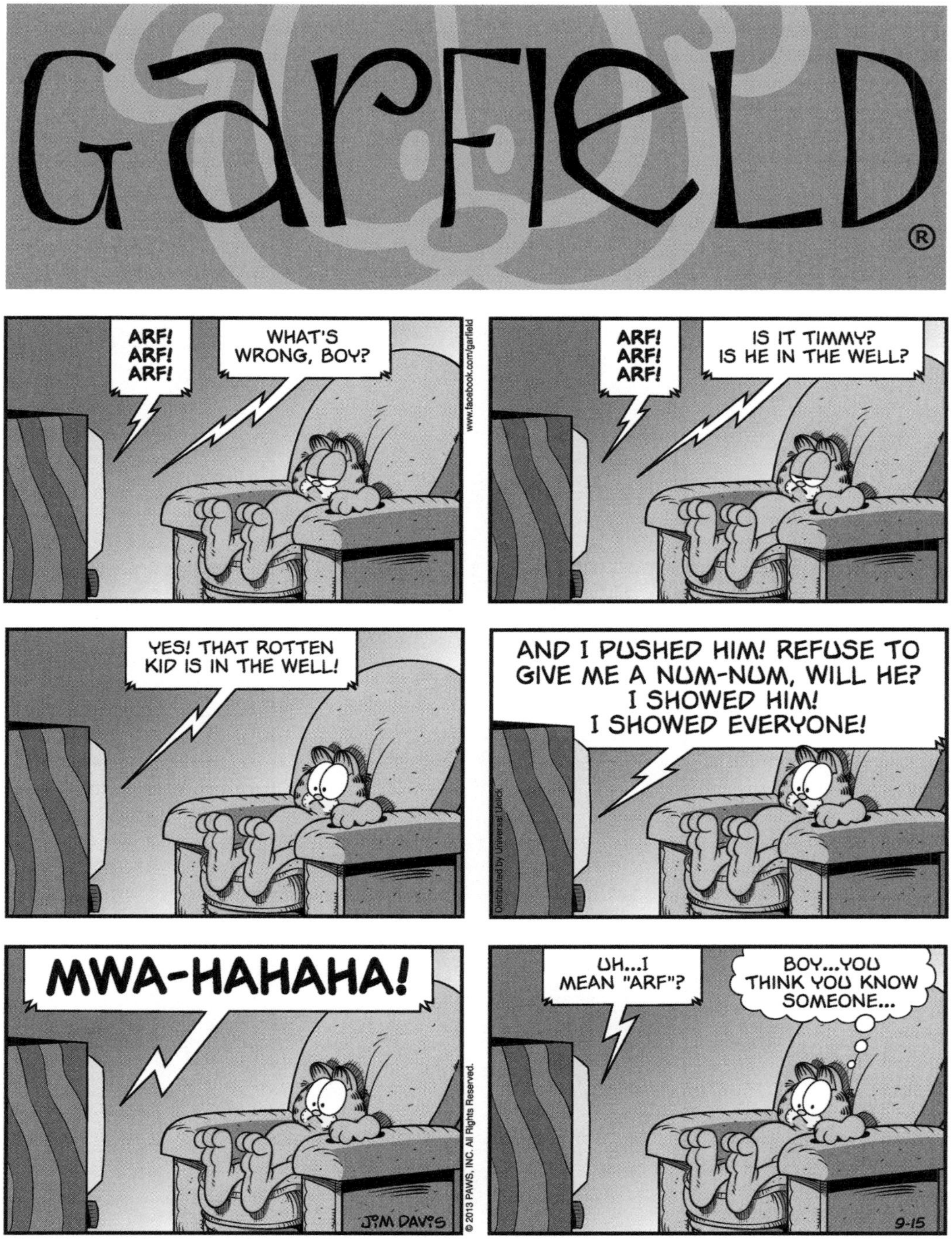
GARFIELD®
ARF! ARF! ARF!
WHAT'S WRONG, BOY?
www.facebook.com/garfield
ARF! ARF! ARF!
IS IT TIMMY? IS HE IN THE WELL?
YES! THAT ROTTEN KID IS IN THE WELL!
AND I PUSHED HIM! REFUSE TO GIVE ME A NUM-NUM, WILL HE? I SHOWED HIM! I SHOWED EVERYONE!
Distributed by Universal Uclick
MWA-HAHAHA!
JIM DAVIS
© 2013 PAWS, INC. All Rights Reserved.
UH...I MEAN "ARF"?
BOY...YOU THINK YOU KNOW SOMEONE...
9-15

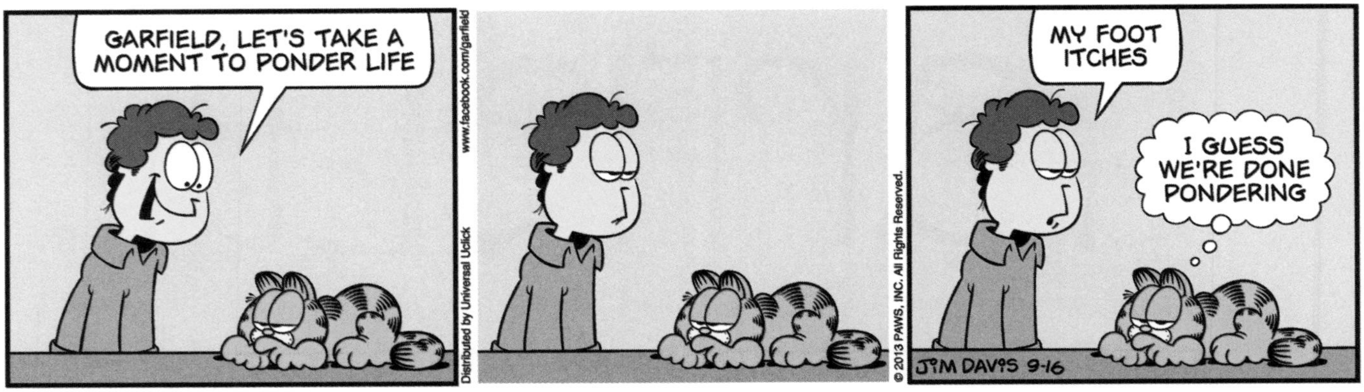
GARFIELD, LET'S TAKE A MOMENT TO PONDER LIFE
MY FOOT ITCHES
I GUESS WE'RE DONE PONDERING
JIM DAVIS 9-16
Distributed by Universal Uclick www.facebook.com/garfield
© 2013 PAWS, INC. All Rights Reserved.

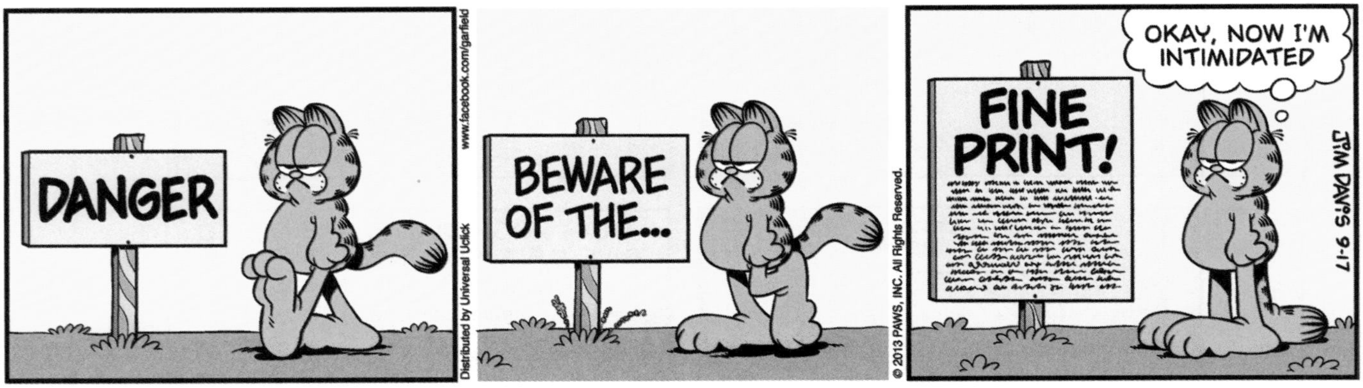
DANGER
BEWARE OF THE...
FINE PRINT!
OKAY, NOW I'M INTIMIDATED
JIM DAVIS 9-17
Distributed by Universal Uclick www.facebook.com/garfield
© 2013 PAWS, INC. All Rights Reserved.

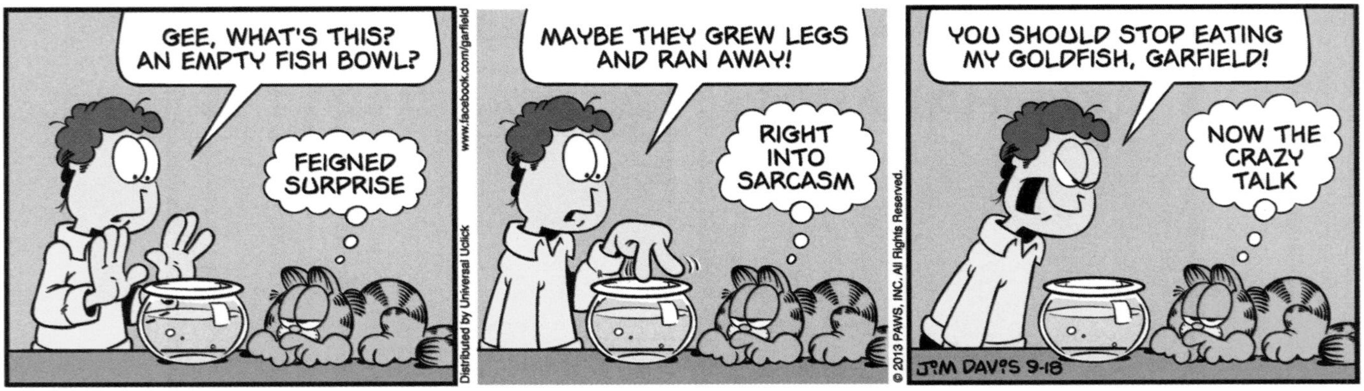
GEE, WHAT'S THIS? AN EMPTY FISH BOWL?
FEIGNED SURPRISE
MAYBE THEY GREW LEGS AND RAN AWAY!
RIGHT INTO SARCASM
YOU SHOULD STOP EATING MY GOLDFISH, GARFIELD!
NOW THE CRAZY TALK
JIM DAVIS 9-18
Distributed by Universal Uclick www.facebook.com/garfield
© 2013 PAWS, INC. All Rights Reserved.

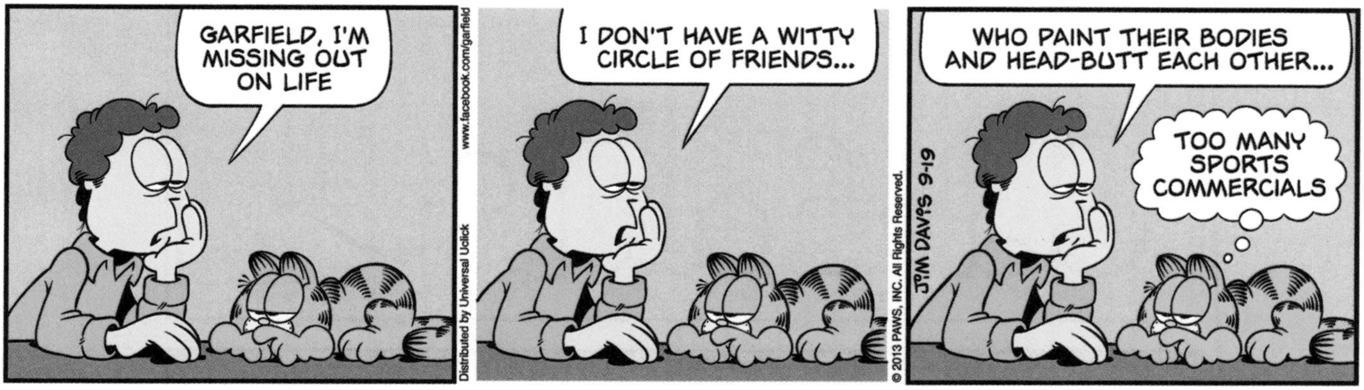
GARFIELD, I'M MISSING OUT ON LIFE
I DON'T HAVE A WITTY CIRCLE OF FRIENDS...
WHO PAINT THEIR BODIES AND HEAD-BUTT EACH OTHER...
TOO MANY SPORTS COMMERCIALS
JIM DAVIS 9-19
Distributed by Universal Uclick
www.facebook.com/garfield
© 2013 PAWS, INC. All Rights Reserved.

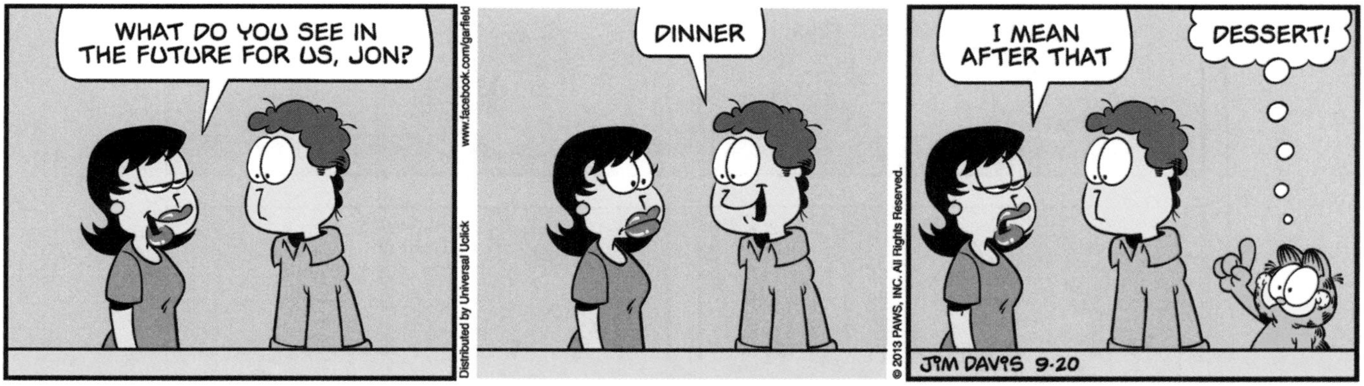
WHAT DO YOU SEE IN THE FUTURE FOR US, JON?
DINNER
I MEAN AFTER THAT
DESSERT!
JIM DAVIS 9-20
Distributed by Universal Uclick
www.facebook.com/garfield
© 2013 PAWS, INC. All Rights Reserved.

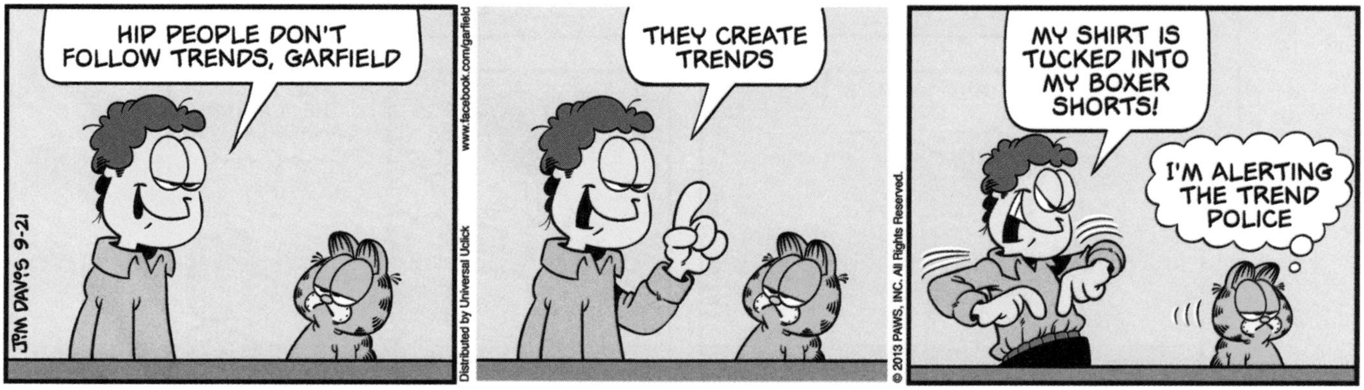
HIP PEOPLE DON'T FOLLOW TRENDS, GARFIELD
THEY CREATE TRENDS
MY SHIRT IS TUCKED INTO MY BOXER SHORTS!
I'M ALERTING THE TREND POLICE
JIM DAVIS 9-21
Distributed by Universal Uclick
www.facebook.com/garfield
© 2013 PAWS, INC. All Rights Reserved.

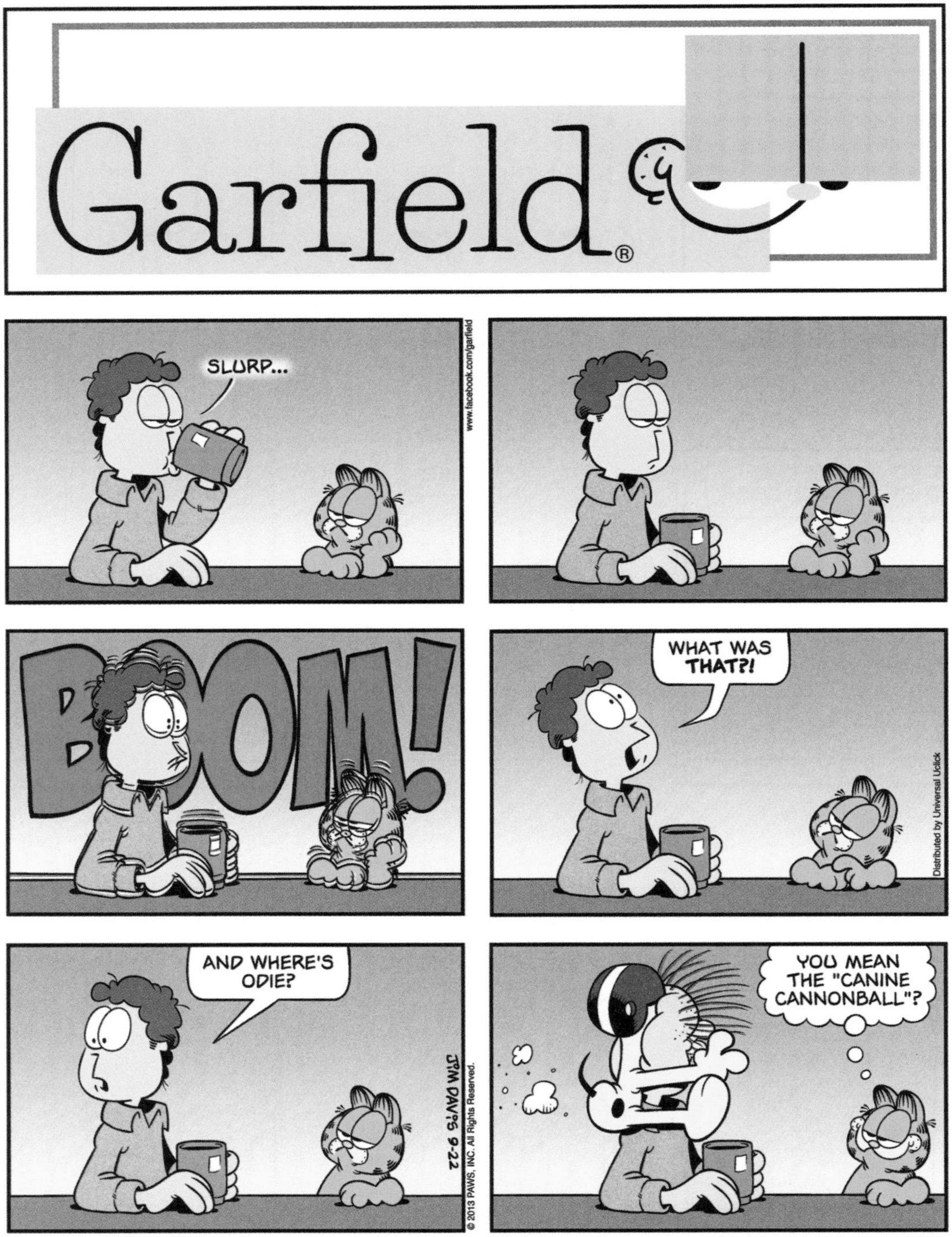
Garfield®
SLURP...
www.facebook.com/garfield
BOOM!
WHAT WAS THAT?!
Distributed by Universal Uclick
AND WHERE'S ODIE?
JIM DAVIS 9-22
© 2013 PAWS, INC. All Rights Reserved.
YOU MEAN THE "CANINE CANNONBALL"?

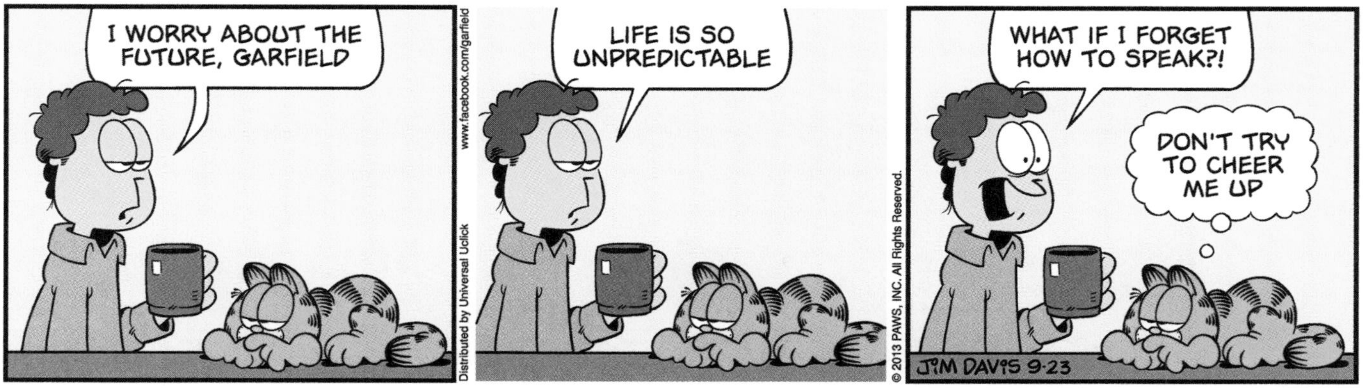
I WORRY ABOUT THE FUTURE, GARFIELD
LIFE IS SO UNPREDICTABLE
WHAT IF I FORGET HOW TO SPEAK?!
DON'T TRY TO CHEER ME UP
JIM DAVIS 9-23
Distributed by Universal Uclick www.facebook.com/garfield
© 2013 PAWS, INC. All Rights Reserved.

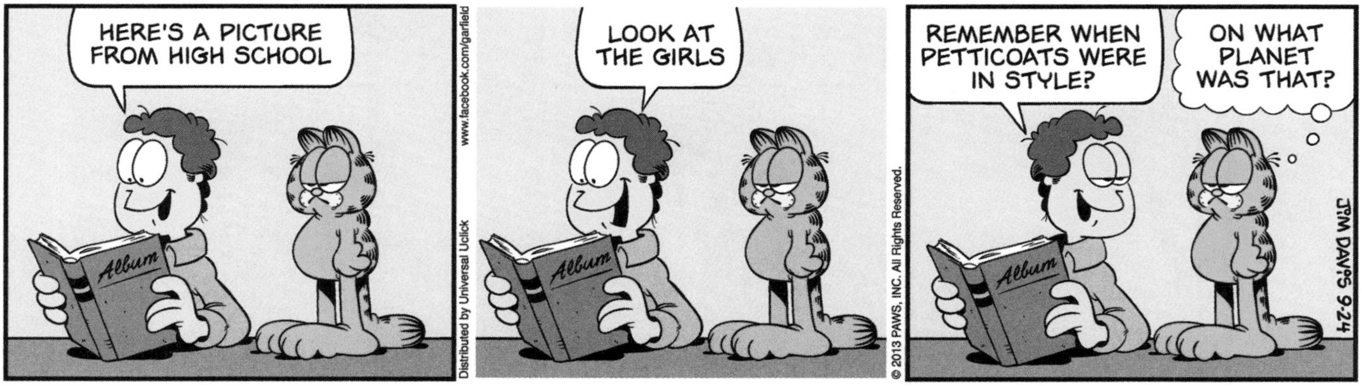
HERE'S A PICTURE FROM HIGH SCHOOL
Album
LOOK AT THE GIRLS
REMEMBER WHEN PETTICOATS WERE IN STYLE?
ON WHAT PLANET WAS THAT?
JIM DAVIS 9-24
Distributed by Universal Uclick www.facebook.com/garfield
© 2013 PAWS, INC. All Rights Reserved.

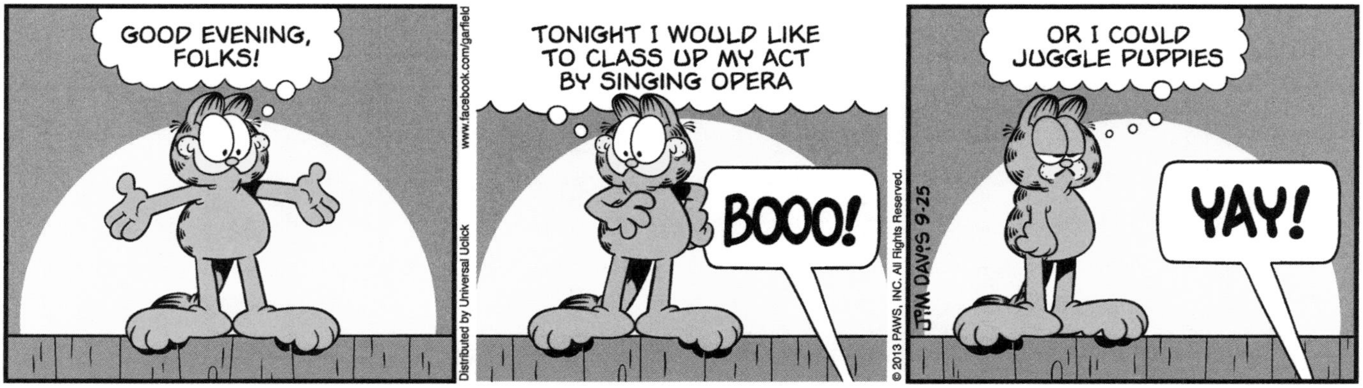
GOOD EVENING, FOLKS!
TONIGHT I WOULD LIKE TO CLASS UP MY ACT BY SINGING OPERA
BOOO!
OR I COULD JUGGLE PUPPIES
YAY!
JIM DAVIS 9-25
Distributed by Universal Uclick www.facebook.com/garfield
© 2013 PAWS, INC. All Rights Reserved.

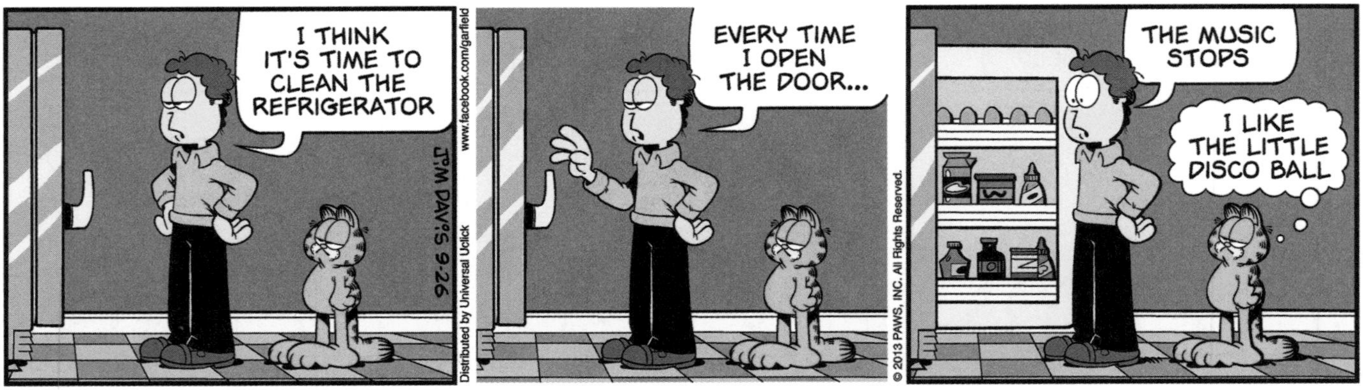
I THINK IT'S TIME TO CLEAN THE REFRIGERATOR
JIM DAVIS 9-26
www.facebook.com/garfield
Distributed by Universal Uclick
EVERY TIME I OPEN THE DOOR...
© 2013 PAWS, INC. All Rights Reserved.
THE MUSIC STOPS
I LIKE THE LITTLE DISCO BALL

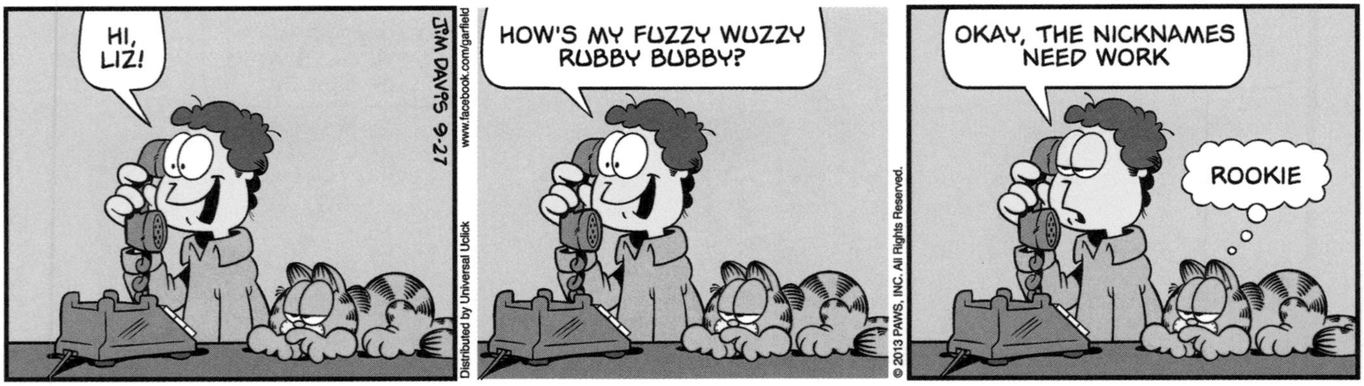
HI, LIZ!
JIM DAVIS 9-27
www.facebook.com/garfield
Distributed by Universal Uclick
HOW'S MY FUZZY WUZZY RUBBY BUBBY?
© 2013 PAWS, INC. All Rights Reserved.
OKAY, THE NICKNAMES NEED WORK
ROOKIE

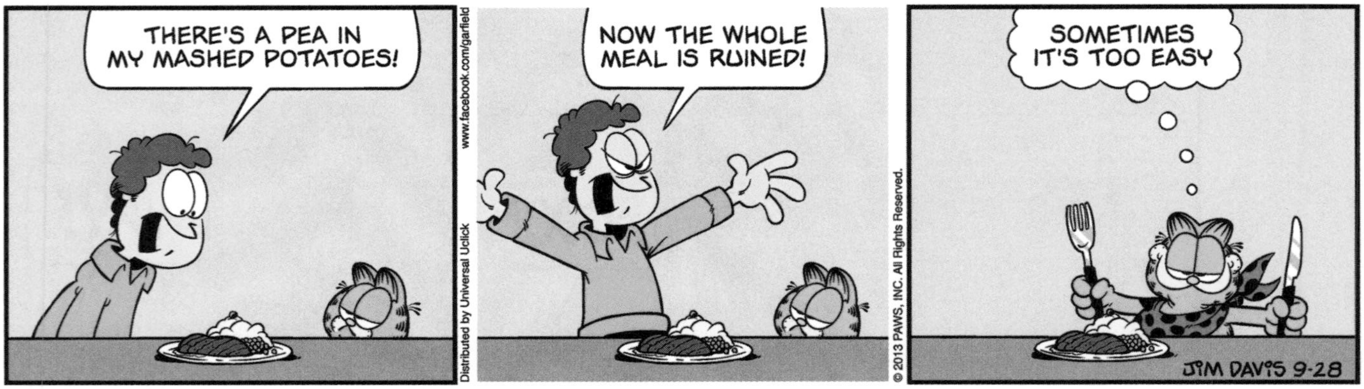
THERE'S A PEA IN MY MASHED POTATOES!
www.facebook.com/garfield
Distributed by Universal Uclick
NOW THE WHOLE MEAL IS RUINED!
© 2013 PAWS, INC. All Rights Reserved.
SOMETIMES IT'S TOO EASY
JIM DAVIS 9-28

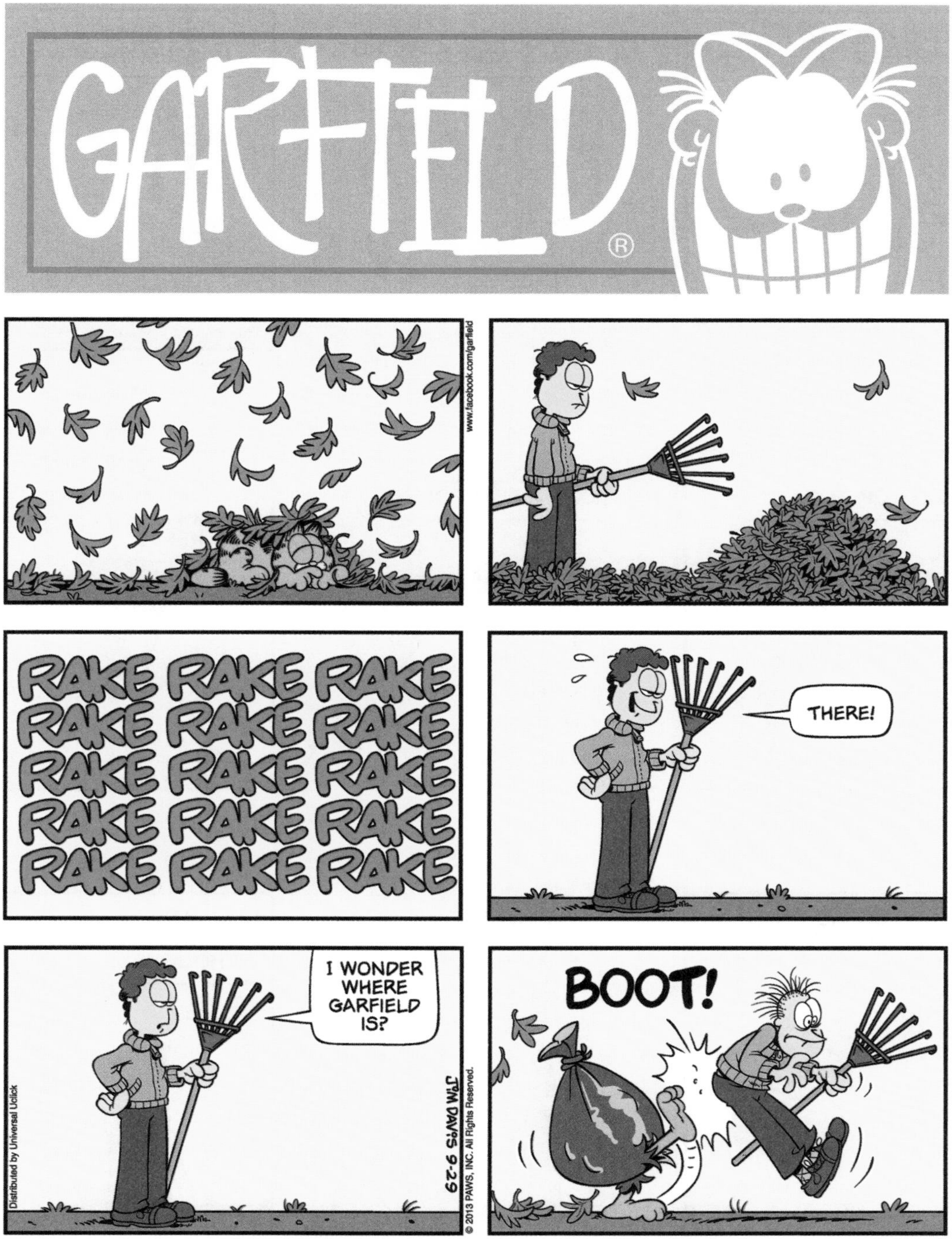
GARFIELD®
www.facebook.com/garfield
RAKE RAKE RAKE RAKE RAKE RAKE RAKE RAKE RAKE RAKE RAKE RAKE RAKE RAKE RAKE
THERE!
I WONDER WHERE GARFIELD IS?
JIM DAVIS 9-29
Distributed by Universal Uclick
© 2013 PAWS, INC. All Rights Reserved.
BOOT!

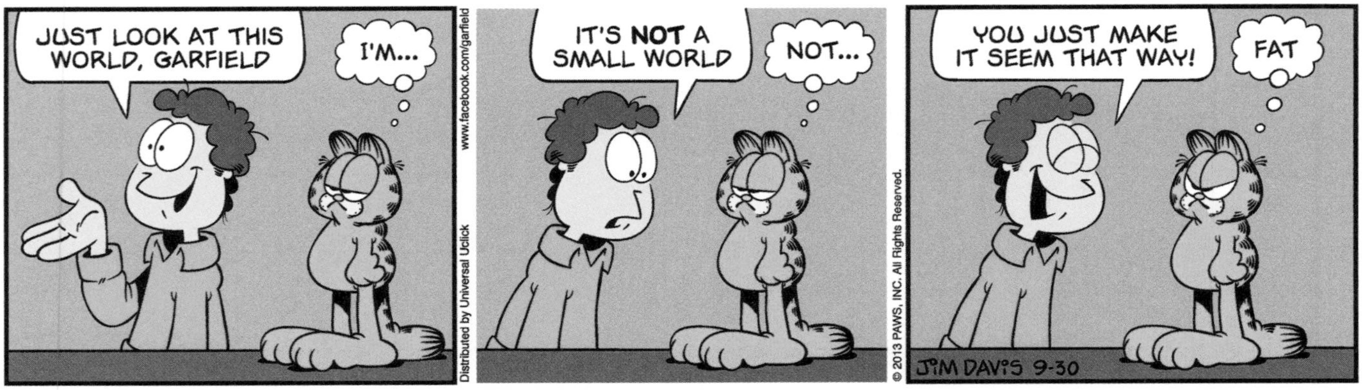
JUST LOOK AT THIS WORLD, GARFIELD
I'M...
IT'S **NOT** A SMALL WORLD
NOT...
YOU JUST MAKE IT SEEM THAT WAY!
FAT
JIM DAVIS 9-30
Distributed by Universal Uclick
www.facebook.com/garfield
© 2013 PAWS, INC. All Rights Reserved.

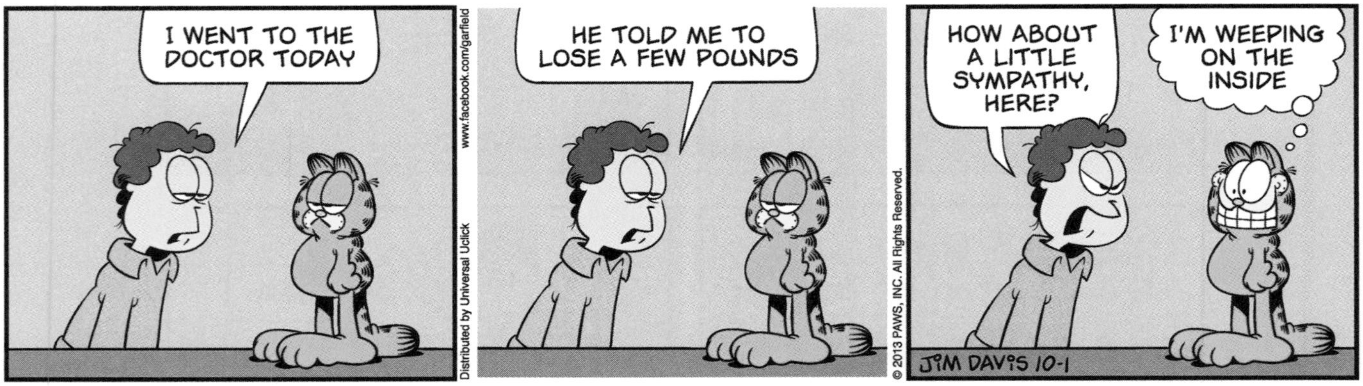
I WENT TO THE DOCTOR TODAY
HE TOLD ME TO LOSE A FEW POUNDS
HOW ABOUT A LITTLE SYMPATHY, HERE?
I'M WEEPING ON THE INSIDE
JIM DAVIS 10-1
Distributed by Universal Uclick
www.facebook.com/garfield
© 2013 PAWS, INC. All Rights Reserved.

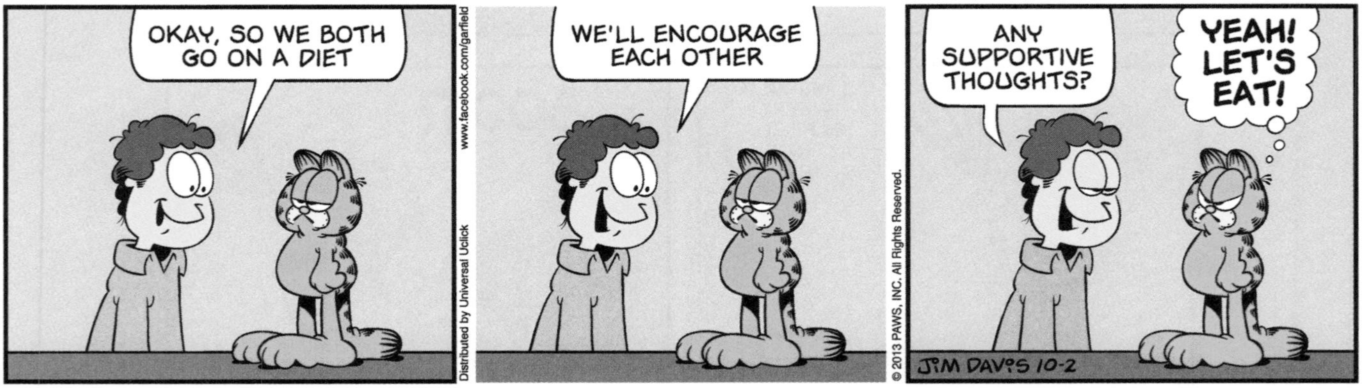
OKAY, SO WE BOTH GO ON A DIET
WE'LL ENCOURAGE EACH OTHER
ANY SUPPORTIVE THOUGHTS?
YEAH! LET'S EAT!
JIM DAVIS 10-2
Distributed by Universal Uclick
www.facebook.com/garfield
© 2013 PAWS, INC. All Rights Reserved.

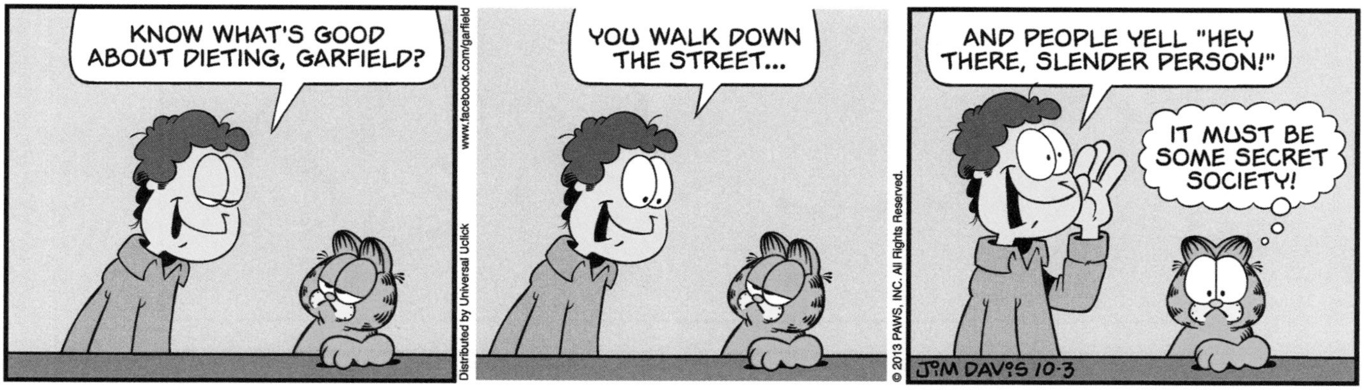
KNOW WHAT'S GOOD ABOUT DIETING, GARFIELD?
www.facebook.com/garfield
Distributed by Universal Uclick
YOU WALK DOWN THE STREET...
© 2013 PAWS, INC. All Rights Reserved.
AND PEOPLE YELL "HEY THERE, SLENDER PERSON!"
IT MUST BE SOME SECRET SOCIETY!
JIM DAVIS 10-3

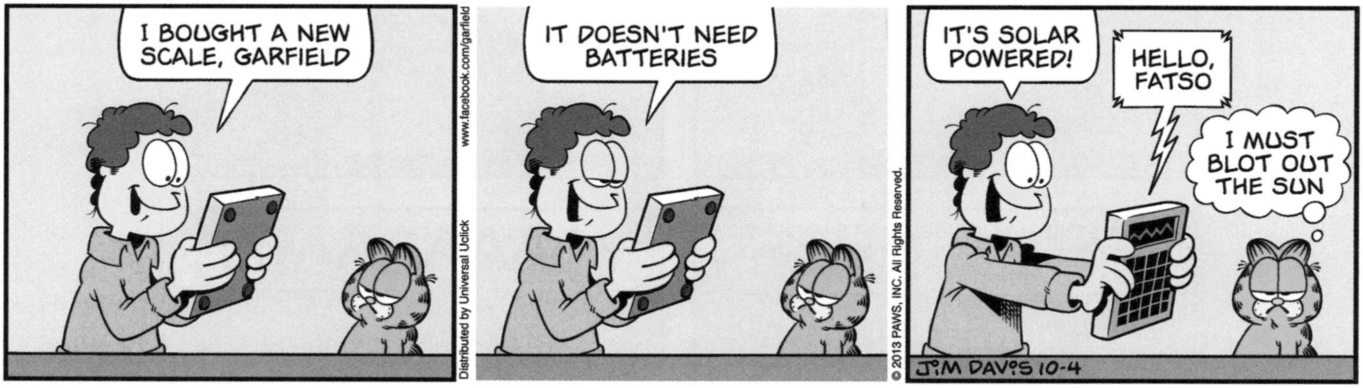
I BOUGHT A NEW SCALE, GARFIELD
www.facebook.com/garfield
Distributed by Universal Uclick
IT DOESN'T NEED BATTERIES
© 2013 PAWS, INC. All Rights Reserved.
IT'S SOLAR POWERED!
HELLO, FATSO
I MUST BLOT OUT THE SUN
JIM DAVIS 10-4

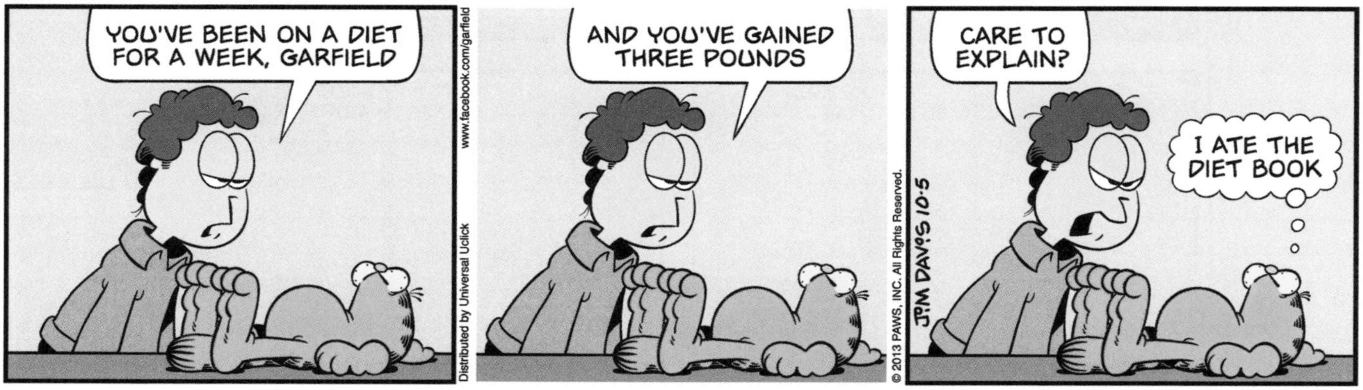
YOU'VE BEEN ON A DIET FOR A WEEK, GARFIELD
www.facebook.com/garfield
Distributed by Universal Uclick
AND YOU'VE GAINED THREE POUNDS
© 2013 PAWS, INC. All Rights Reserved.
JIM DAVIS 10-5
CARE TO EXPLAIN?
I ATE THE DIET BOOK

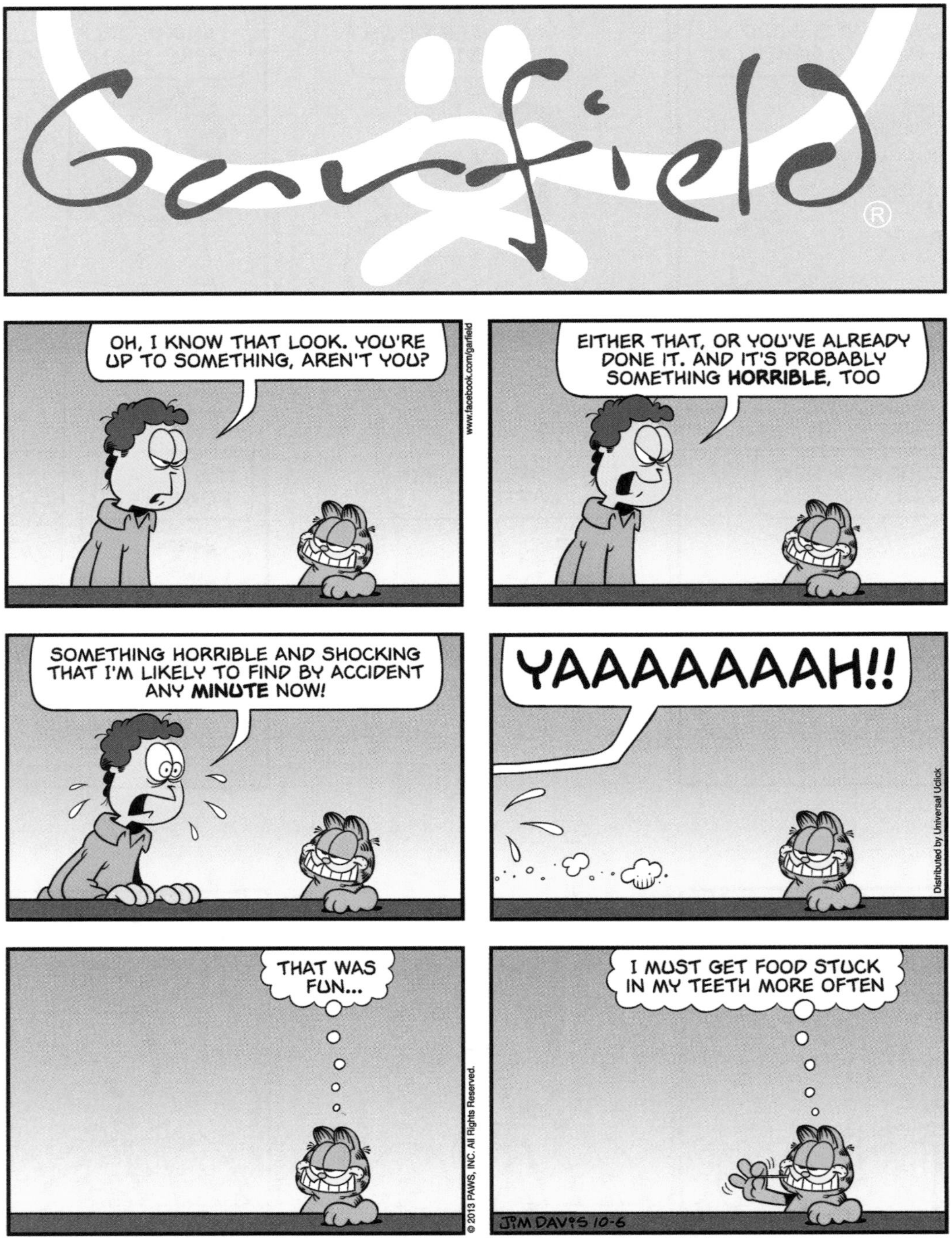
Garfield®
OH, I KNOW THAT LOOK. YOU'RE UP TO SOMETHING, AREN'T YOU?
www.facebook.com/garfield
EITHER THAT, OR YOU'VE ALREADY DONE IT. AND IT'S PROBABLY SOMETHING HORRIBLE, TOO
SOMETHING HORRIBLE AND SHOCKING THAT I'M LIKELY TO FIND BY ACCIDENT ANY MINUTE NOW!
YAAAAAAAH!!
Distributed by Universal Uclick
THAT WAS FUN...
© 2013 PAWS, INC. All Rights Reserved.
I MUST GET FOOD STUCK IN MY TEETH MORE OFTEN
JIM DAVIS 10-6

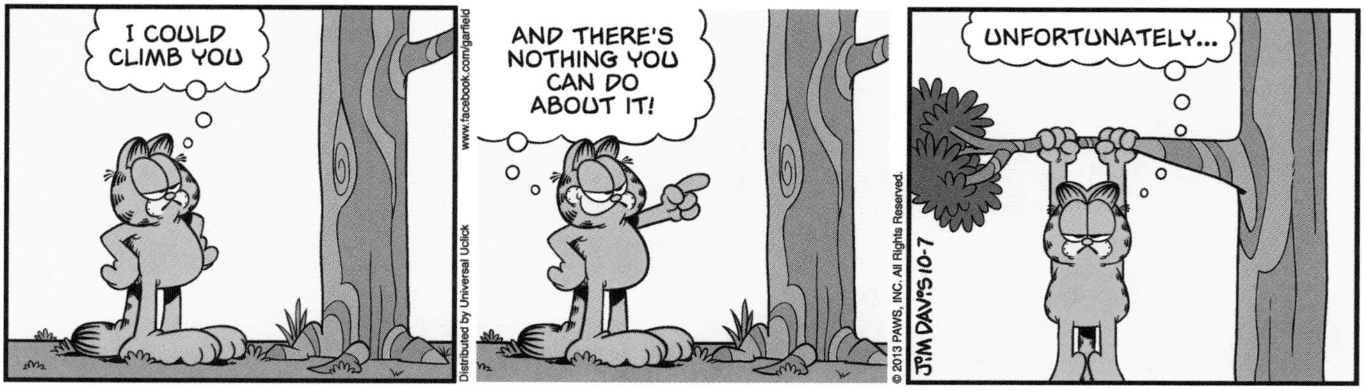
I COULD CLIMB YOU
AND THERE'S NOTHING YOU CAN DO ABOUT IT!
UNFORTUNATELY...
www.facebook.com/garfield
Distributed by Universal Uclick
© 2013 PAWS, INC. All Rights Reserved.
JIM DAVIS 10-7

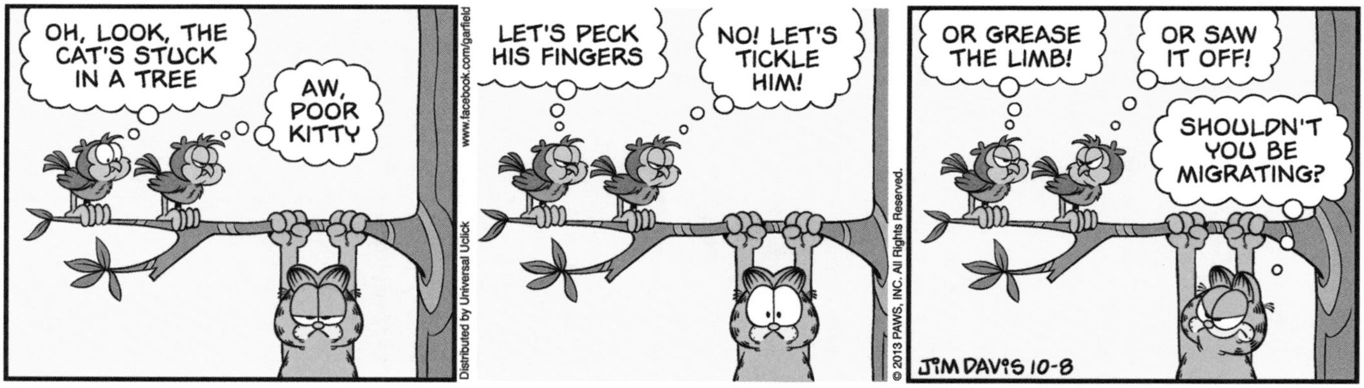
OH, LOOK, THE CAT'S STUCK IN A TREE
AW, POOR KITTY
LET'S PECK HIS FINGERS
NO! LET'S TICKLE HIM!
OR GREASE THE LIMB!
OR SAW IT OFF!
SHOULDN'T YOU BE MIGRATING?
www.facebook.com/garfield
Distributed by Universal Uclick
© 2013 PAWS, INC. All Rights Reserved.
JIM DAVIS 10-8

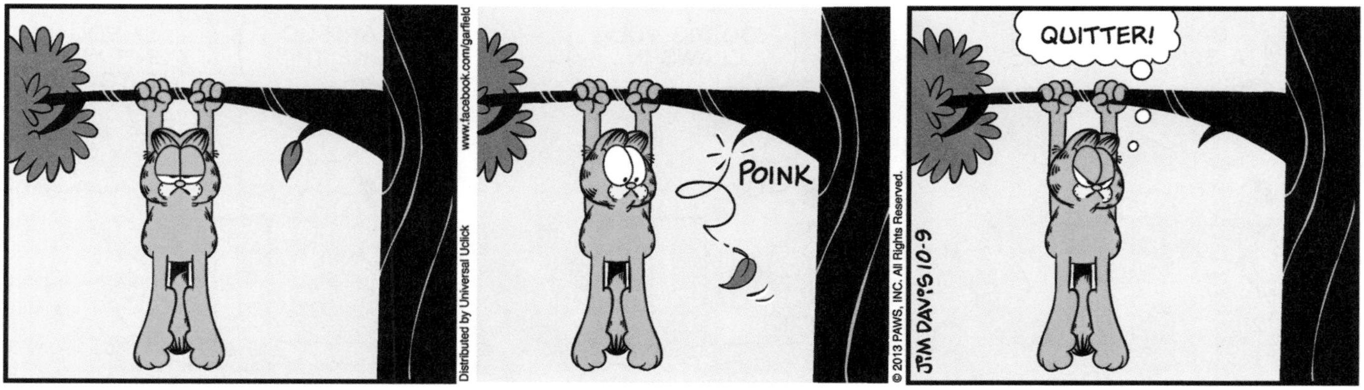
POINK
QUITTER!
www.facebook.com/garfield
Distributed by Universal Uclick
© 2013 PAWS, INC. All Rights Reserved.
JIM DAVIS 10-9

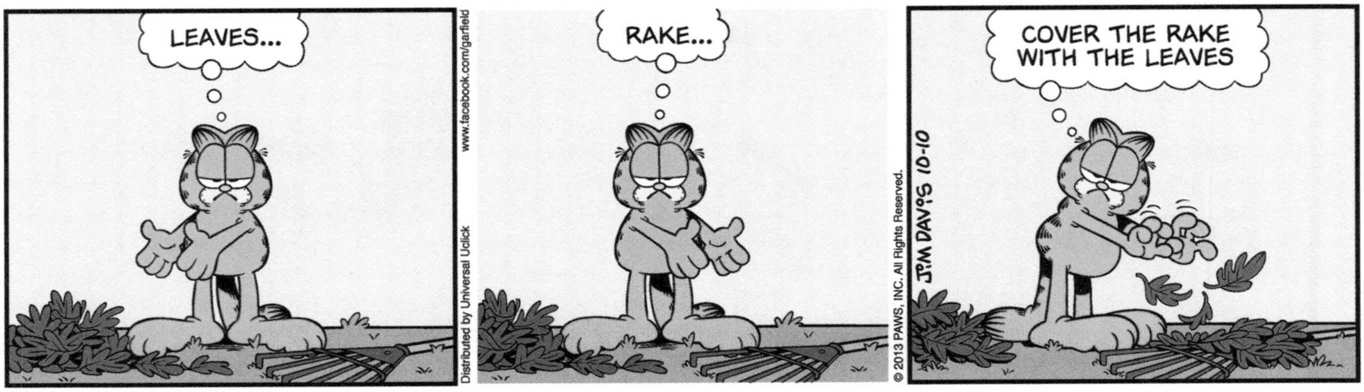
LEAVES...
RAKE...
COVER THE RAKE WITH THE LEAVES
JIM DAVIS 10-10
Distributed by Universal Uclick www.facebook.com/garfield
© 2013 PAWS, INC. All Rights Reserved.

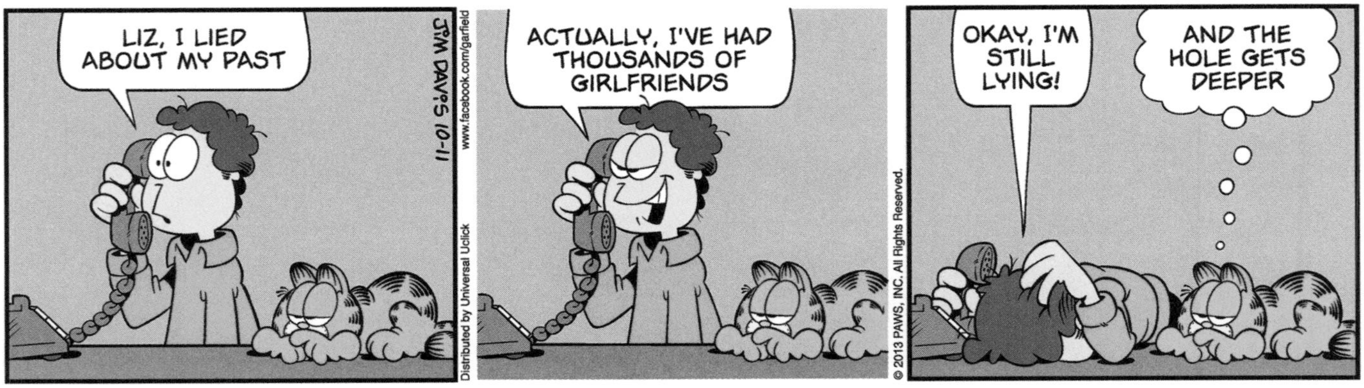
LIZ, I LIED ABOUT MY PAST
JIM DAVIS 10-11
ACTUALLY, I'VE HAD THOUSANDS OF GIRLFRIENDS
OKAY, I'M STILL LYING!
AND THE HOLE GETS DEEPER
Distributed by Universal Uclick www.facebook.com/garfield
© 2013 PAWS, INC. All Rights Reserved.

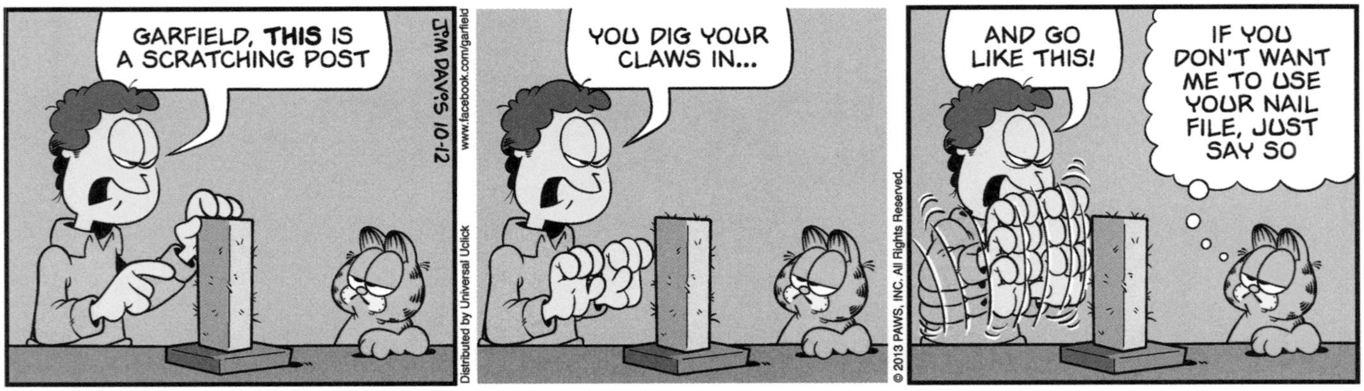
GARFIELD, THIS IS A SCRATCHING POST
JIM DAVIS 10-12
YOU DIG YOUR CLAWS IN...
AND GO LIKE THIS!
IF YOU DON'T WANT ME TO USE YOUR NAIL FILE, JUST SAY SO
Distributed by Universal Uclick www.facebook.com/garfield
© 2013 PAWS, INC. All Rights Reserved.

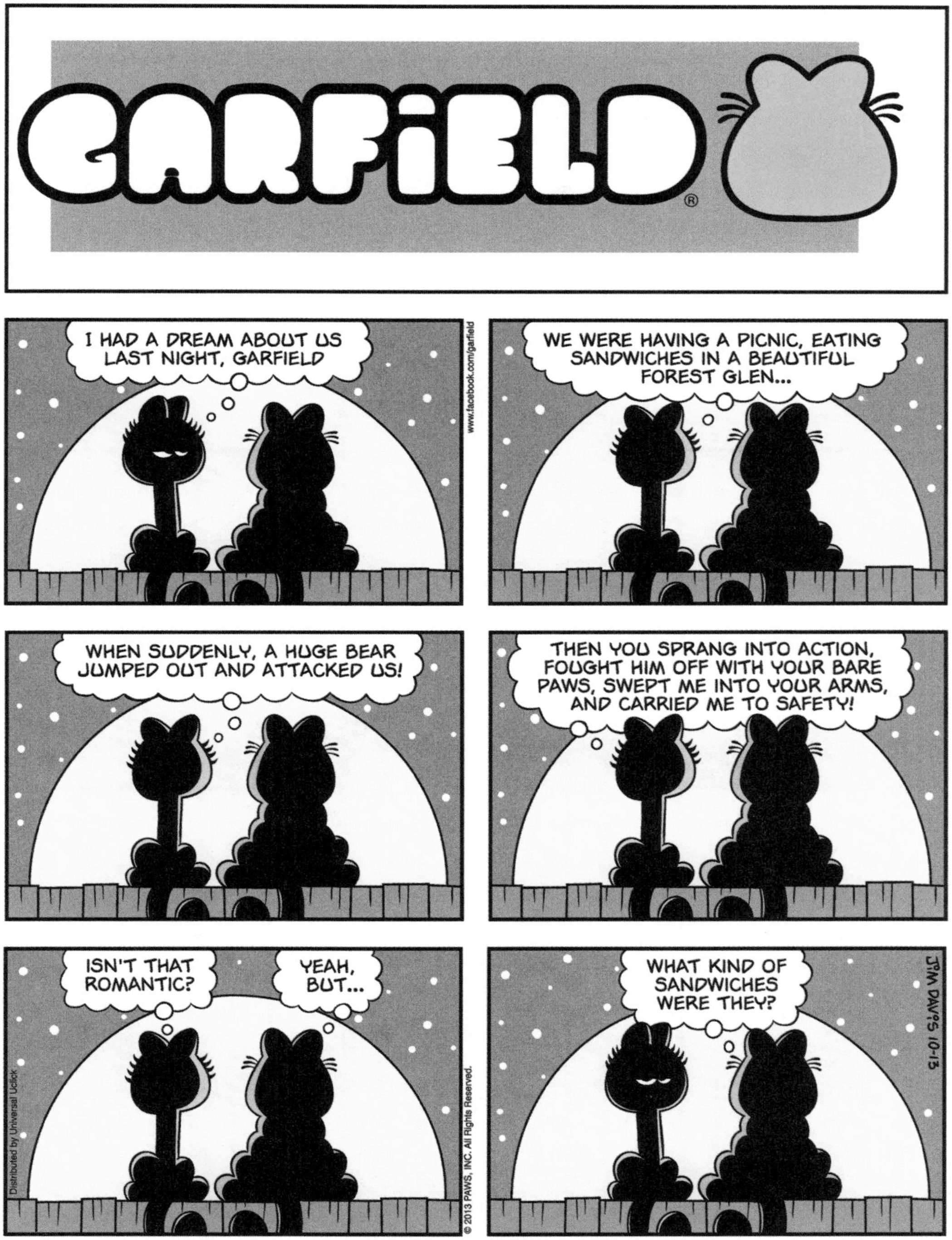
GARFIELD
I HAD A DREAM ABOUT US LAST NIGHT, GARFIELD
www.facebook.com/garfield
WE WERE HAVING A PICNIC, EATING SANDWICHES IN A BEAUTIFUL FOREST GLEN...
WHEN SUDDENLY, A HUGE BEAR JUMPED OUT AND ATTACKED US!
THEN YOU SPRANG INTO ACTION, FOUGHT HIM OFF WITH YOUR BARE PAWS, SWEPT ME INTO YOUR ARMS, AND CARRIED ME TO SAFETY!
ISN'T THAT ROMANTIC?
YEAH, BUT...
Distributed by Universal Uclick
© 2013 PAWS, INC. All Rights Reserved.
WHAT KIND OF SANDWICHES WERE THEY?
JIM DAVIS 10-13

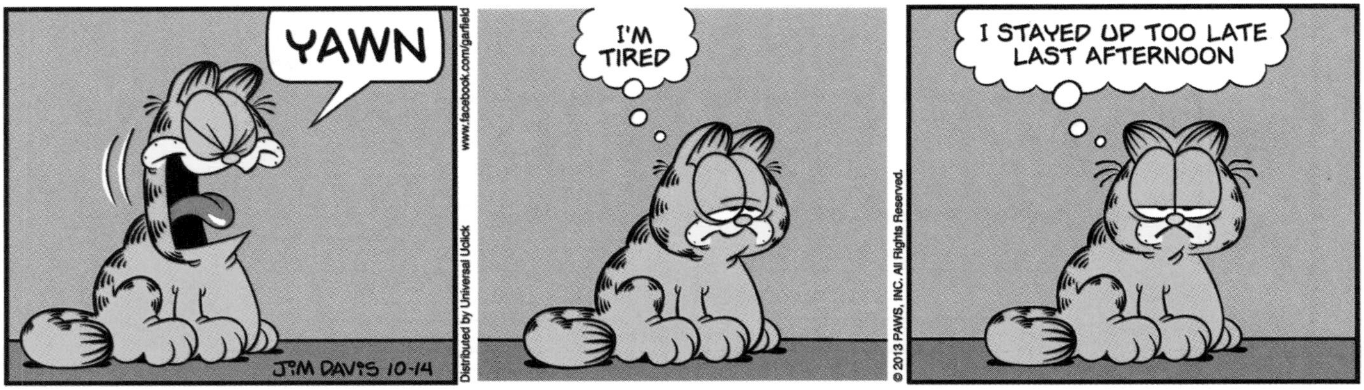
YAWN
JIM DAVIS 10-14
www.facebook.com/garfield
Distributed by Universal Uclick
I'M TIRED
© 2013 PAWS, INC. All Rights Reserved.
I STAYED UP TOO LATE LAST AFTERNOON

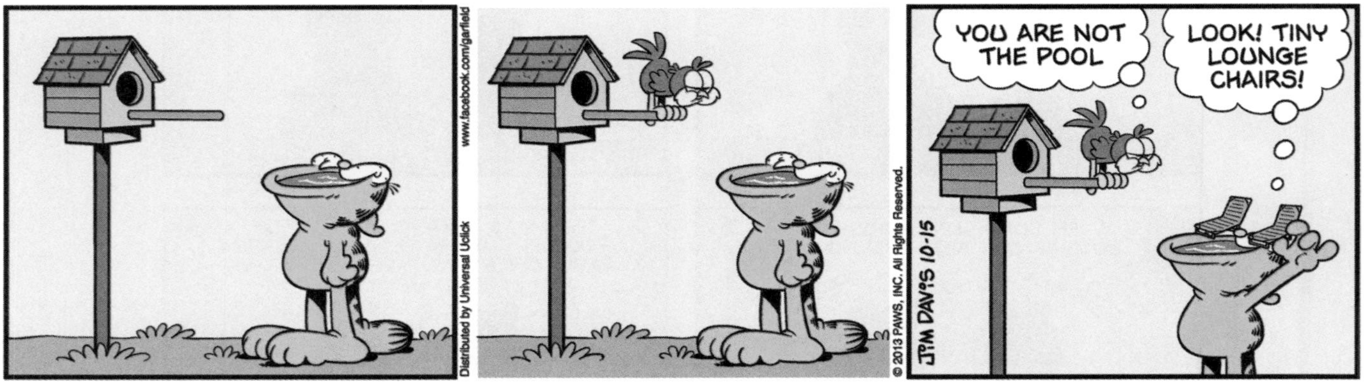
www.facebook.com/garfield
Distributed by Universal Uclick
© 2013 PAWS, INC. All Rights Reserved.
JIM DAVIS 10-15
YOU ARE NOT THE POOL
LOOK! TINY LOUNGE CHAIRS!

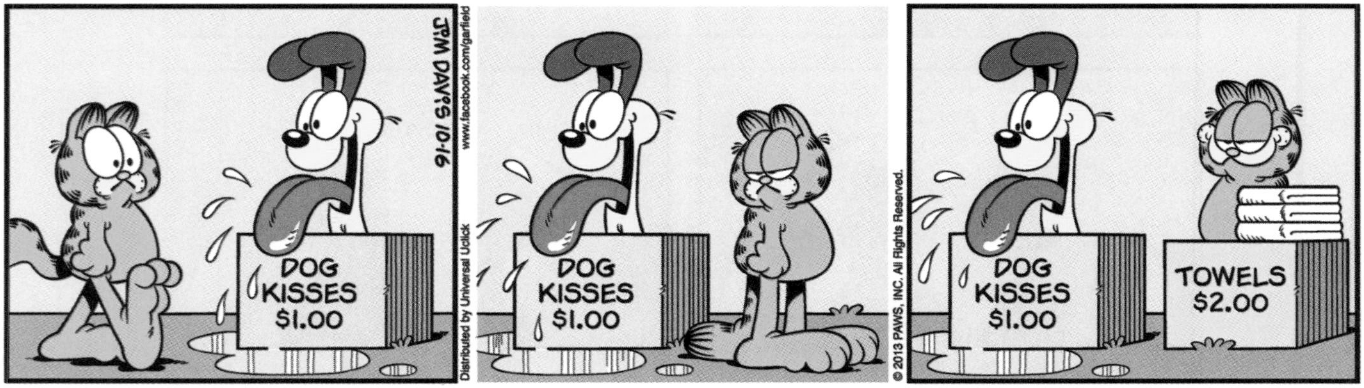
JIM DAVIS 10-16
DOG KISSES $1.00
www.facebook.com/garfield
Distributed by Universal Uclick
DOG KISSES $1.00
© 2013 PAWS, INC. All Rights Reserved.
DOG KISSES $1.00
TOWELS $2.00

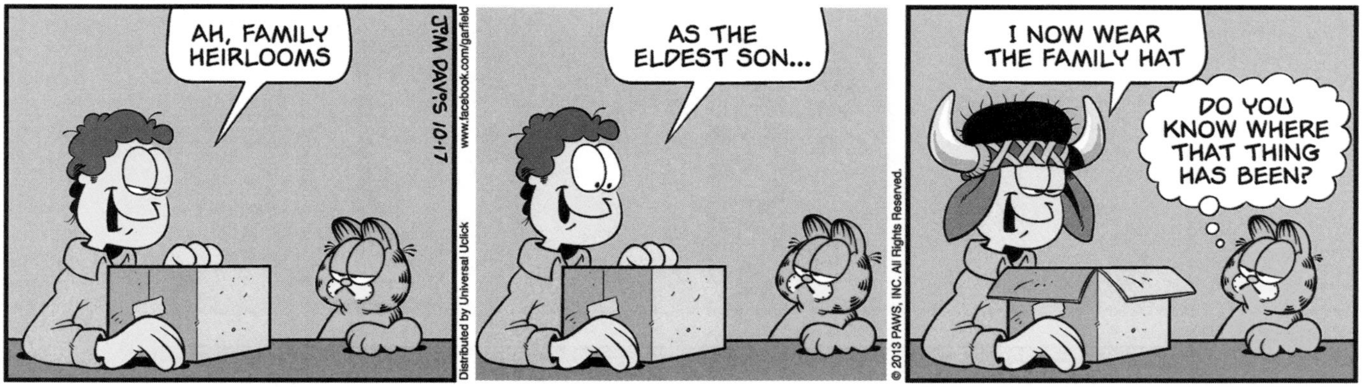
AH, FAMILY HEIRLOOMS
JIM DAVIS 10-17
www.facebook.com/garfield
Distributed by Universal Uclick
AS THE ELDEST SON...
© 2013 PAWS, INC. All Rights Reserved.
I NOW WEAR THE FAMILY HAT
DO YOU KNOW WHERE THAT THING HAS BEEN?

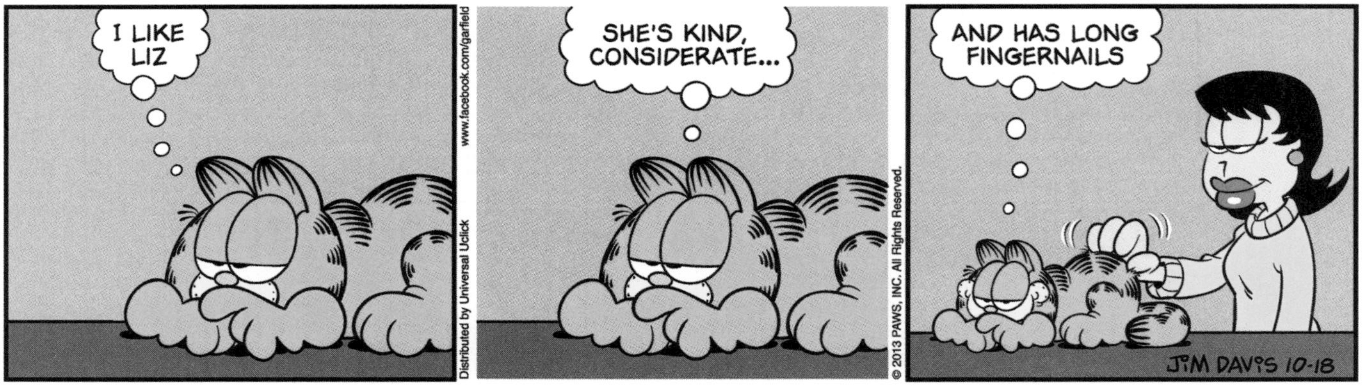
I LIKE LIZ
www.facebook.com/garfield
Distributed by Universal Uclick
SHE'S KIND, CONSIDERATE...
© 2013 PAWS, INC. All Rights Reserved.
AND HAS LONG FINGERNAILS
JIM DAVIS 10-18

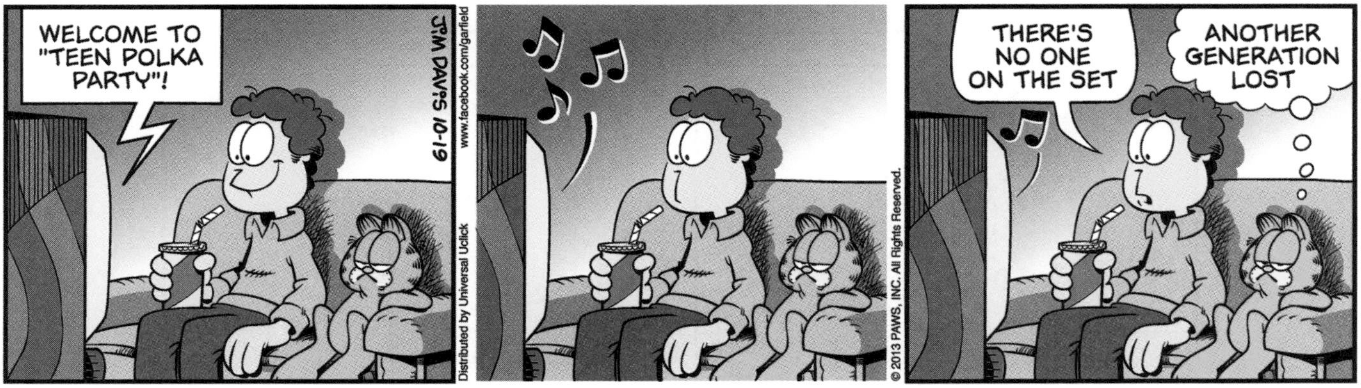
WELCOME TO "TEEN POLKA PARTY"!
JIM DAVIS 10-19
www.facebook.com/garfield
Distributed by Universal Uclick
© 2013 PAWS, INC. All Rights Reserved.
THERE'S NO ONE ON THE SET
ANOTHER GENERATION LOST

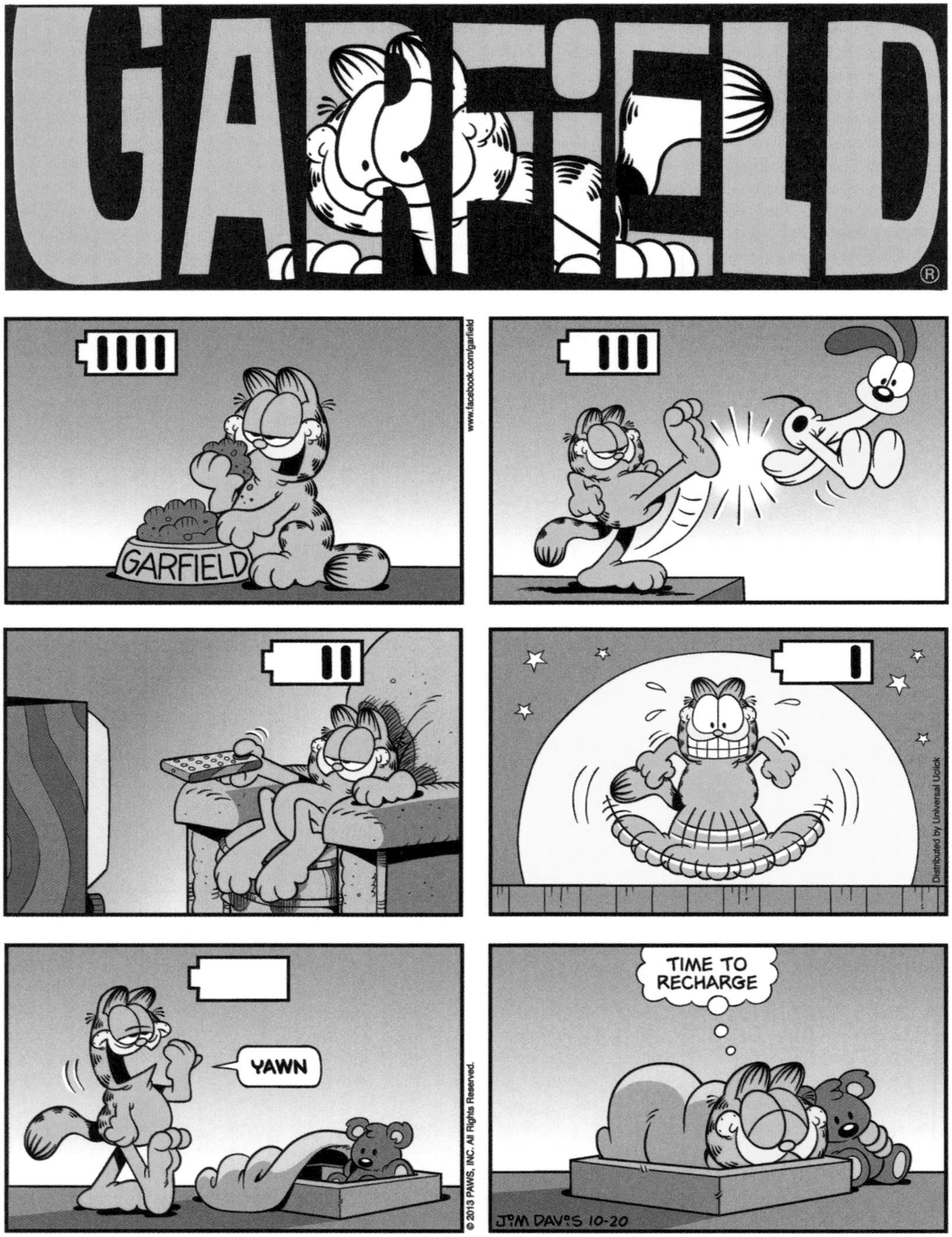
GARFIELD
GARFIELD
www.facebook.com/garfield
Distributed by Universal Uclick
YAWN
© 2013 PAWS, INC. All Rights Reserved.
TIME TO RECHARGE
JIM DAVIS 10-20

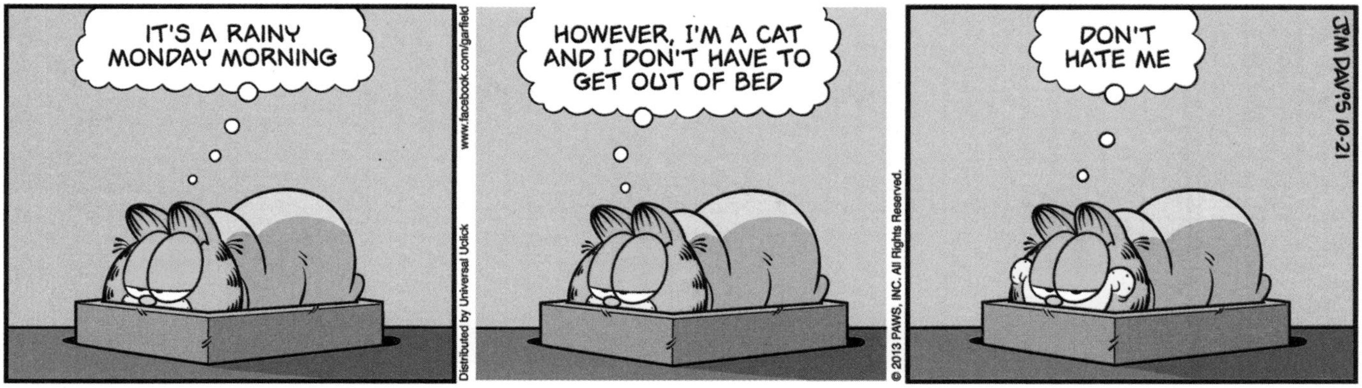
IT'S A RAINY MONDAY MORNING
HOWEVER, I'M A CAT AND I DON'T HAVE TO GET OUT OF BED
DON'T HATE ME
JIM DAVIS 10-21
Distributed by Universal Uclick www.facebook.com/garfield
© 2013 PAWS, INC. All Rights Reserved.

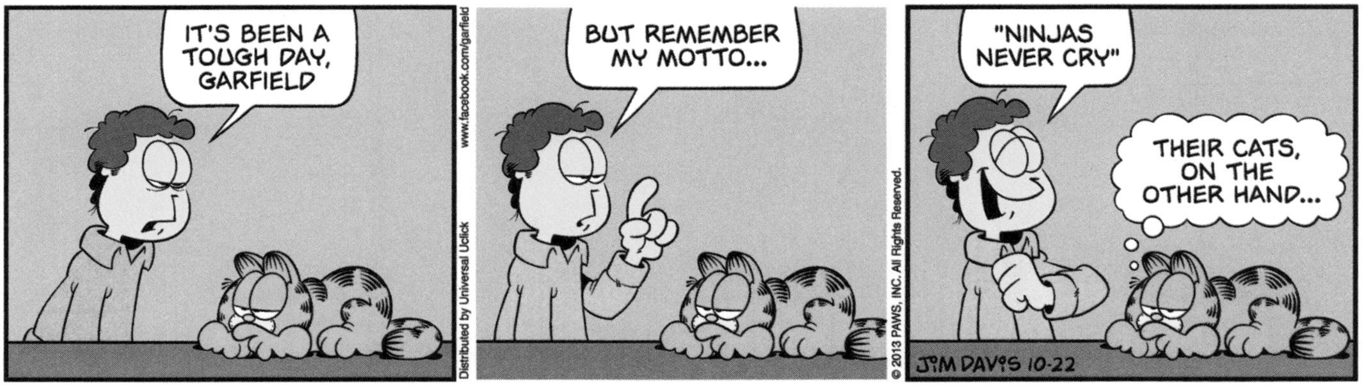
IT'S BEEN A TOUGH DAY, GARFIELD
BUT REMEMBER MY MOTTO...
"NINJAS NEVER CRY"
THEIR CATS, ON THE OTHER HAND...
JIM DAVIS 10-22
Distributed by Universal Uclick www.facebook.com/garfield
© 2013 PAWS, INC. All Rights Reserved.

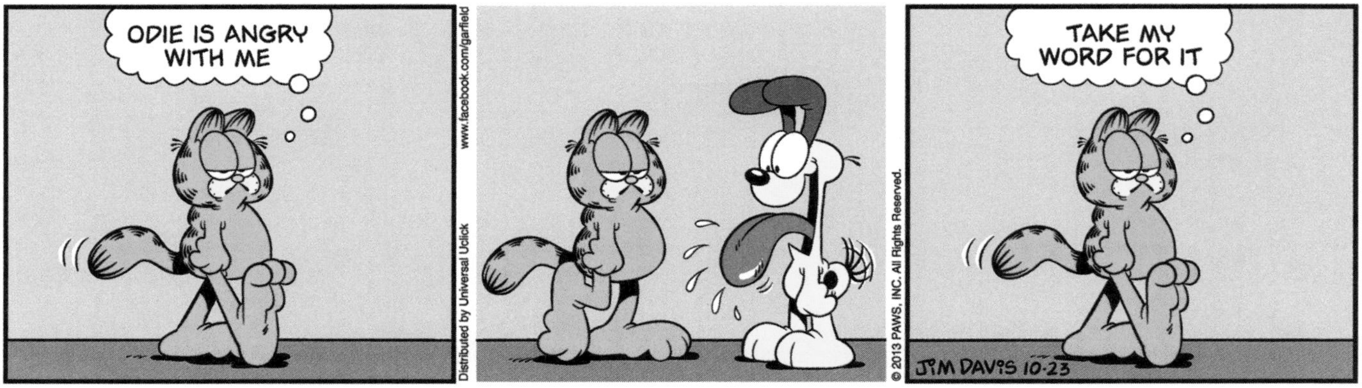
ODIE IS ANGRY WITH ME
TAKE MY WORD FOR IT
JIM DAVIS 10-23
Distributed by Universal Uclick www.facebook.com/garfield
© 2013 PAWS, INC. All Rights Reserved.

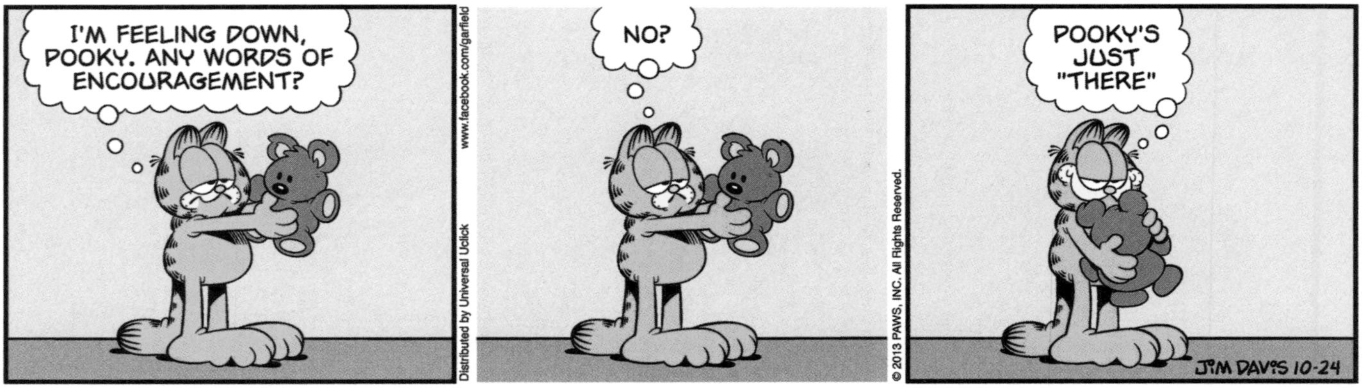
I'M FEELING DOWN, POOKY. ANY WORDS OF ENCOURAGEMENT?
NO?
POOKY'S JUST "THERE"
Distributed by Universal Uclick
www.facebook.com/garfield
© 2013 PAWS, INC. All Rights Reserved.
JIM DAVIS 10-24

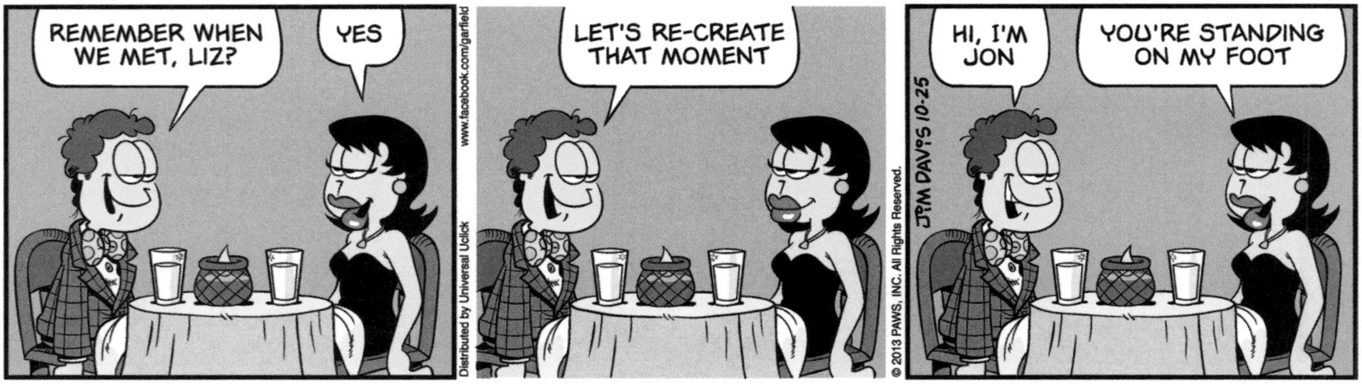
REMEMBER WHEN WE MET, LIZ?
YES
LET'S RE-CREATE THAT MOMENT
HI, I'M JON
YOU'RE STANDING ON MY FOOT
Distributed by Universal Uclick
www.facebook.com/garfield
© 2013 PAWS, INC. All Rights Reserved.
JIM DAVIS 10-25

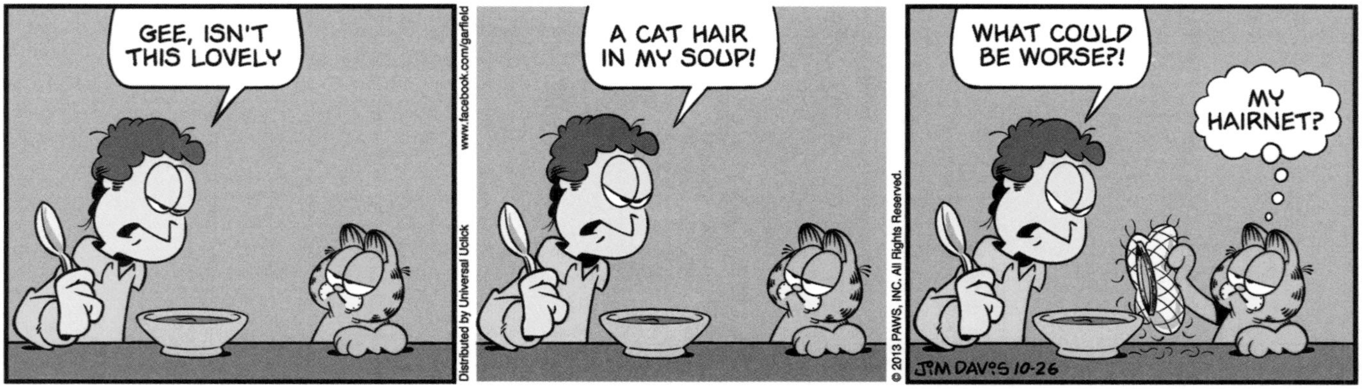
GEE, ISN'T THIS LOVELY
A CAT HAIR IN MY SOUP!
WHAT COULD BE WORSE?!
MY HAIRNET?
Distributed by Universal Uclick
www.facebook.com/garfield
© 2013 PAWS, INC. All Rights Reserved.
JIM DAVIS 10-26

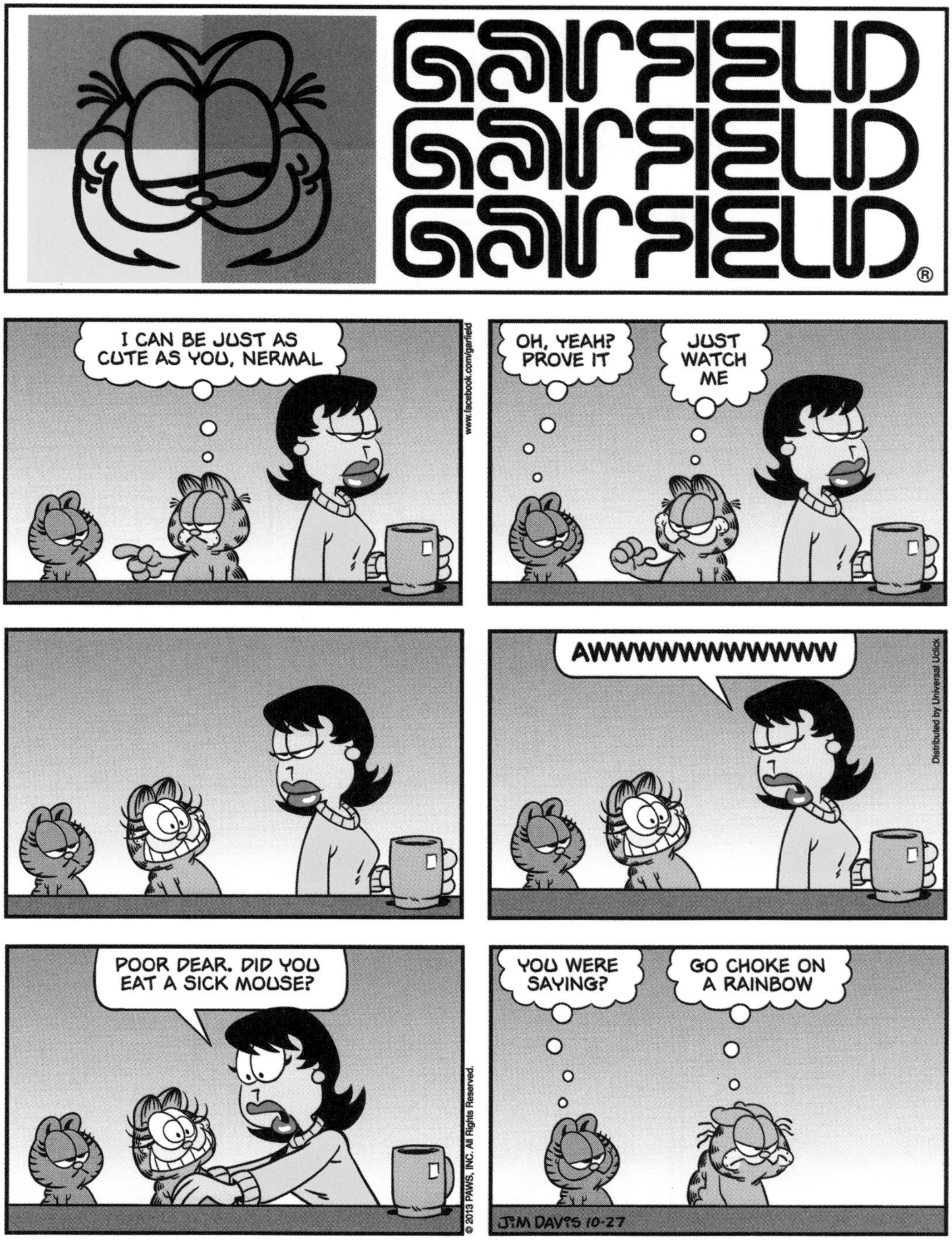
GARFIELD
GARFIELD
GARFIELD
I CAN BE JUST AS CUTE AS YOU, NERMAL
www.facebook.com/garfield
OH, YEAH? PROVE IT
JUST WATCH ME
AWWWWWWWWWWWW
Distributed by Universal Uclick
POOR DEAR. DID YOU EAT A SICK MOUSE?
© 2013 PAWS, INC. All Rights Reserved.
YOU WERE SAYING?
GO CHOKE ON A RAINBOW
JIM DAVIS 10-27

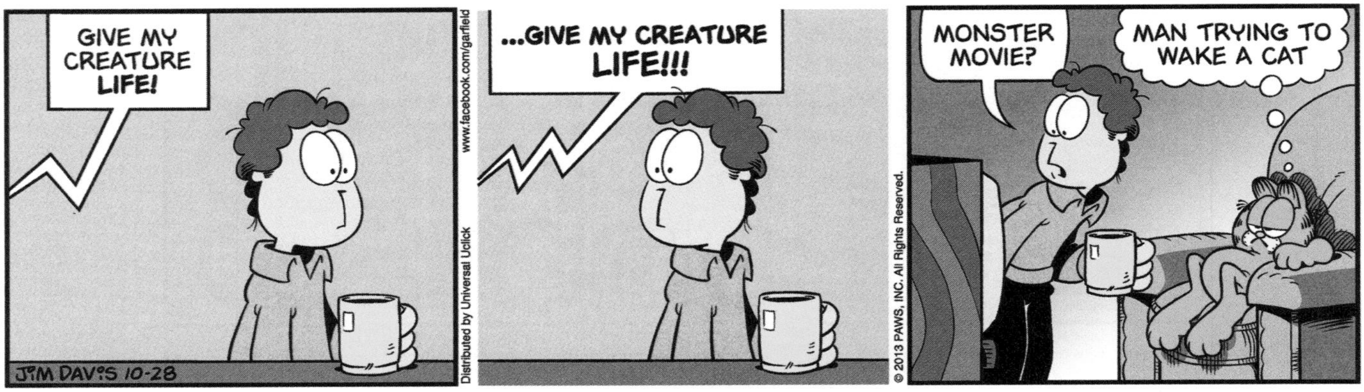
GIVE MY CREATURE LIFE!
JIM DAVIS 10-28
www.facebook.com/garfield
Distributed by Universal Uclick
...GIVE MY CREATURE LIFE!!!
© 2013 PAWS, INC. All Rights Reserved.
MONSTER MOVIE?
MAN TRYING TO WAKE A CAT

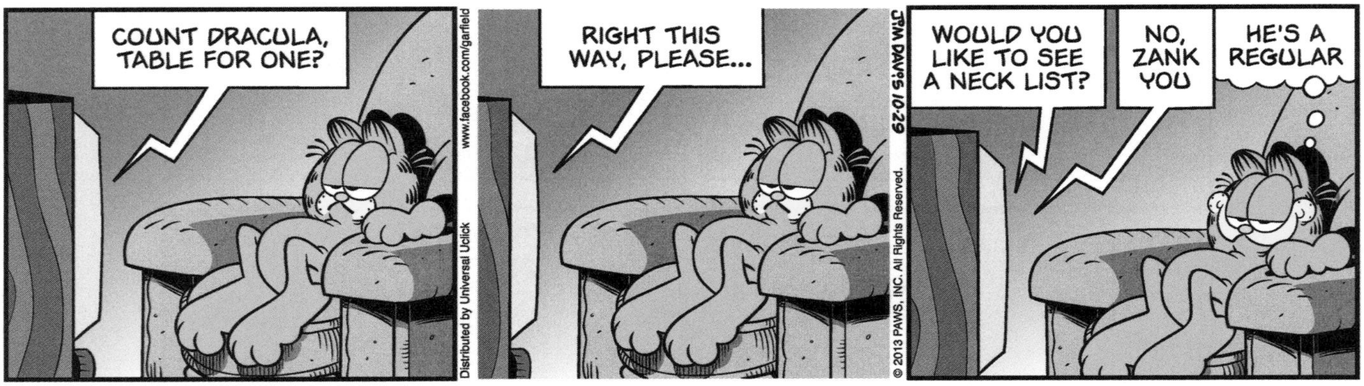
COUNT DRACULA, TABLE FOR ONE?
www.facebook.com/garfield
Distributed by Universal Uclick
RIGHT THIS WAY, PLEASE...
JIM DAVIS 10-29
© 2013 PAWS, INC. All Rights Reserved.
WOULD YOU LIKE TO SEE A NECK LIST?
NO, ZANK YOU
HE'S A REGULAR

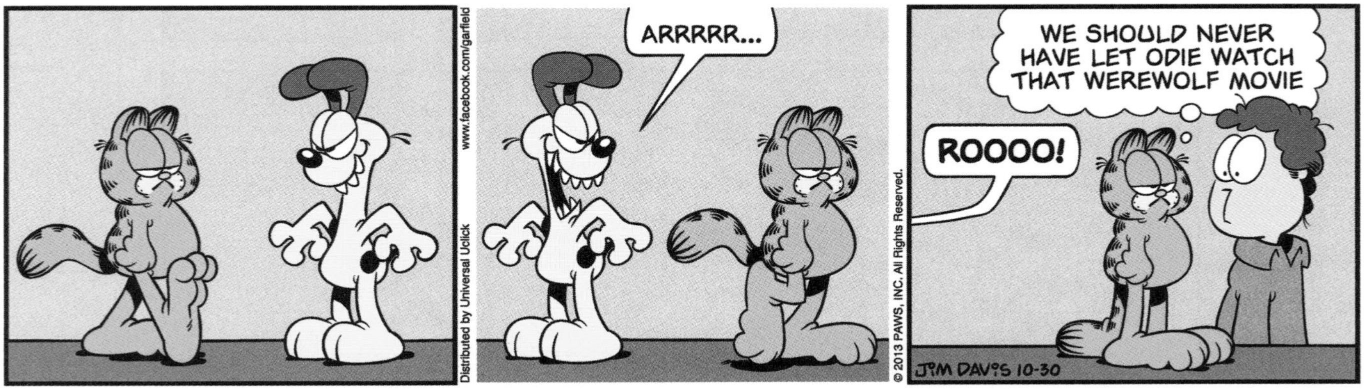
www.facebook.com/garfield
Distributed by Universal Uclick
ARRRRR...
© 2013 PAWS, INC. All Rights Reserved.
WE SHOULD NEVER HAVE LET ODIE WATCH THAT WEREWOLF MOVIE
ROOOO!
JIM DAVIS 10-30

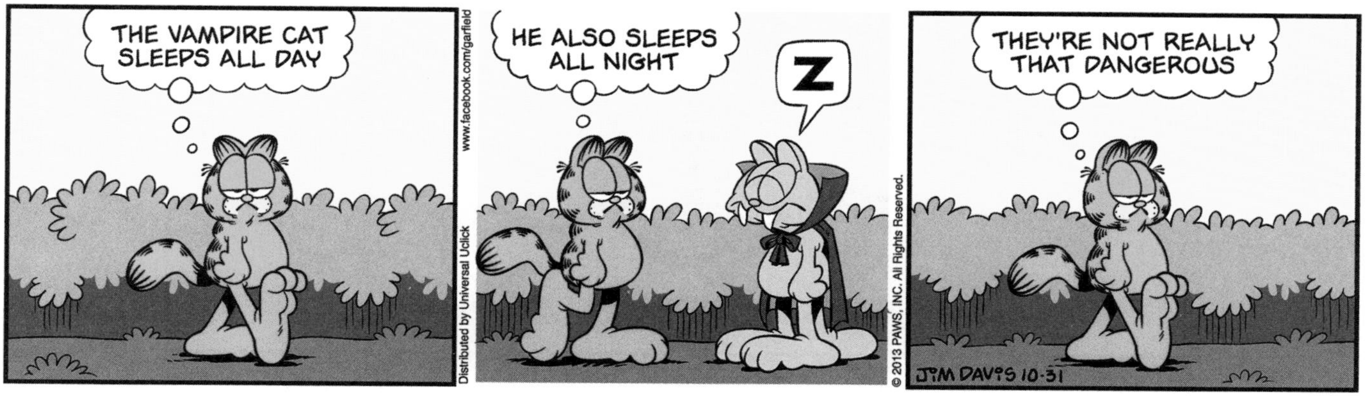
THE VAMPIRE CAT SLEEPS ALL DAY
Distributed by Universal Uclick
www.facebook.com/garfield
HE ALSO SLEEPS ALL NIGHT
Z
© 2013 PAWS, INC. All Rights Reserved.
THEY'RE NOT REALLY THAT DANGEROUS
JIM DAVIS 10-31

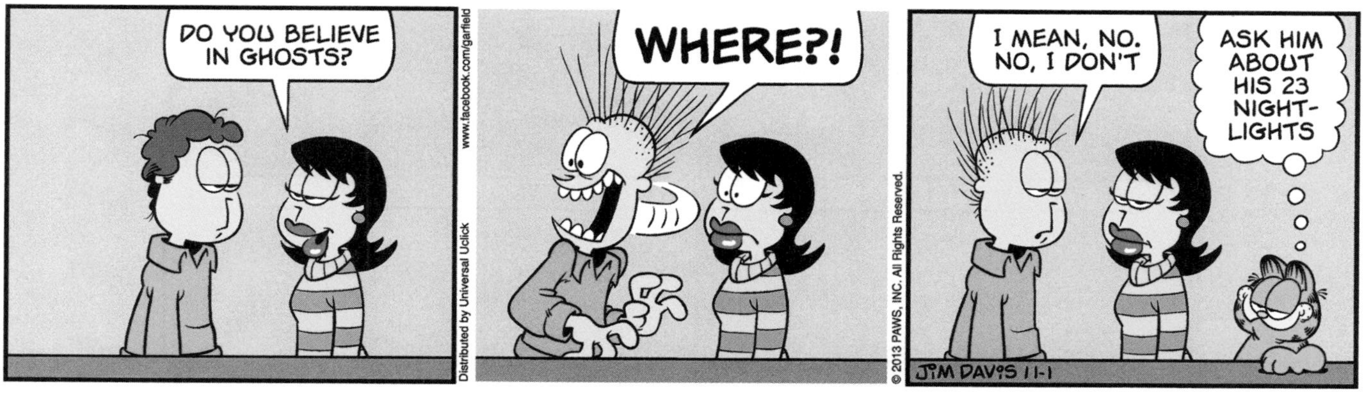
DO YOU BELIEVE IN GHOSTS?
Distributed by Universal Uclick
www.facebook.com/garfield
WHERE?!
© 2013 PAWS, INC. All Rights Reserved.
I MEAN, NO. NO, I DON'T
ASK HIM ABOUT HIS 23 NIGHT-LIGHTS
JIM DAVIS 11-1

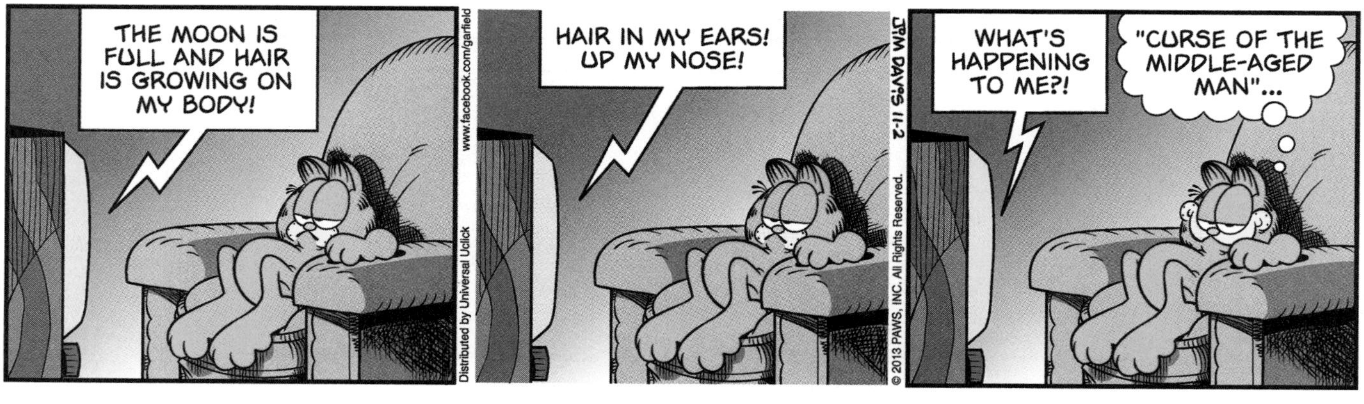
THE MOON IS FULL AND HAIR IS GROWING ON MY BODY!
Distributed by Universal Uclick
www.facebook.com/garfield
HAIR IN MY EARS! UP MY NOSE!
JIM DAVIS 11-2
© 2013 PAWS, INC. All Rights Reserved.
WHAT'S HAPPENING TO ME?!
"CURSE OF THE MIDDLE-AGED MAN"...

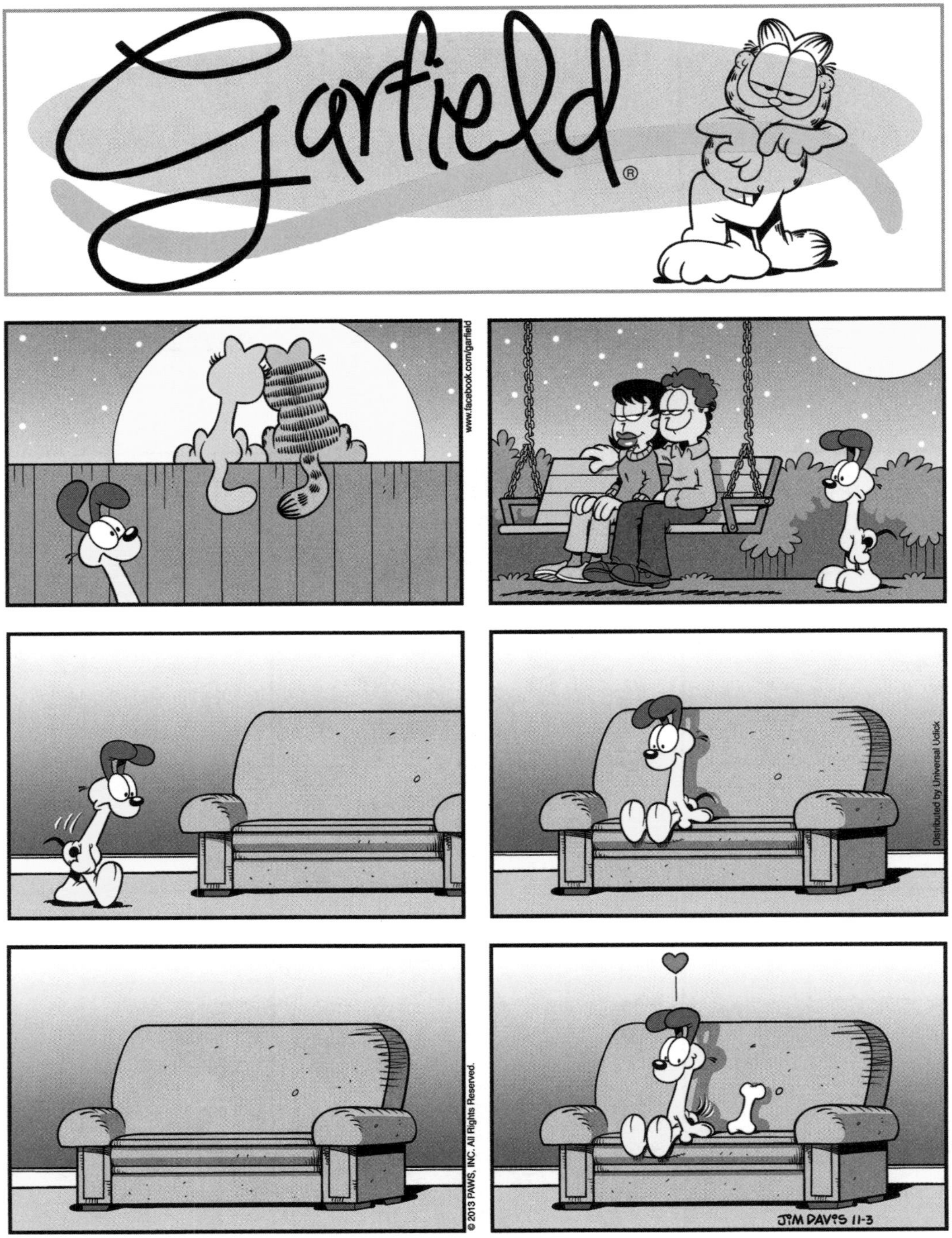
Garfield®
www.facebook.com/garfield
Distributed by Universal Uclick
© 2013 PAWS, INC. All Rights Reserved.
JIM DAVIS 11-3

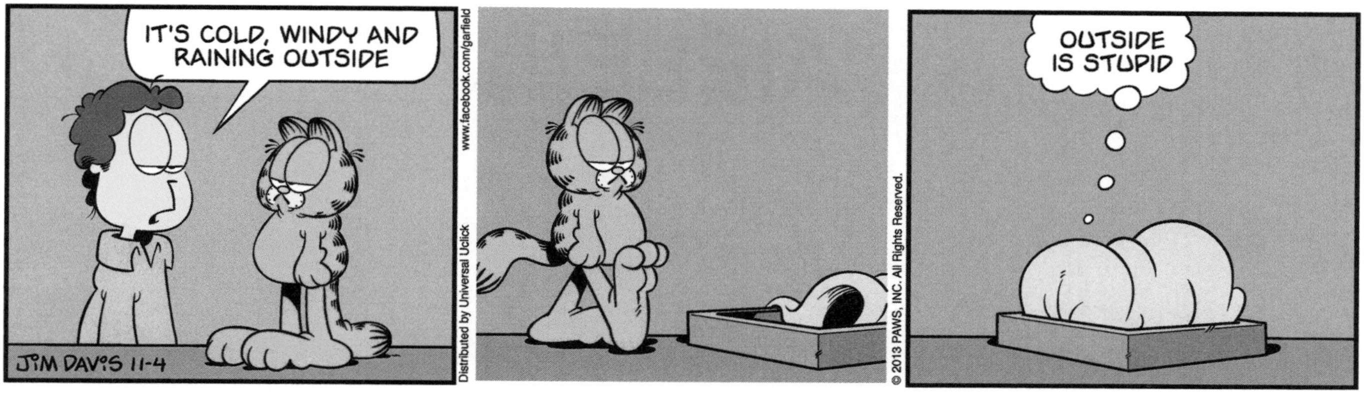
IT'S COLD, WINDY AND RAINING OUTSIDE
OUTSIDE IS STUPID
JIM DAVIS 11-4
Distributed by Universal Uclick www.facebook.com/garfield
© 2013 PAWS, INC. All Rights Reserved.

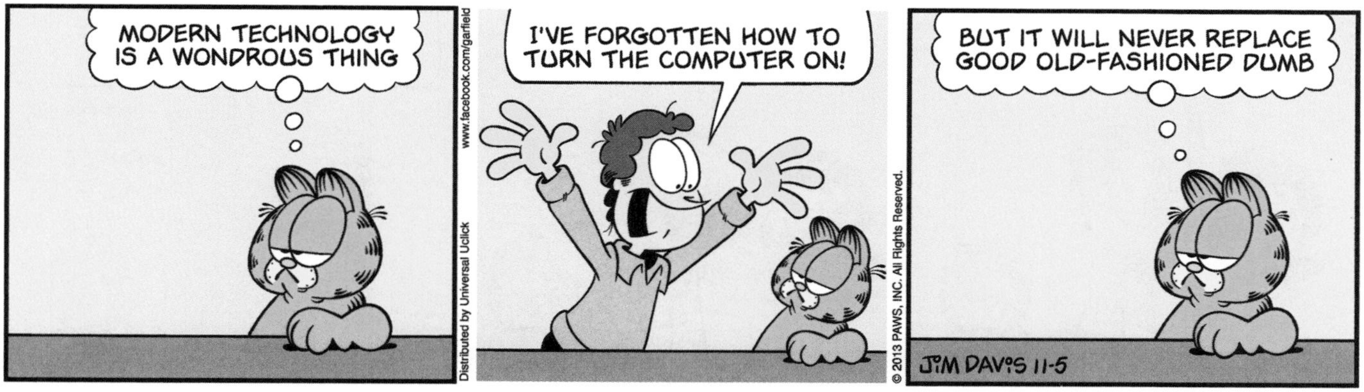
MODERN TECHNOLOGY IS A WONDROUS THING
I'VE FORGOTTEN HOW TO TURN THE COMPUTER ON!
BUT IT WILL NEVER REPLACE GOOD OLD-FASHIONED DUMB
JIM DAVIS 11-5
Distributed by Universal Uclick www.facebook.com/garfield
© 2013 PAWS, INC. All Rights Reserved.

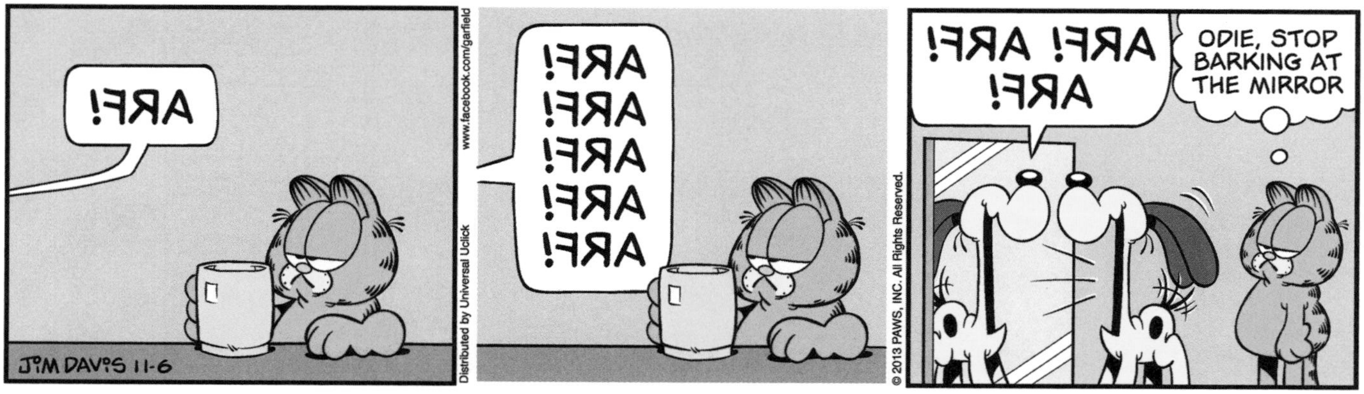
ARF!
ARF! ARF! ARF! ARF! ARF!
ARF! ARF! ARF!
ODIE, STOP BARKING AT THE MIRROR
JIM DAVIS 11-6
Distributed by Universal Uclick www.facebook.com/garfield
© 2013 PAWS, INC. All Rights Reserved.

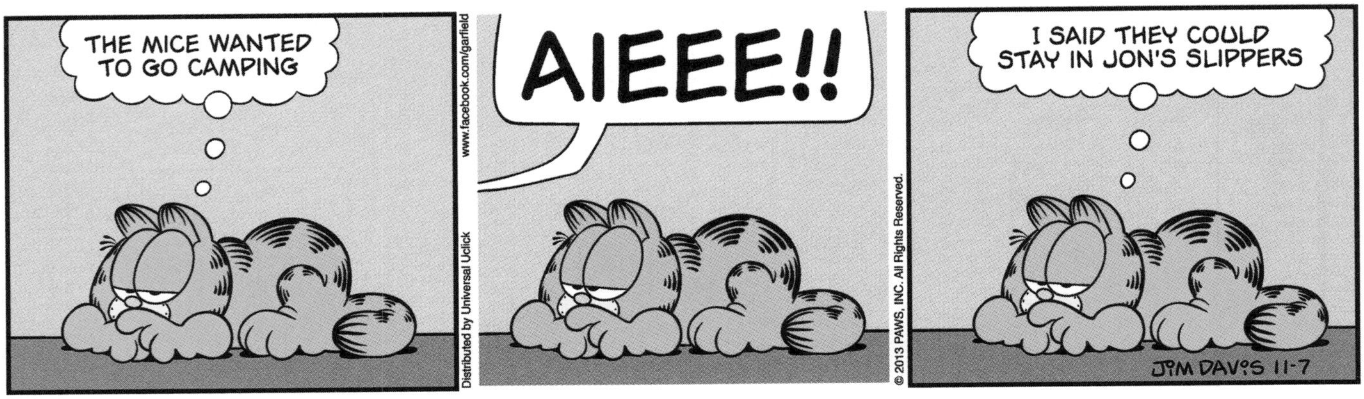
THE MICE WANTED TO GO CAMPING
Distributed by Universal Uclick www.facebook.com/garfield
AIEEE!!
© 2013 PAWS, INC. All Rights Reserved.
I SAID THEY COULD STAY IN JON'S SLIPPERS
JIM DAVIS 11-7

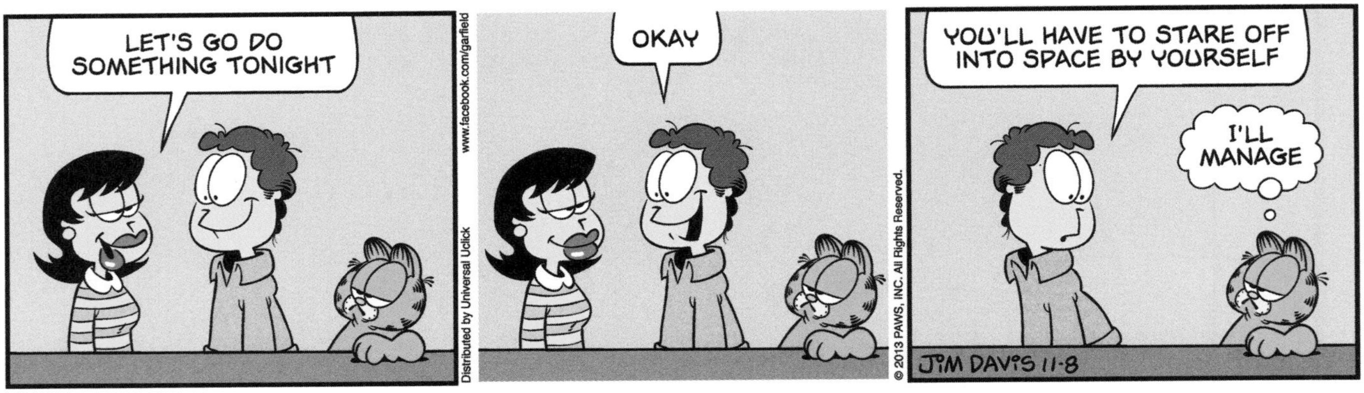
LET'S GO DO SOMETHING TONIGHT
Distributed by Universal Uclick www.facebook.com/garfield
OKAY
© 2013 PAWS, INC. All Rights Reserved.
YOU'LL HAVE TO STARE OFF INTO SPACE BY YOURSELF
I'LL MANAGE
JIM DAVIS 11-8

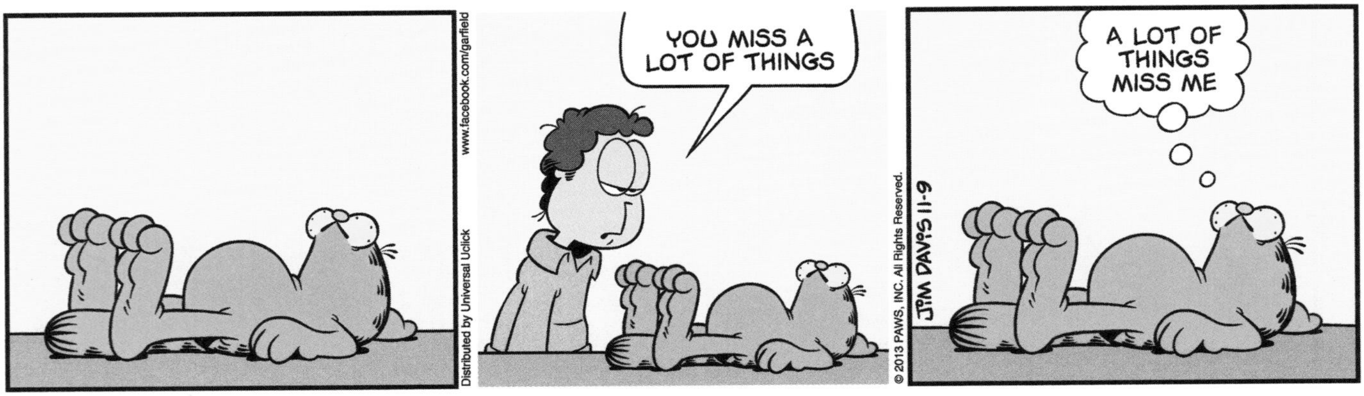
Distributed by Universal Uclick www.facebook.com/garfield
YOU MISS A LOT OF THINGS
© 2013 PAWS, INC. All Rights Reserved.
JIM DAVIS 11-9
A LOT OF THINGS MISS ME

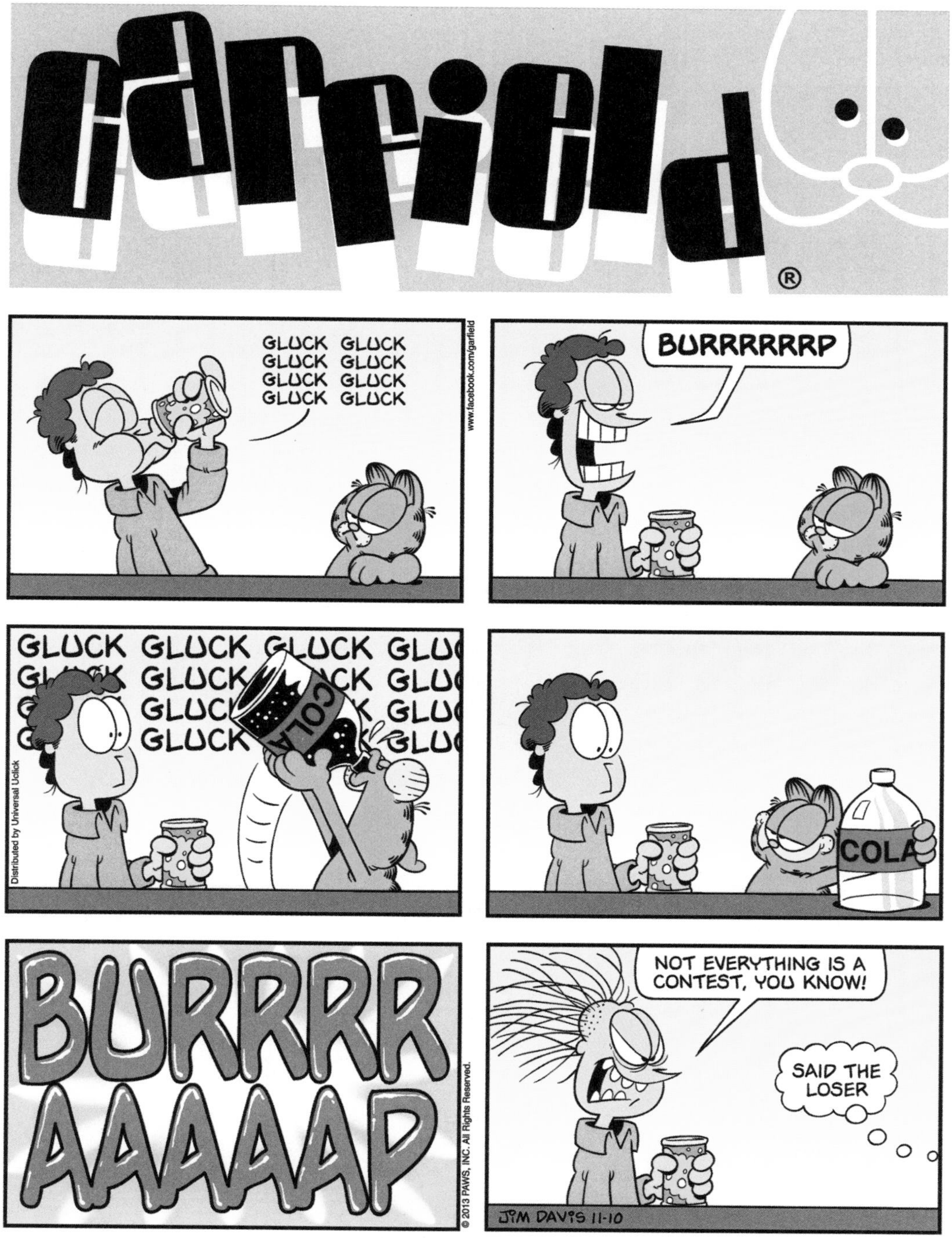
Garfield®
GLUCK GLUCK
GLUCK GLUCK
GLUCK GLUCK
GLUCK GLUCK
www.facebook.com/garfield
BURRRRRRP
GLUCK GLUCK GLUCK GLU
COLA
Distributed by Universal Uclick
COLA
BURRRR
AAAAAP
© 2013 PAWS, INC. All Rights Reserved.
NOT EVERYTHING IS A CONTEST, YOU KNOW!
SAID THE LOSER
JIM DAVIS 11-10

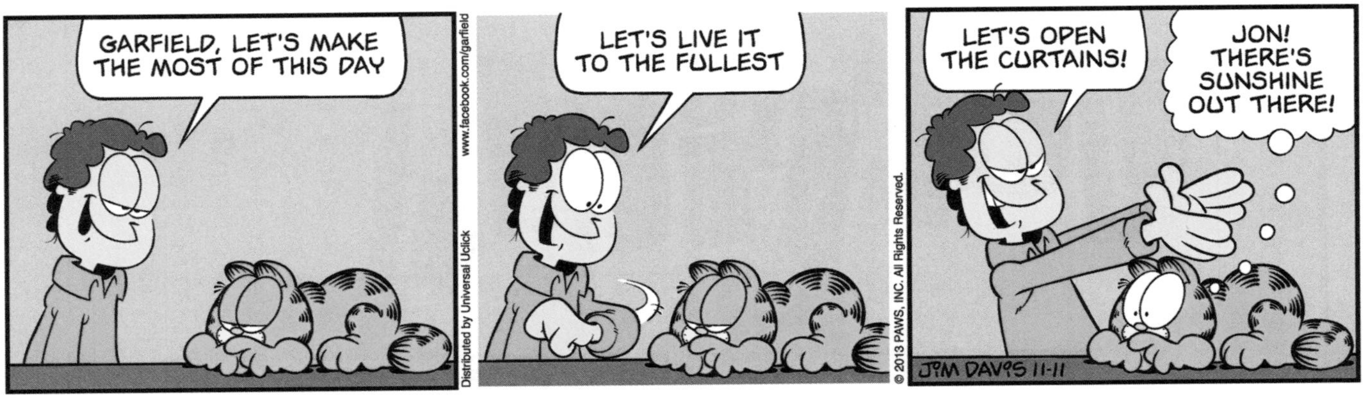
GARFIELD, LET'S MAKE THE MOST OF THIS DAY
LET'S LIVE IT TO THE FULLEST
LET'S OPEN THE CURTAINS!
JON! THERE'S SUNSHINE OUT THERE!
JIM DAVIS 11-11
Distributed by Universal Uclick www.facebook.com/garfield
© 2013 PAWS, INC. All Rights Reserved.

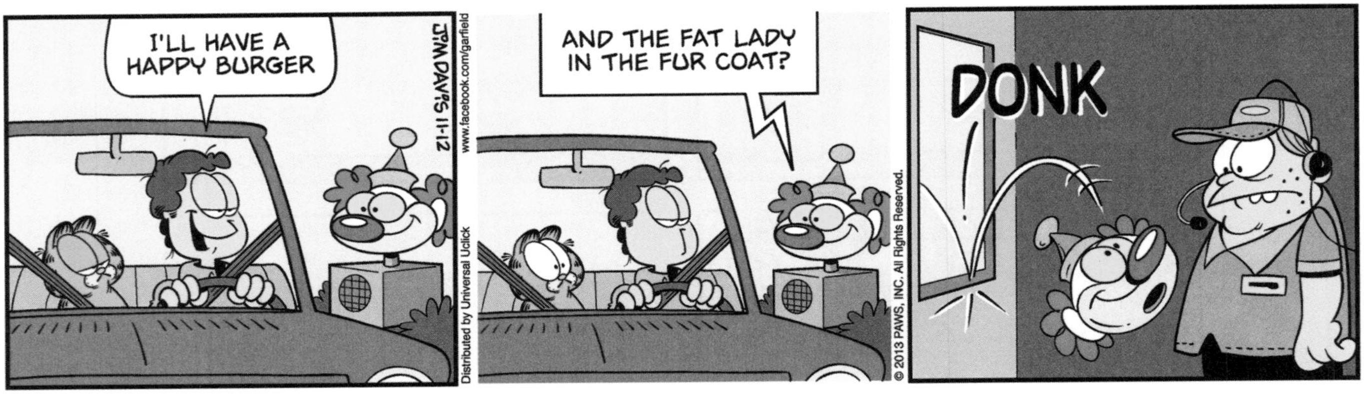
I'LL HAVE A HAPPY BURGER
JIM DAVIS 11-12
Distributed by Universal Uclick www.facebook.com/garfield
AND THE FAT LADY IN THE FUR COAT?
© 2013 PAWS, INC. All Rights Reserved.
DONK

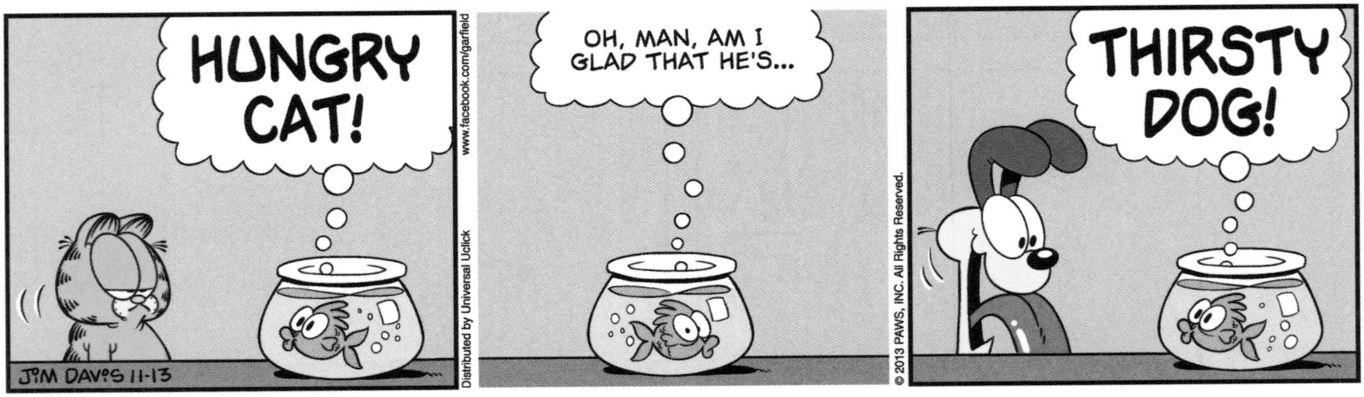
HUNGRY CAT!
JIM DAVIS 11-13
Distributed by Universal Uclick www.facebook.com/garfield
OH, MAN, AM I GLAD THAT HE'S...
© 2013 PAWS, INC. All Rights Reserved.
THIRSTY DOG!

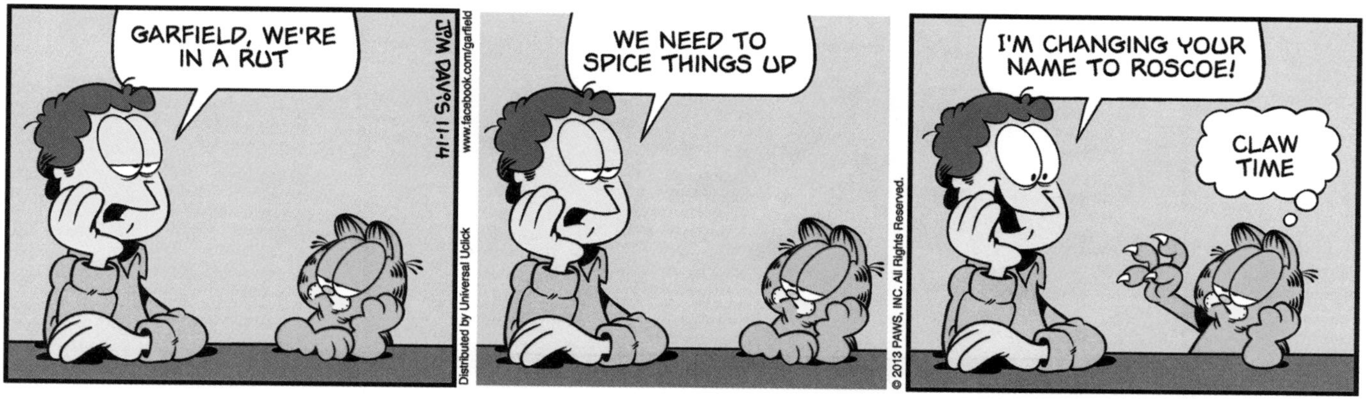
GARFIELD, WE'RE IN A RUT
JIM DAVIS 11-14
www.facebook.com/garfield
Distributed by Universal Uclick
WE NEED TO SPICE THINGS UP
© 2013 PAWS, INC. All Rights Reserved.
I'M CHANGING YOUR NAME TO ROSCOE!
CLAW TIME

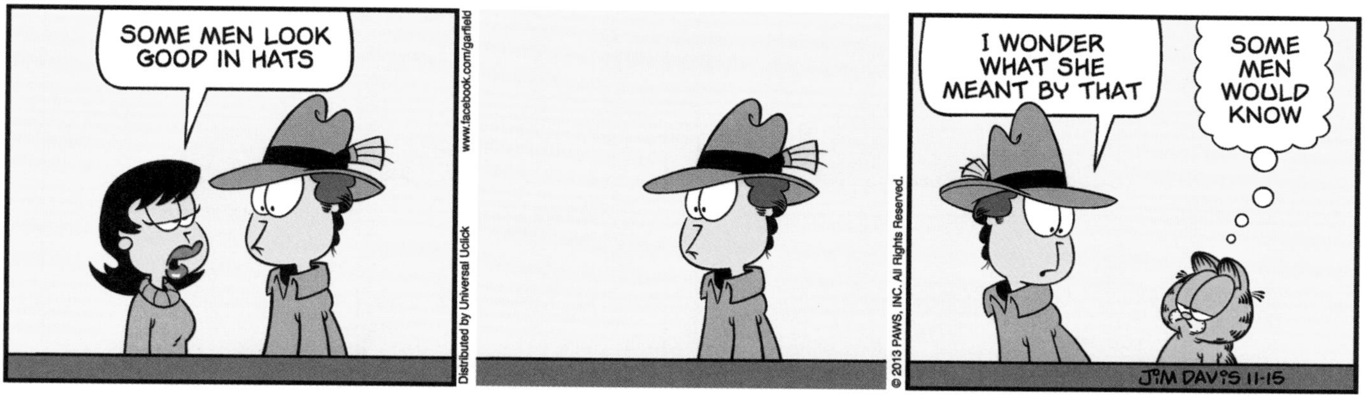
SOME MEN LOOK GOOD IN HATS
www.facebook.com/garfield
Distributed by Universal Uclick
© 2013 PAWS, INC. All Rights Reserved.
I WONDER WHAT SHE MEANT BY THAT
SOME MEN WOULD KNOW
JIM DAVIS 11-15

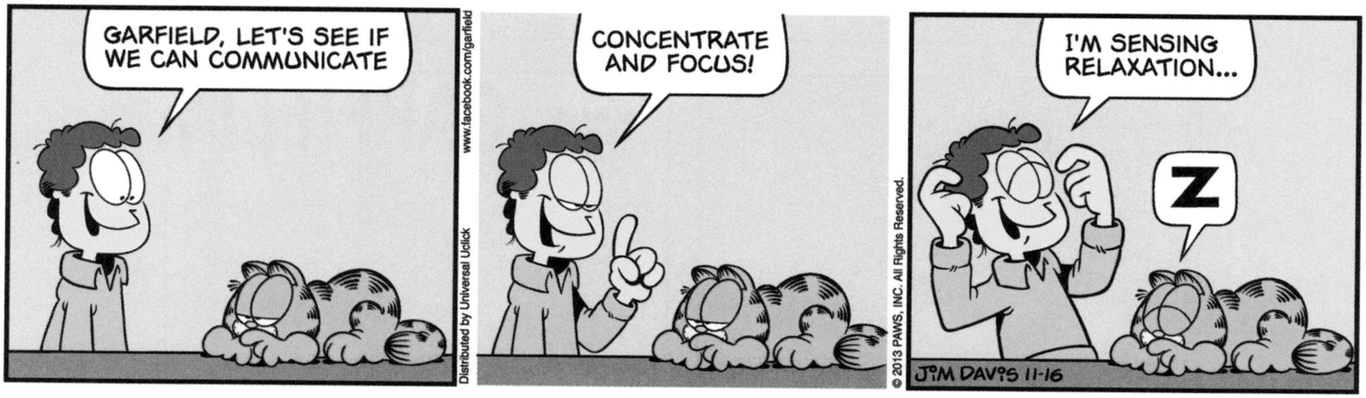
GARFIELD, LET'S SEE IF WE CAN COMMUNICATE
www.facebook.com/garfield
Distributed by Universal Uclick
CONCENTRATE AND FOCUS!
© 2013 PAWS, INC. All Rights Reserved.
I'M SENSING RELAXATION...
Z
JIM DAVIS 11-16

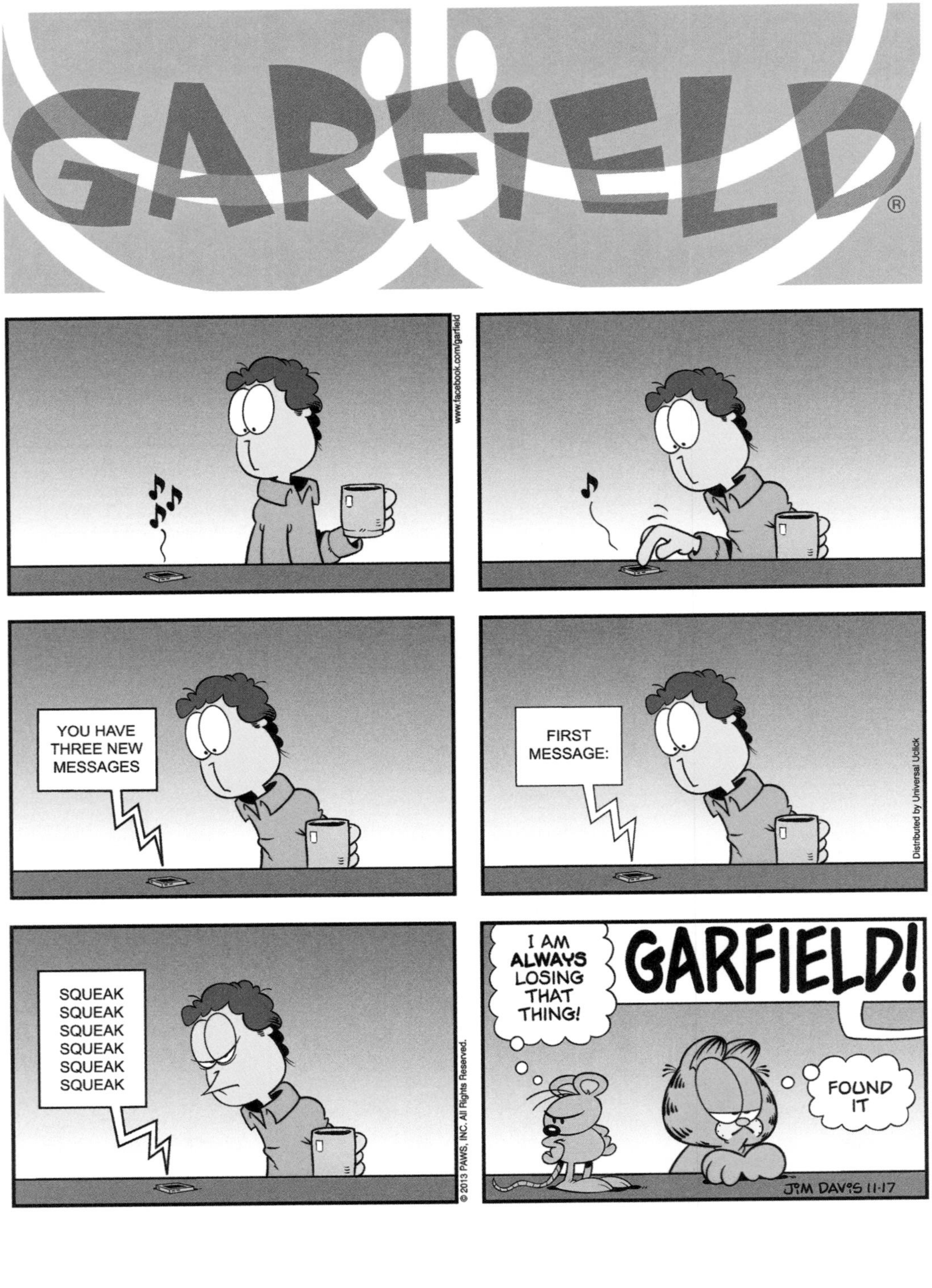

GARFIELD®
www.facebook.com/garfield
YOU HAVE THREE NEW MESSAGES
FIRST MESSAGE:
Distributed by Universal Uclick
SQUEAK SQUEAK SQUEAK SQUEAK SQUEAK SQUEAK
© 2013 PAWS, INC. All Rights Reserved.
I AM ALWAYS LOSING THAT THING!
GARFIELD!
FOUND IT
JIM DAVIS 11-17

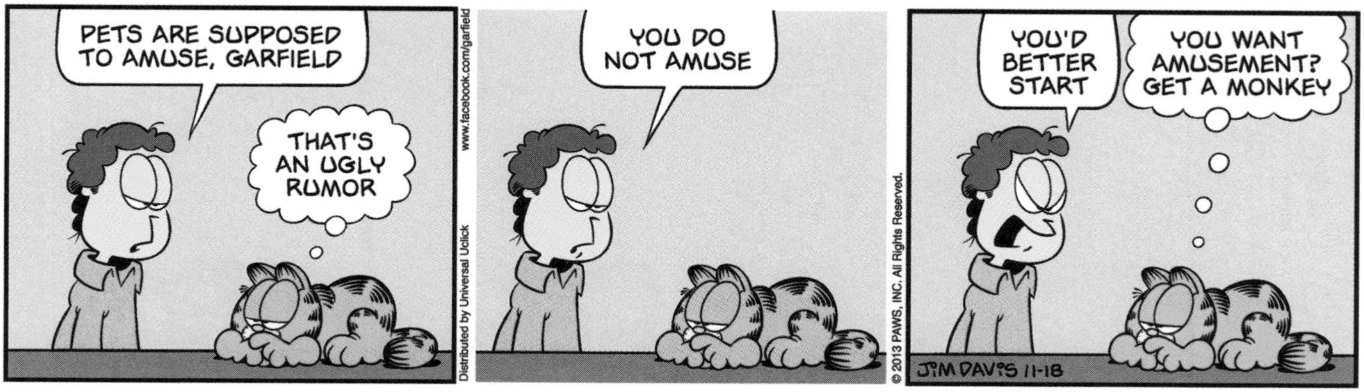
PETS ARE SUPPOSED TO AMUSE, GARFIELD
THAT'S AN UGLY RUMOR
YOU DO NOT AMUSE
YOU'D BETTER START
YOU WANT AMUSEMENT? GET A MONKEY
www.facebook.com/garfield
Distributed by Universal Uclick
© 2013 PAWS, INC. All Rights Reserved.
JIM DAVIS 11-18

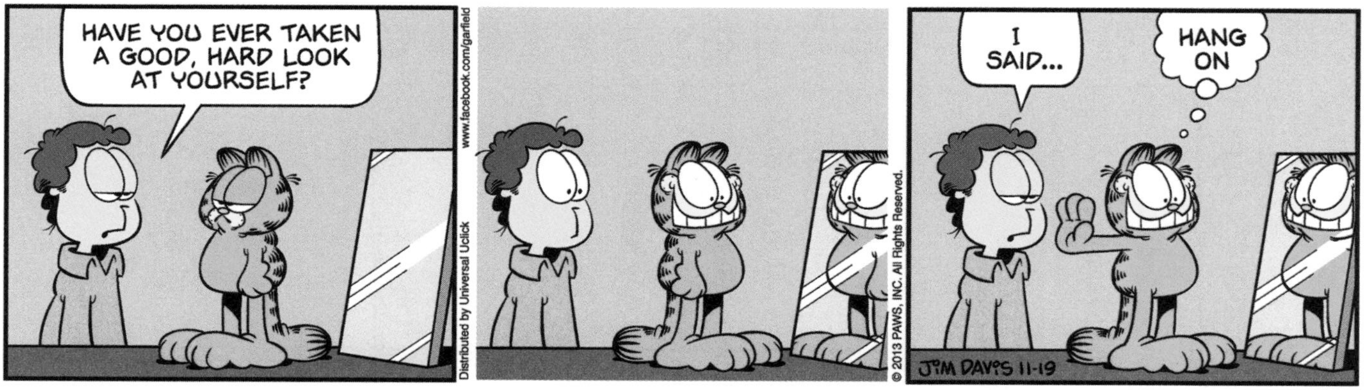
HAVE YOU EVER TAKEN A GOOD, HARD LOOK AT YOURSELF?
I SAID...
HANG ON
www.facebook.com/garfield
Distributed by Universal Uclick
© 2013 PAWS, INC. All Rights Reserved.
JIM DAVIS 11-19

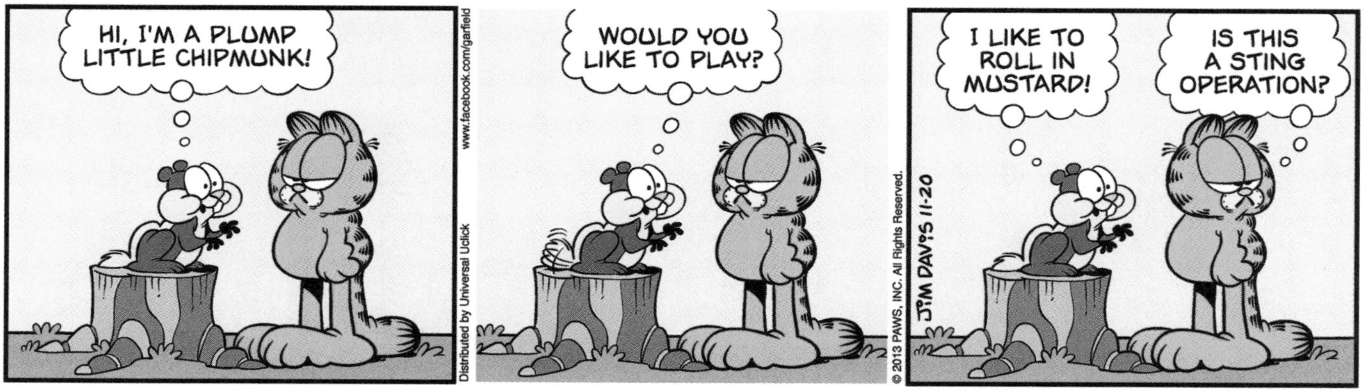
HI, I'M A PLUMP LITTLE CHIPMUNK!
WOULD YOU LIKE TO PLAY?
I LIKE TO ROLL IN MUSTARD!
IS THIS A STING OPERATION?
www.facebook.com/garfield
Distributed by Universal Uclick
© 2013 PAWS, INC. All Rights Reserved.
JIM DAVIS 11-20

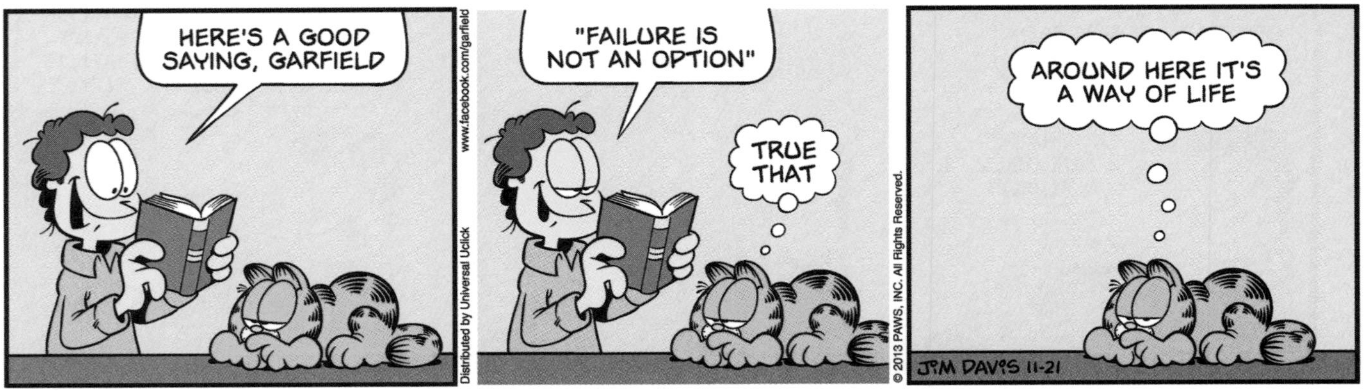
HERE'S A GOOD SAYING, GARFIELD
"FAILURE IS NOT AN OPTION"
TRUE THAT
AROUND HERE IT'S A WAY OF LIFE
JIM DAVIS 11-21
Distributed by Universal Uclick
www.facebook.com/garfield
© 2013 PAWS, INC. All Rights Reserved.

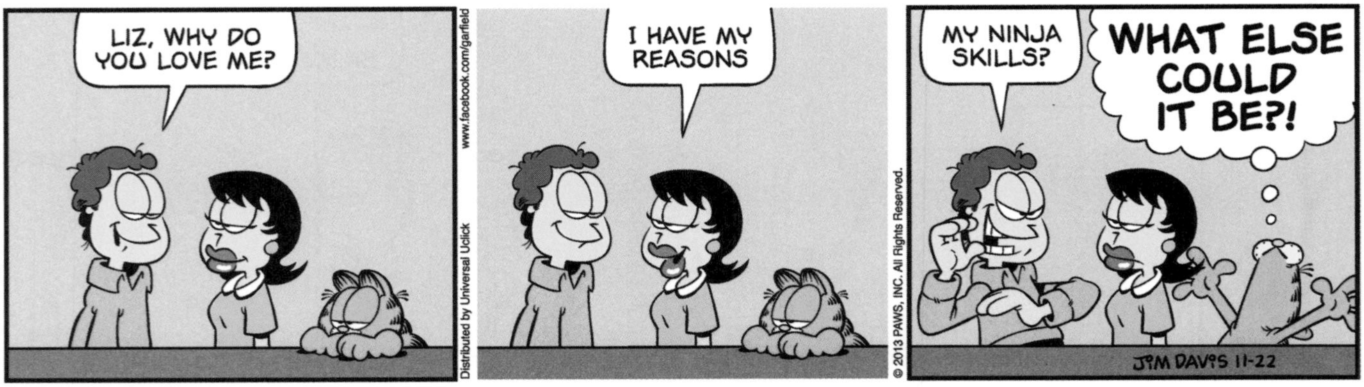
LIZ, WHY DO YOU LOVE ME?
I HAVE MY REASONS
MY NINJA SKILLS?
WHAT ELSE COULD IT BE?!
JIM DAVIS 11-22
Distributed by Universal Uclick
www.facebook.com/garfield
© 2013 PAWS, INC. All Rights Reserved.

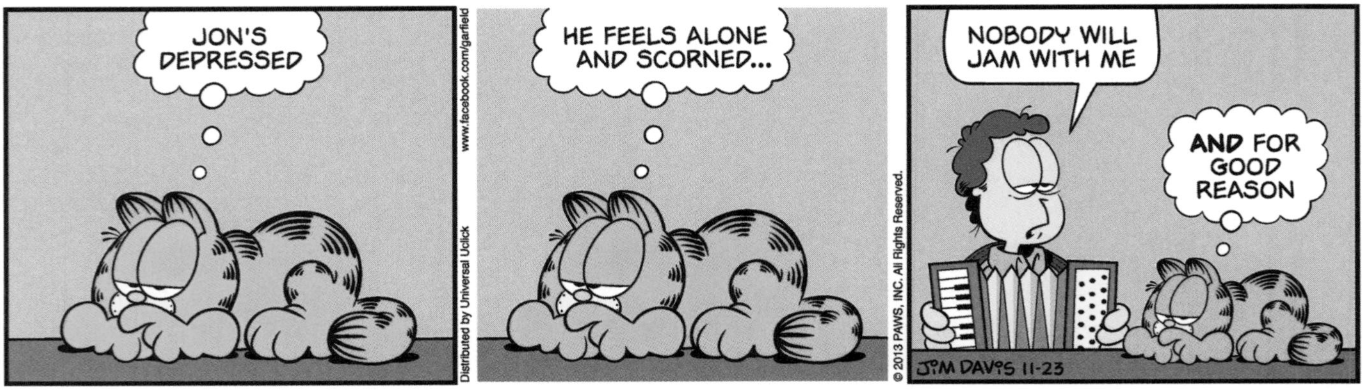
JON'S DEPRESSED
HE FEELS ALONE AND SCORNED...
NOBODY WILL JAM WITH ME
AND FOR GOOD REASON
JIM DAVIS 11-23
Distributed by Universal Uclick
www.facebook.com/garfield
© 2013 PAWS, INC. All Rights Reserved.

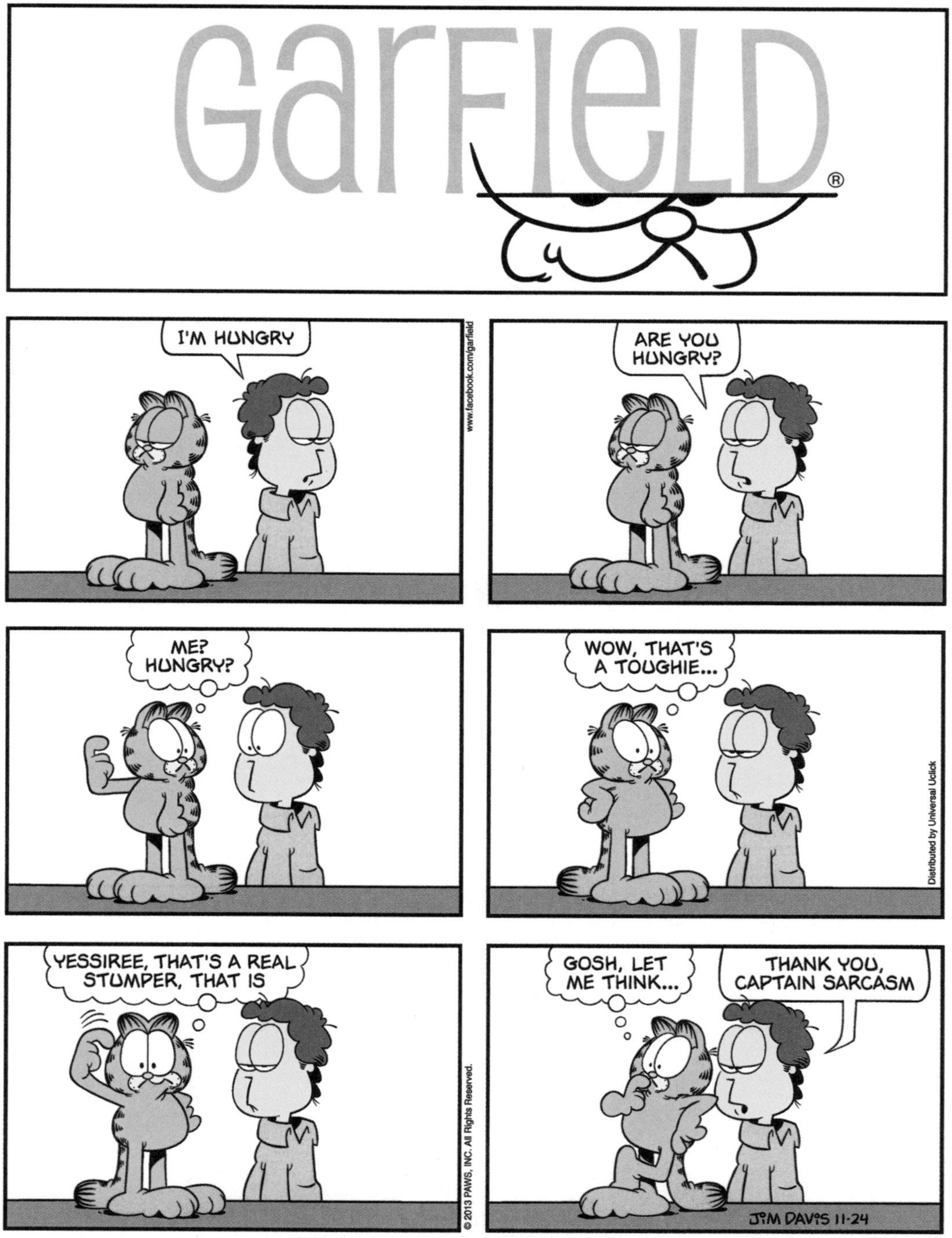
GARFIELD
I'M HUNGRY
www.facebook.com/garfield
ARE YOU HUNGRY?
ME? HUNGRY?
WOW, THAT'S A TOUGHIE...
Distributed by Universal Uclick
YESSIREE, THAT'S A REAL STUMPER, THAT IS
© 2013 PAWS, INC. All Rights Reserved.
GOSH, LET ME THINK...
THANK YOU, CAPTAIN SARCASM
JIM DAVIS 11-24

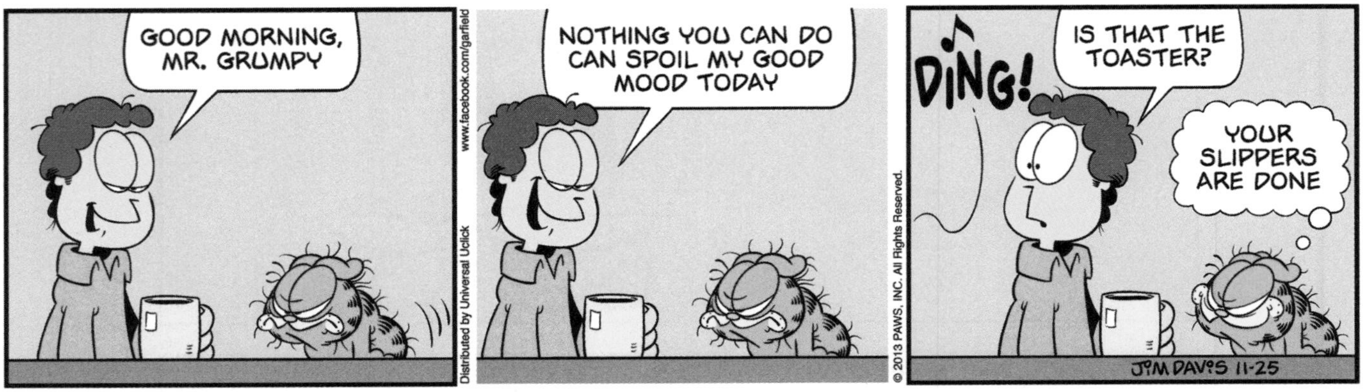
GOOD MORNING, MR. GRUMPY
NOTHING YOU CAN DO CAN SPOIL MY GOOD MOOD TODAY
DING!
IS THAT THE TOASTER?
YOUR SLIPPERS ARE DONE
JIM DAVIS 11-25
www.facebook.com/garfield
Distributed by Universal Uclick
© 2013 PAWS, INC. All Rights Reserved.

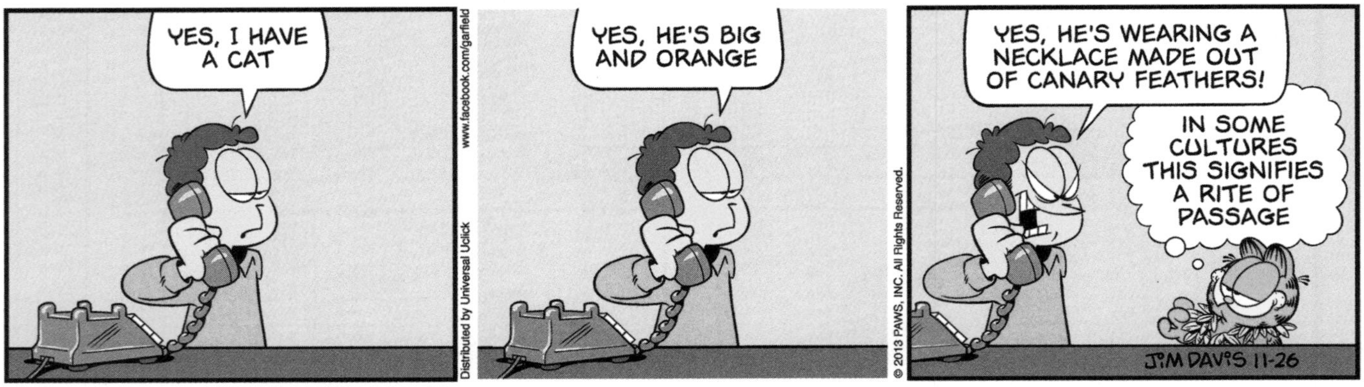
YES, I HAVE A CAT
YES, HE'S BIG AND ORANGE
YES, HE'S WEARING A NECKLACE MADE OUT OF CANARY FEATHERS!
IN SOME CULTURES THIS SIGNIFIES A RITE OF PASSAGE
JIM DAVIS 11-26
www.facebook.com/garfield
Distributed by Universal Uclick
© 2013 PAWS, INC. All Rights Reserved.

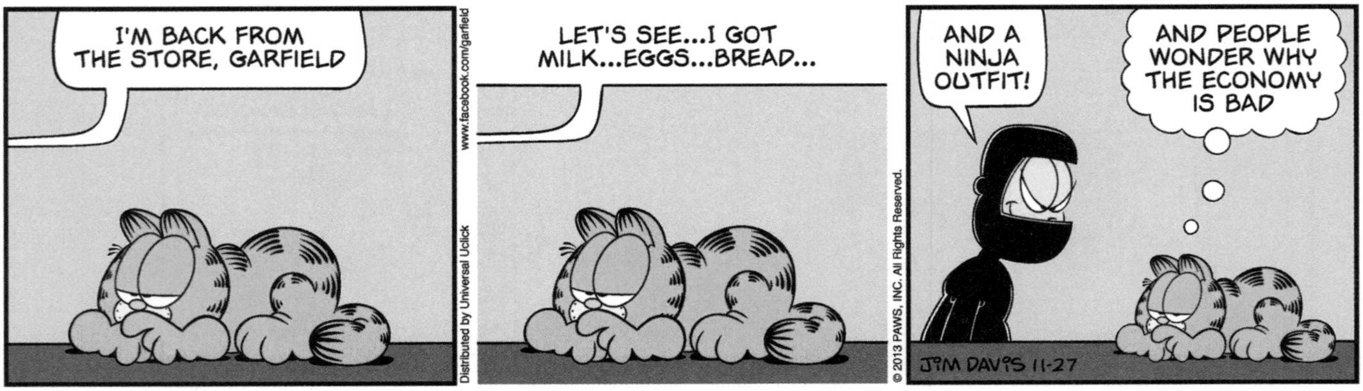
I'M BACK FROM THE STORE, GARFIELD
LET'S SEE...I GOT MILK...EGGS...BREAD...
AND A NINJA OUTFIT!
AND PEOPLE WONDER WHY THE ECONOMY IS BAD
JIM DAVIS 11-27
www.facebook.com/garfield
Distributed by Universal Uclick
© 2013 PAWS, INC. All Rights Reserved.

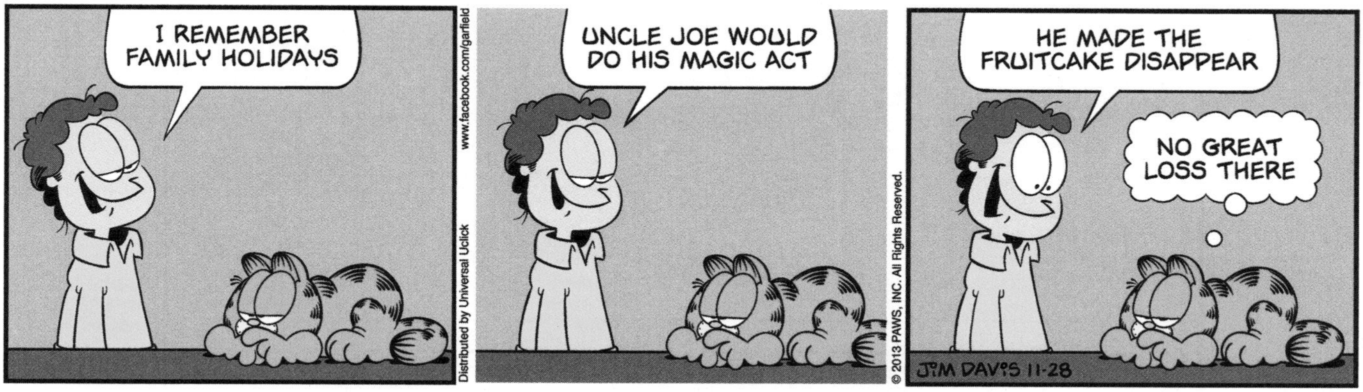
I REMEMBER FAMILY HOLIDAYS
UNCLE JOE WOULD DO HIS MAGIC ACT
HE MADE THE FRUITCAKE DISAPPEAR
NO GREAT LOSS THERE
JIM DAVIS 11-28
Distributed by Universal Uclick
www.facebook.com/garfield
© 2013 PAWS, INC. All Rights Reserved.

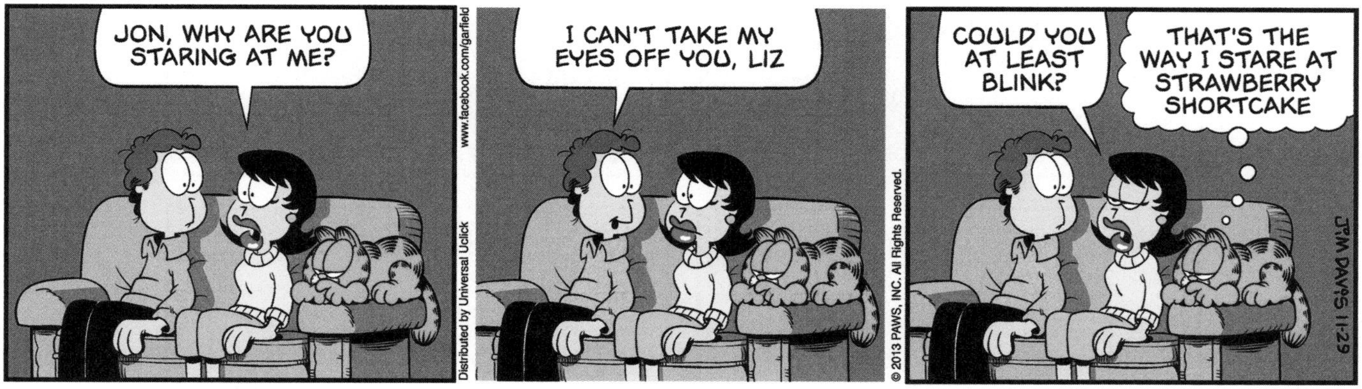
JON, WHY ARE YOU STARING AT ME?
I CAN'T TAKE MY EYES OFF YOU, LIZ
COULD YOU AT LEAST BLINK?
THAT'S THE WAY I STARE AT STRAWBERRY SHORTCAKE
JIM DAVIS 11-29
Distributed by Universal Uclick
www.facebook.com/garfield
© 2013 PAWS, INC. All Rights Reserved.

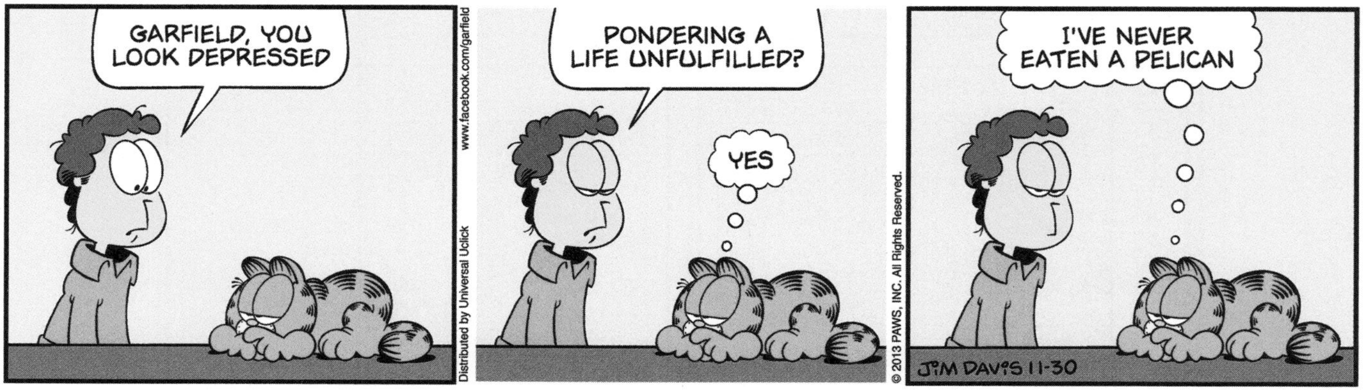
GARFIELD, YOU LOOK DEPRESSED
PONDERING A LIFE UNFULFILLED?
YES
I'VE NEVER EATEN A PELICAN
JIM DAVIS 11-30
Distributed by Universal Uclick
www.facebook.com/garfield
© 2013 PAWS, INC. All Rights Reserved.

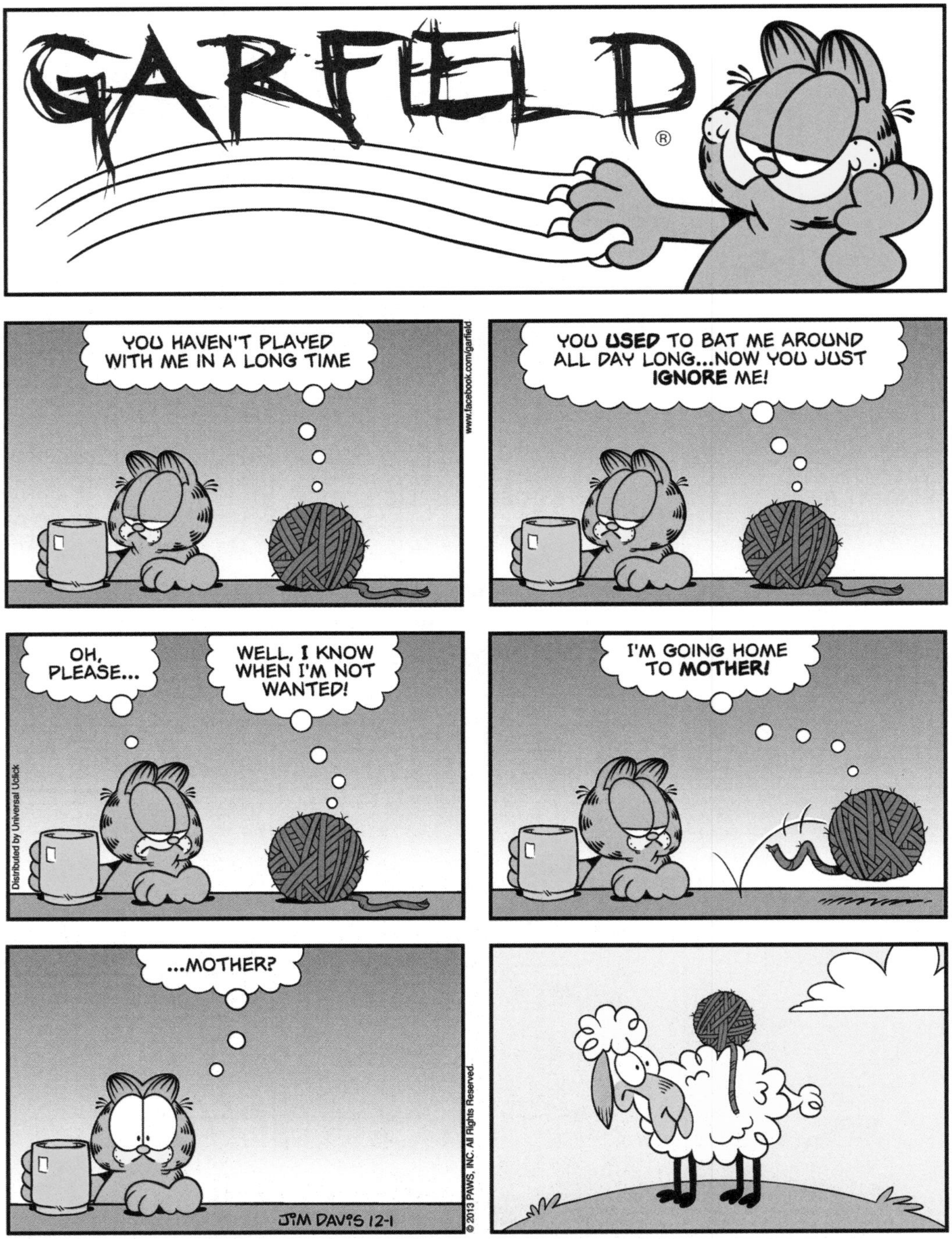
GARFIELD®
YOU HAVEN'T PLAYED WITH ME IN A LONG TIME
YOU **USED** TO BAT ME AROUND ALL DAY LONG...NOW YOU JUST **IGNORE** ME!
OH, PLEASE...
WELL, **I** KNOW WHEN I'M NOT WANTED!
I'M GOING HOME TO **MOTHER!**
...MOTHER?
JIM DAVIS 12-1
www.facebook.com/garfield
Distributed by Universal Uclick
© 2013 PAWS, INC. All Rights Reserved.

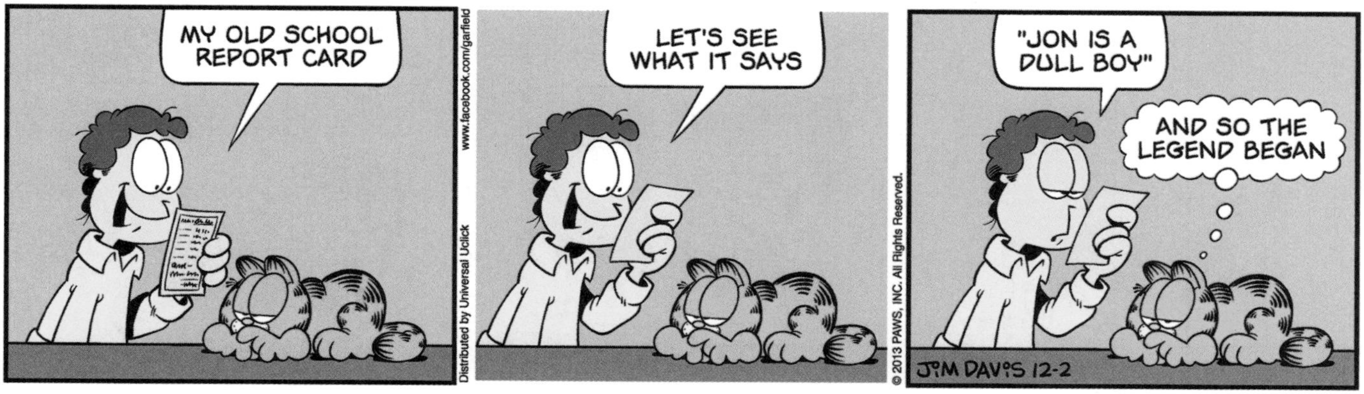
MY OLD SCHOOL REPORT CARD
LET'S SEE WHAT IT SAYS
"JON IS A DULL BOY"
AND SO THE LEGEND BEGAN
Distributed by Universal Uclick www.facebook.com/garfield
© 2013 PAWS, INC. All Rights Reserved.
JIM DAVIS 12-2

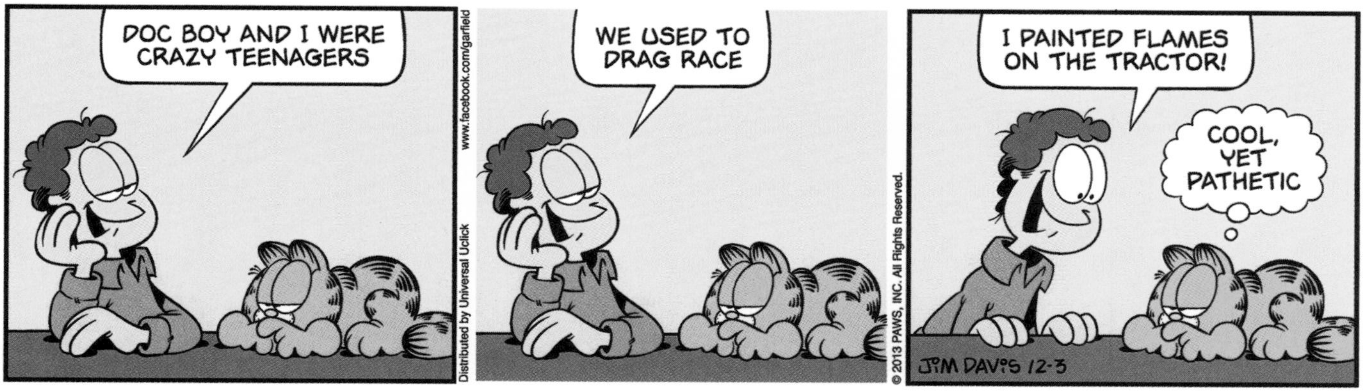
DOC BOY AND I WERE CRAZY TEENAGERS
WE USED TO DRAG RACE
I PAINTED FLAMES ON THE TRACTOR!
COOL, YET PATHETIC
Distributed by Universal Uclick www.facebook.com/garfield
© 2013 PAWS, INC. All Rights Reserved.
JIM DAVIS 12-3

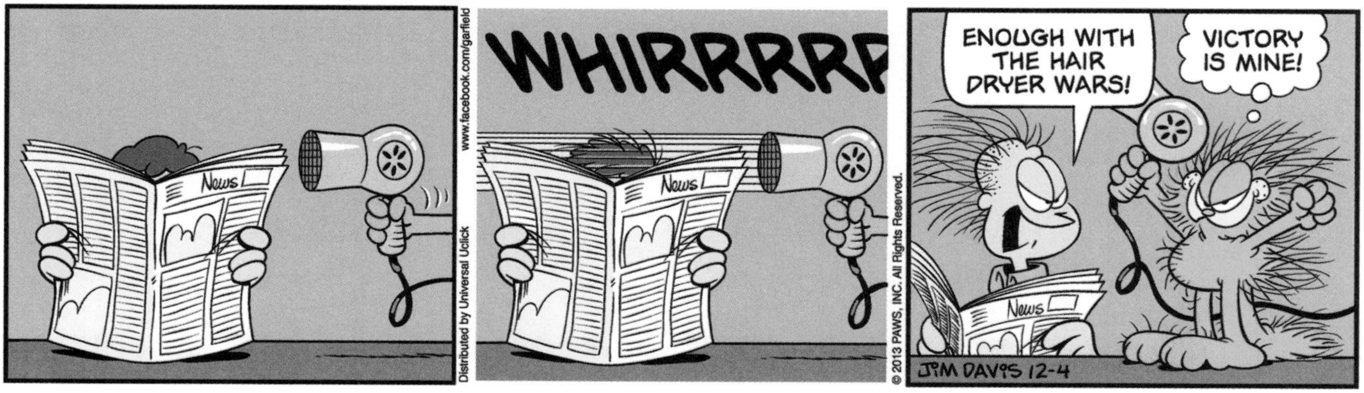
News
WHIRRRRR
News
ENOUGH WITH THE HAIR DRYER WARS!
VICTORY IS MINE!
News
Distributed by Universal Uclick www.facebook.com/garfield
© 2013 PAWS, INC. All Rights Reserved.
JIM DAVIS 12-4

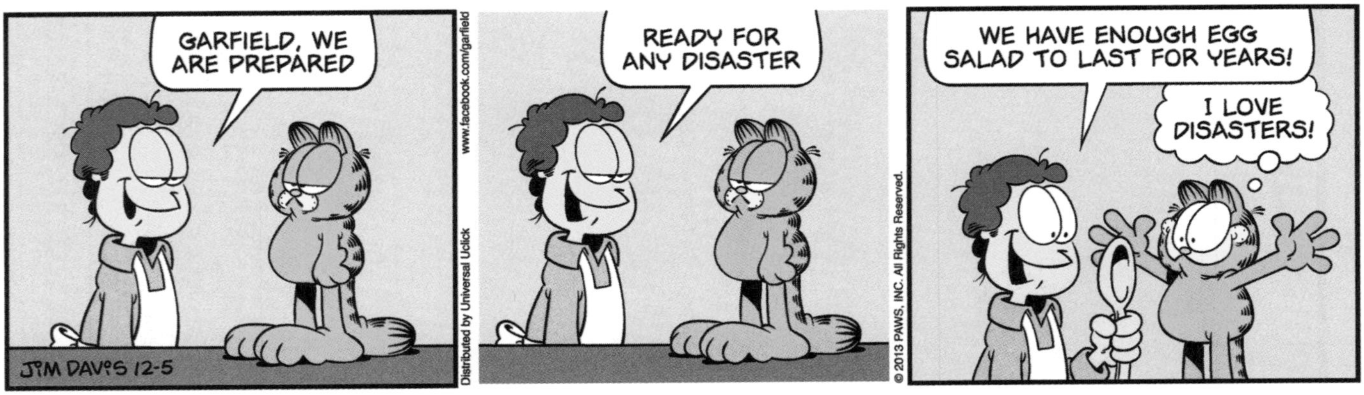
GARFIELD, WE ARE PREPARED
JIM DAVIS 12-5
www.facebook.com/garfield
Distributed by Universal Uclick
READY FOR ANY DISASTER
© 2013 PAWS, INC. All Rights Reserved.
WE HAVE ENOUGH EGG SALAD TO LAST FOR YEARS!
I LOVE DISASTERS!

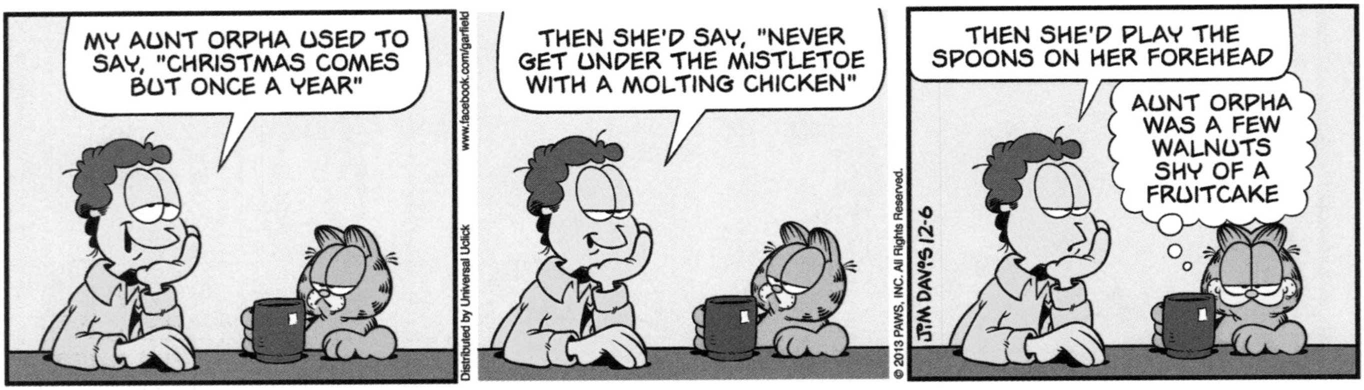
MY AUNT ORPHA USED TO SAY, "CHRISTMAS COMES BUT ONCE A YEAR"
www.facebook.com/garfield
Distributed by Universal Uclick
THEN SHE'D SAY, "NEVER GET UNDER THE MISTLETOE WITH A MOLTING CHICKEN"
© 2013 PAWS, INC. All Rights Reserved.
JIM DAVIS 12-6
THEN SHE'D PLAY THE SPOONS ON HER FOREHEAD
AUNT ORPHA WAS A FEW WALNUTS SHY OF A FRUITCAKE

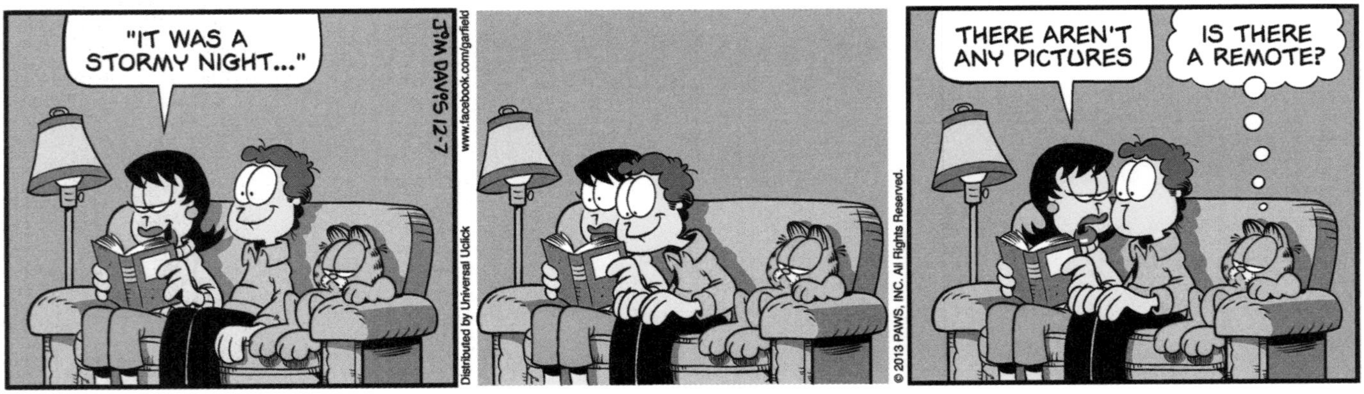
"IT WAS A STORMY NIGHT..."
JIM DAVIS 12-7
www.facebook.com/garfield
Distributed by Universal Uclick
© 2013 PAWS, INC. All Rights Reserved.
THERE AREN'T ANY PICTURES
IS THERE A REMOTE?

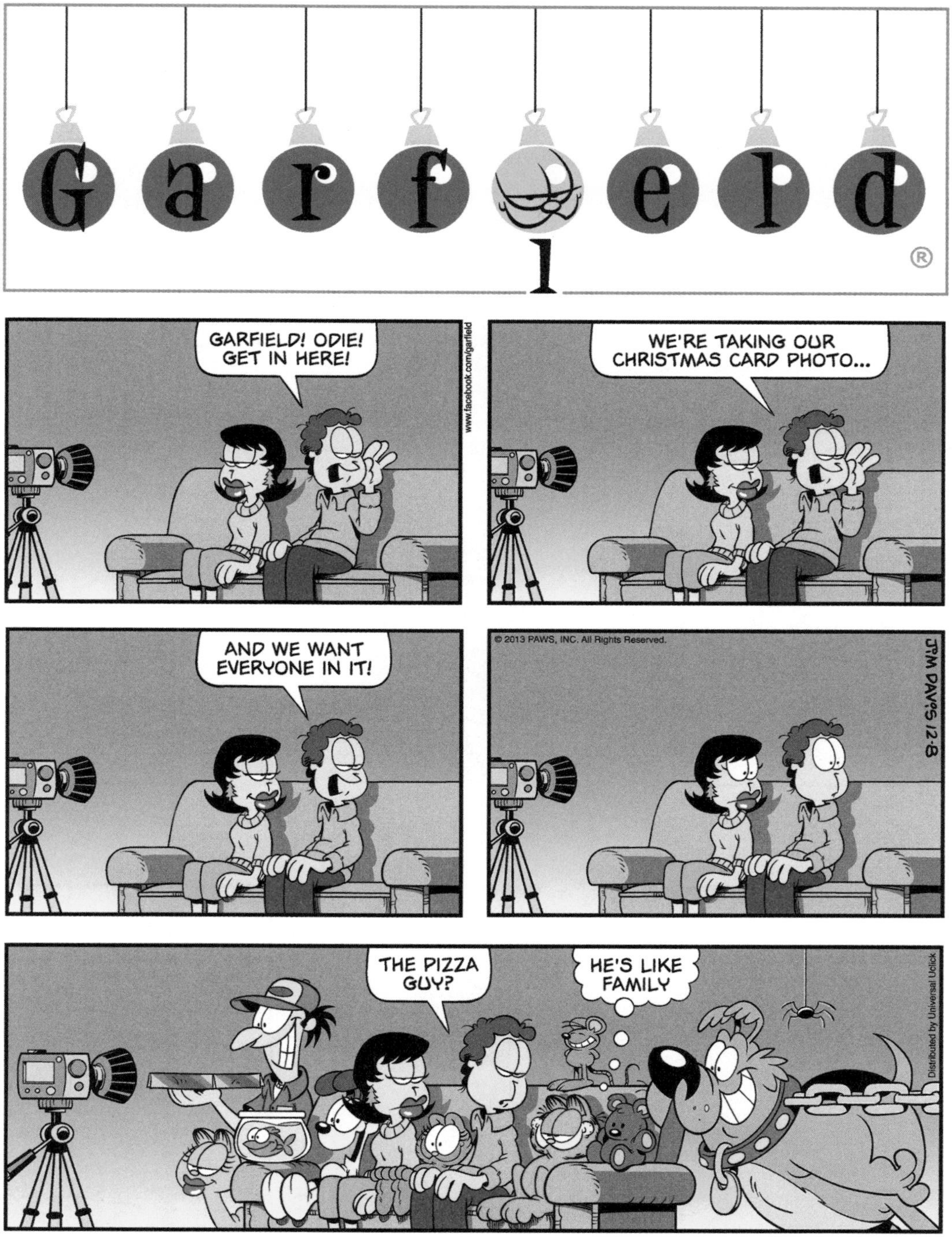
Garfield
GARFIELD! ODIE! GET IN HERE!
www.facebook.com/garfield
WE'RE TAKING OUR CHRISTMAS CARD PHOTO...
AND WE WANT EVERYONE IN IT!
© 2013 PAWS, INC. All Rights Reserved.
JIM DAVIS 12-8
THE PIZZA GUY?
HE'S LIKE FAMILY
Distributed by Universal Uclick

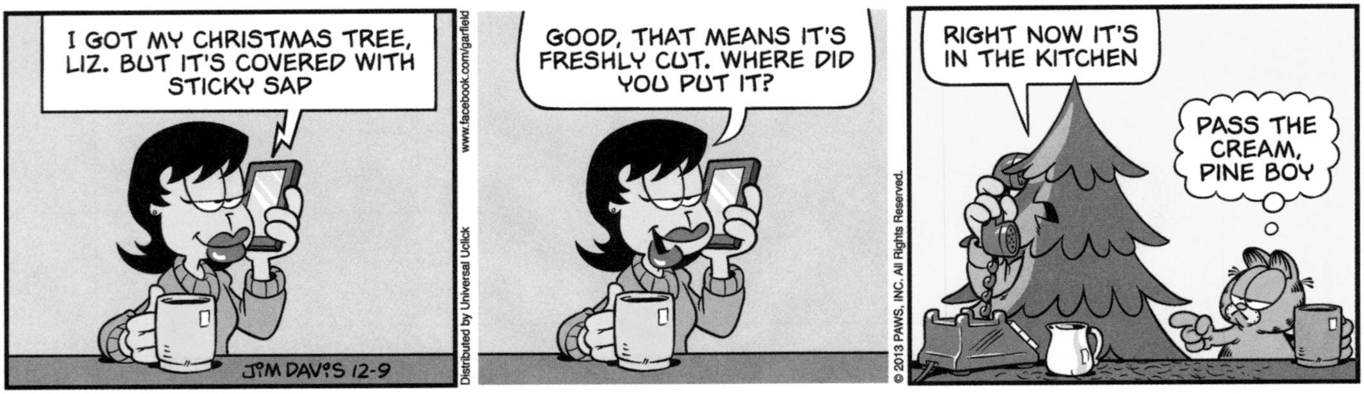
I GOT MY CHRISTMAS TREE, LIZ. BUT IT'S COVERED WITH STICKY SAP
JIM DAVIS 12-9
www.facebook.com/garfield
Distributed by Universal Uclick
GOOD, THAT MEANS IT'S FRESHLY CUT. WHERE DID YOU PUT IT?
© 2013 PAWS, INC. All Rights Reserved.
RIGHT NOW IT'S IN THE KITCHEN
PASS THE CREAM, PINE BOY

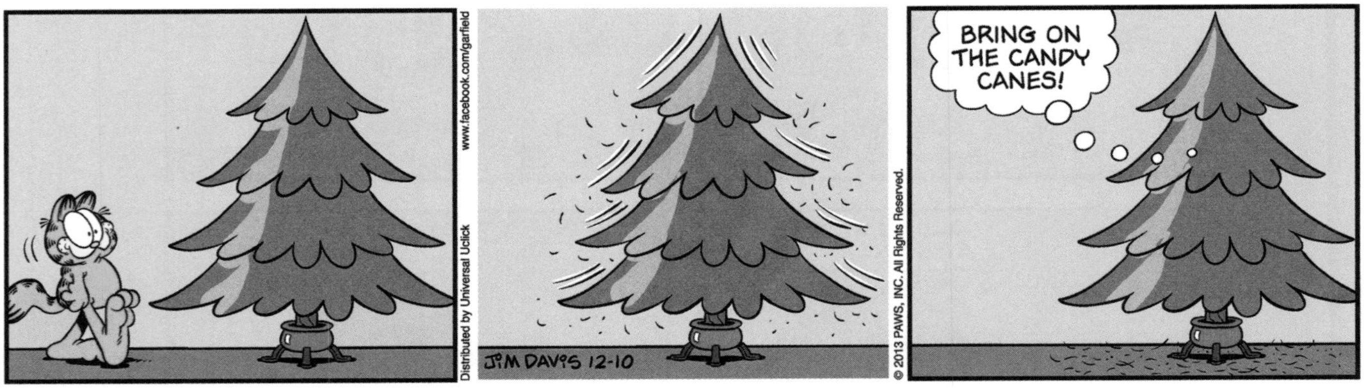
www.facebook.com/garfield
Distributed by Universal Uclick
JIM DAVIS 12-10
© 2013 PAWS, INC. All Rights Reserved.
BRING ON THE CANDY CANES!

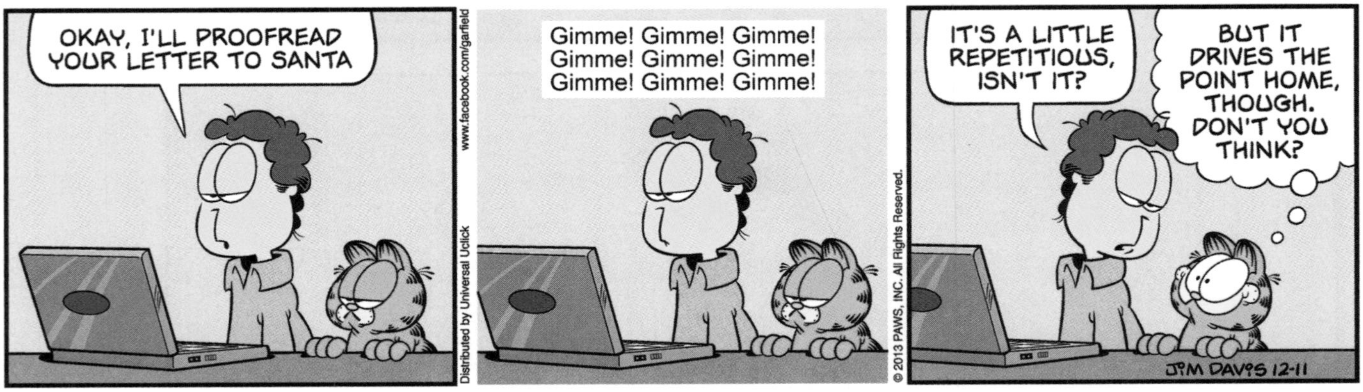
OKAY, I'LL PROOFREAD YOUR LETTER TO SANTA
www.facebook.com/garfield
Distributed by Universal Uclick
Gimme! Gimme! Gimme!
Gimme! Gimme! Gimme!
Gimme! Gimme! Gimme!
© 2013 PAWS, INC. All Rights Reserved.
IT'S A LITTLE REPETITIOUS, ISN'T IT?
BUT IT DRIVES THE POINT HOME, THOUGH. DON'T YOU THINK?
JIM DAVIS 12-11

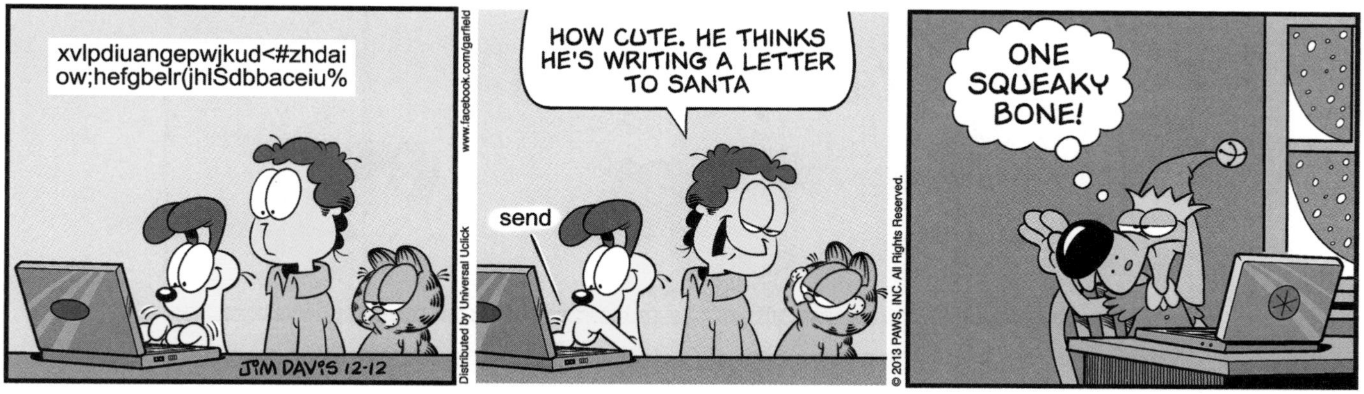
xvlpdiuangepwjkud<#zhdai
ow;hefgbelr(jhlSdbbaceiu%
JIM DAVIS 12-12
www.facebook.com/garfield
Distributed by Universal Uclick
HOW CUTE. HE THINKS HE'S WRITING A LETTER TO SANTA
send
© 2013 PAWS, INC. All Rights Reserved.
ONE SQUEAKY BONE!

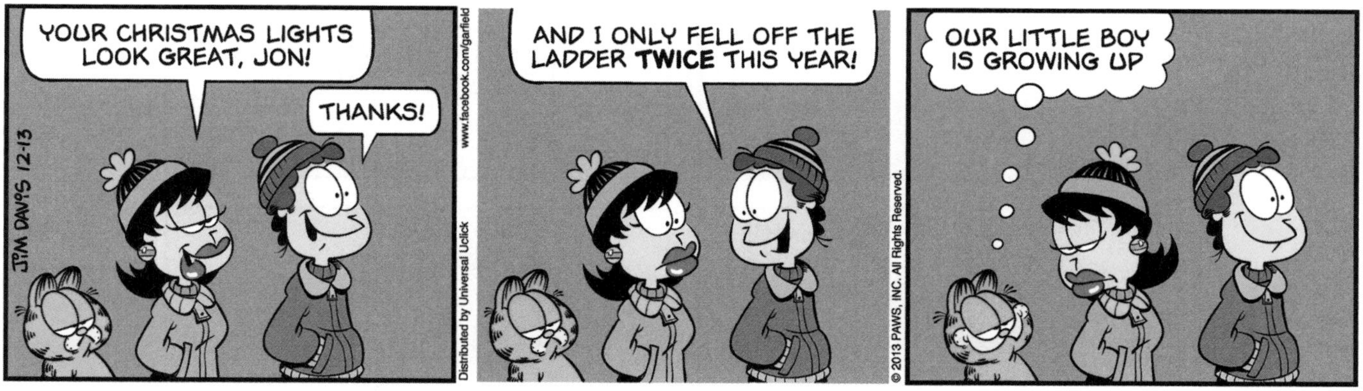
YOUR CHRISTMAS LIGHTS LOOK GREAT, JON!
THANKS!
JIM DAVIS 12-13
www.facebook.com/garfield
Distributed by Universal Uclick
AND I ONLY FELL OFF THE LADDER **TWICE** THIS YEAR!
© 2013 PAWS, INC. All Rights Reserved.
OUR LITTLE BOY IS GROWING UP

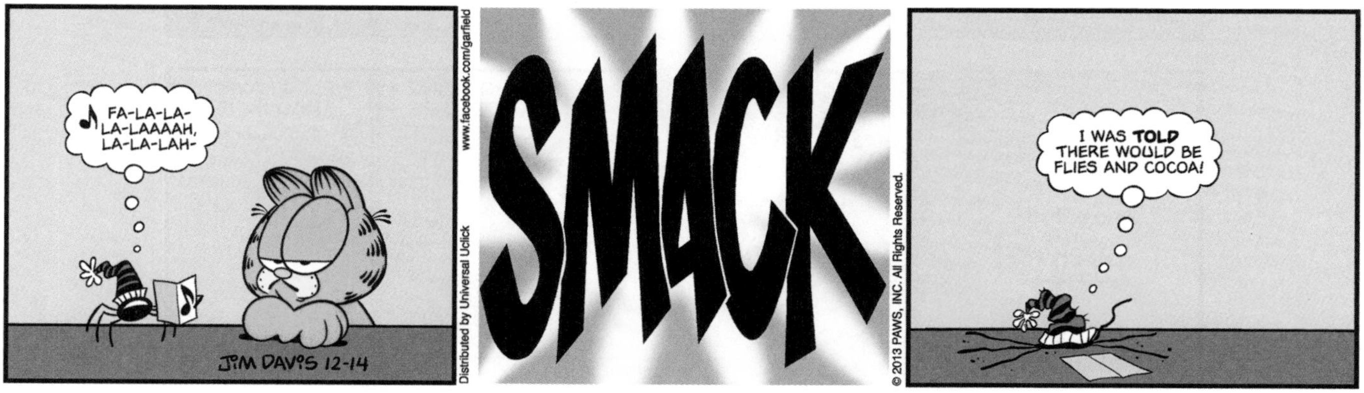
FA-LA-LA-LA-LAAAAH, LA-LA-LAH-
JIM DAVIS 12-14
www.facebook.com/garfield
Distributed by Universal Uclick
SMACK
© 2013 PAWS, INC. All Rights Reserved.
I WAS **TOLD** THERE WOULD BE FLIES AND COCOA!

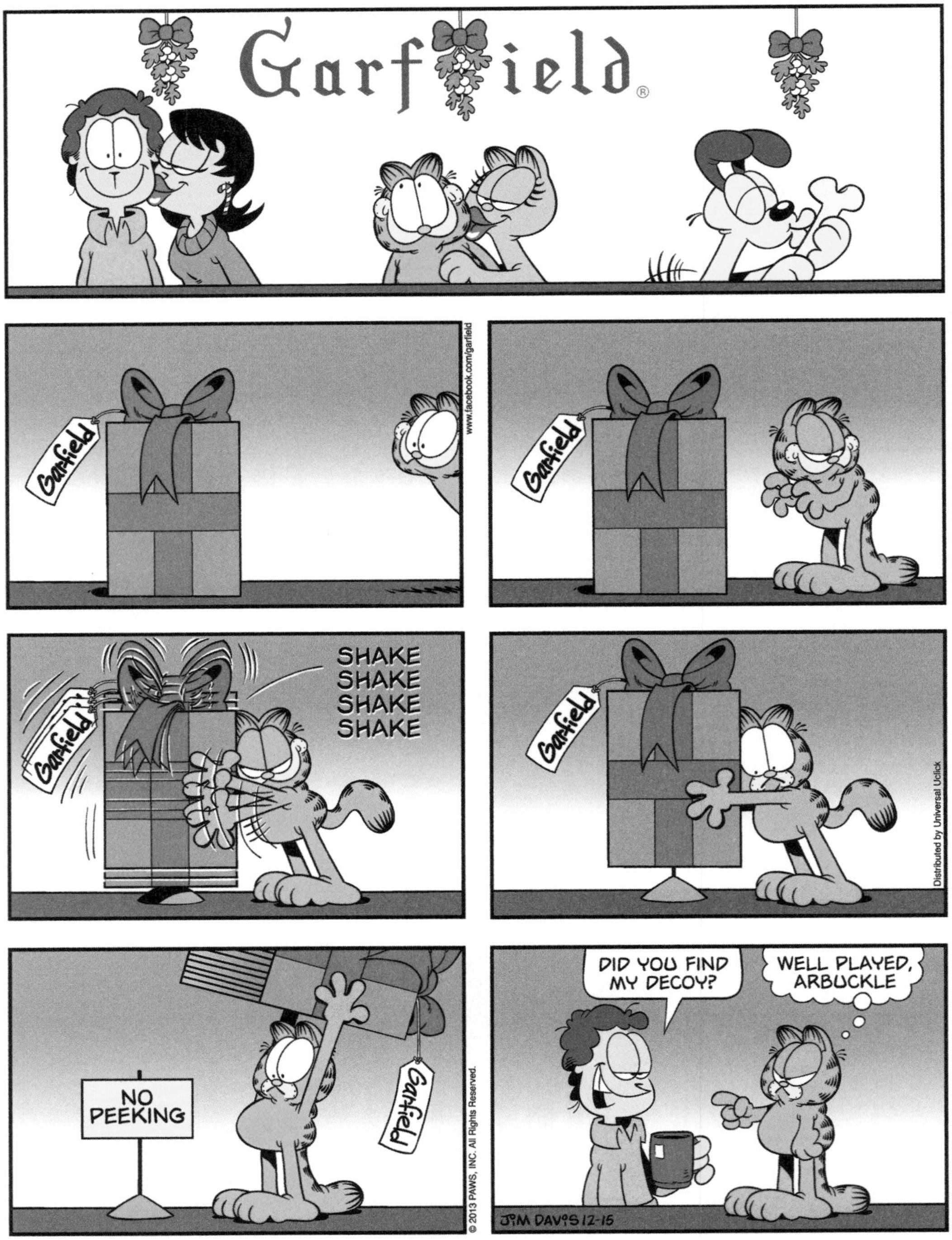
Garfield
www.facebook.com/garfield
Garfield
Garfield
Garfield
SHAKE
SHAKE
SHAKE
SHAKE
Garfield
Distributed by Universal Uclick
NO PEEKING
Garfield
© 2013 PAWS, INC. All Rights Reserved.
DID YOU FIND MY DECOY?
WELL PLAYED, ARBUCKLE
JIM DAVIS 12-15

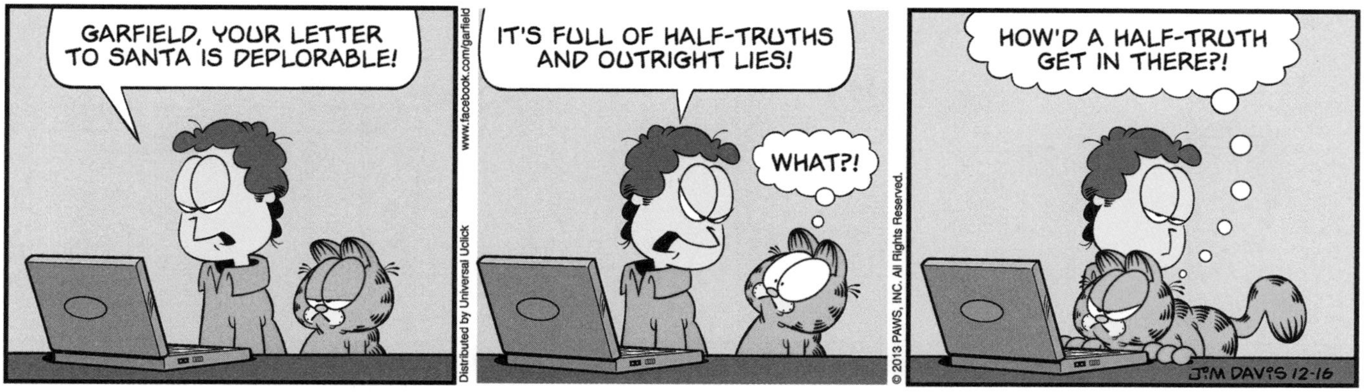
GARFIELD, YOUR LETTER TO SANTA IS DEPLORABLE!
IT'S FULL OF HALF-TRUTHS AND OUTRIGHT LIES!
WHAT?!
HOW'D A HALF-TRUTH GET IN THERE?!
JIM DAVIS 12-16
Distributed by Universal Uclick www.facebook.com/garfield
© 2013 PAWS, INC. All Rights Reserved.

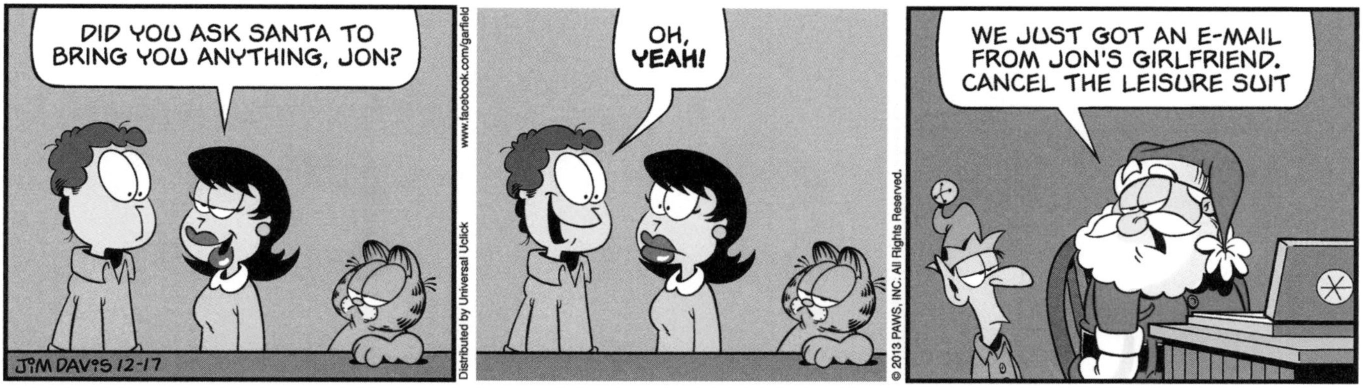
DID YOU ASK SANTA TO BRING YOU ANYTHING, JON?
OH, **YEAH!**
WE JUST GOT AN E-MAIL FROM JON'S GIRLFRIEND. CANCEL THE LEISURE SUIT
JIM DAVIS 12-17
Distributed by Universal Uclick www.facebook.com/garfield
© 2013 PAWS, INC. All Rights Reserved.

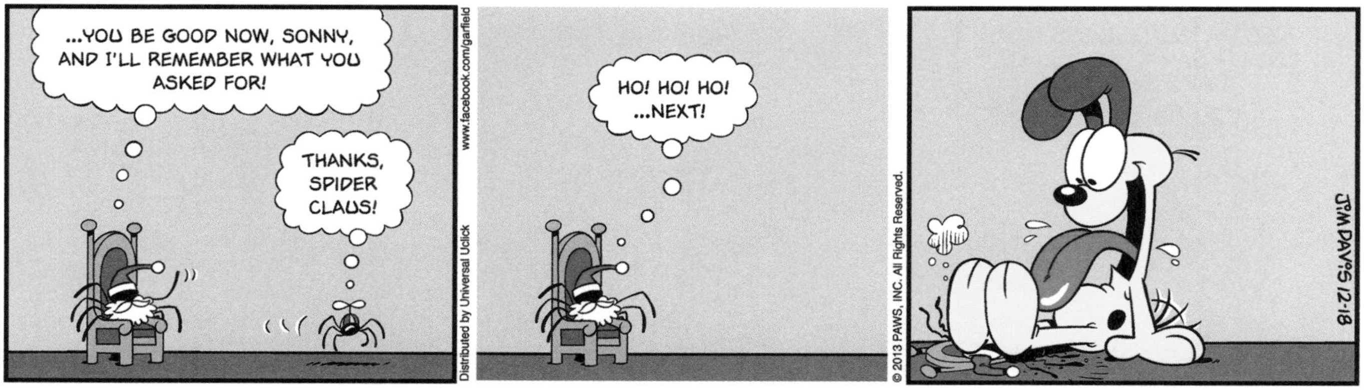
...YOU BE GOOD NOW, SONNY, AND I'LL REMEMBER WHAT YOU ASKED FOR!
THANKS, SPIDER CLAUS!
HO! HO! HO! ...NEXT!
JIM DAVIS 12-18
Distributed by Universal Uclick www.facebook.com/garfield
© 2013 PAWS, INC. All Rights Reserved.

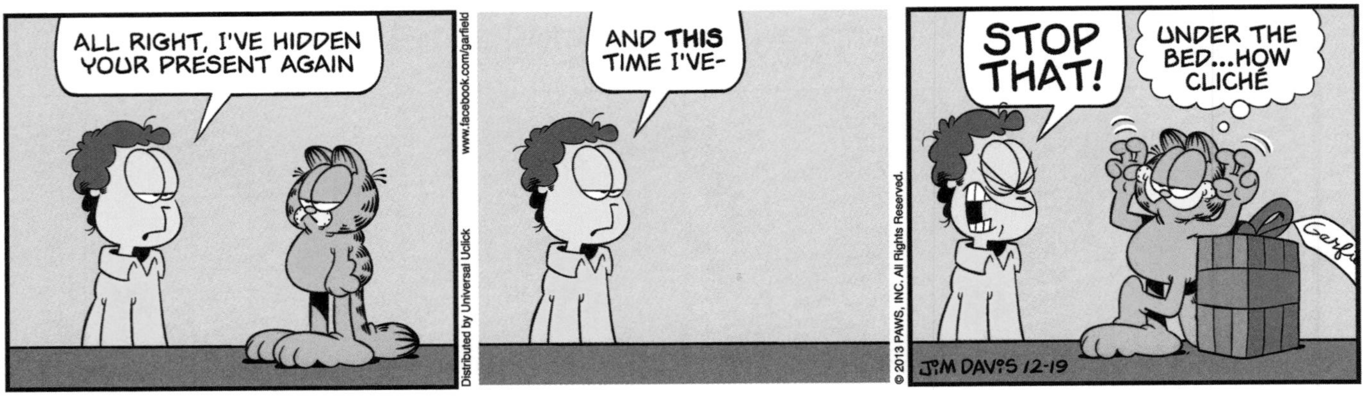
ALL RIGHT, I'VE HIDDEN YOUR PRESENT AGAIN
AND THIS TIME I'VE-
STOP THAT!
UNDER THE BED...HOW CLICHÉ
www.facebook.com/garfield
Distributed by Universal Uclick
© 2013 PAWS, INC. All Rights Reserved.
JIM DAVIS 12-19

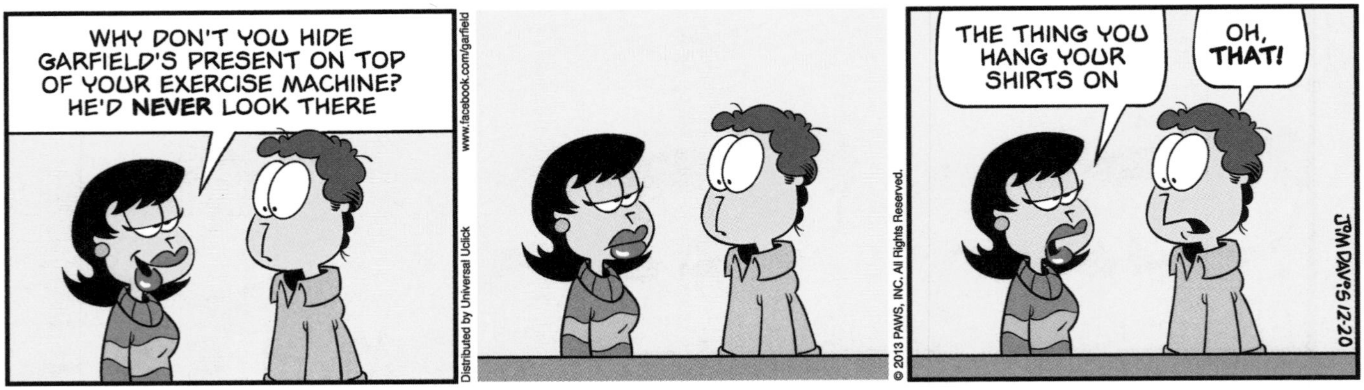
WHY DON'T YOU HIDE GARFIELD'S PRESENT ON TOP OF YOUR EXERCISE MACHINE? HE'D NEVER LOOK THERE
THE THING YOU HANG YOUR SHIRTS ON
OH, THAT!
www.facebook.com/garfield
Distributed by Universal Uclick
© 2013 PAWS, INC. All Rights Reserved.
JIM DAVIS 12-20

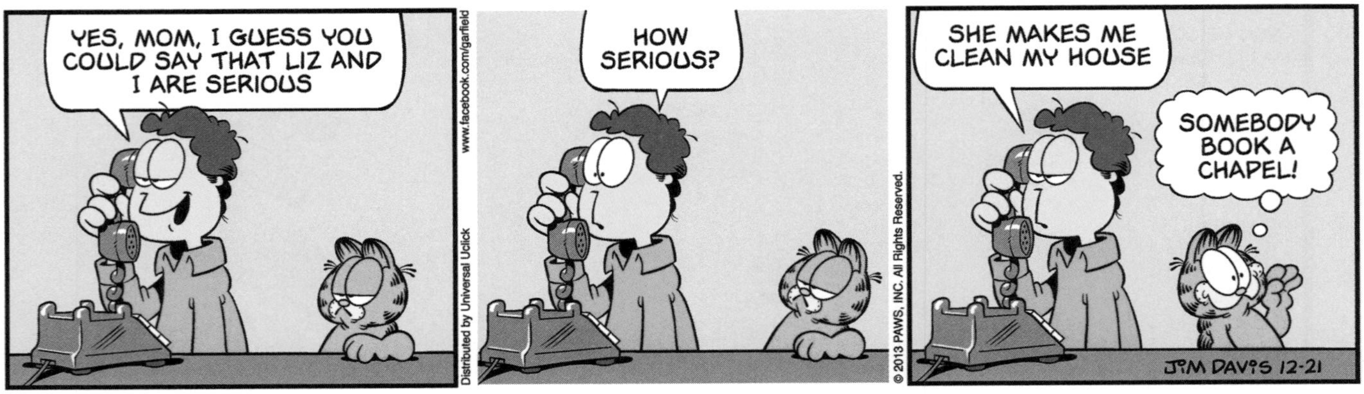
YES, MOM, I GUESS YOU COULD SAY THAT LIZ AND I ARE SERIOUS
HOW SERIOUS?
SHE MAKES ME CLEAN MY HOUSE
SOMEBODY BOOK A CHAPEL!
www.facebook.com/garfield
Distributed by Universal Uclick
© 2013 PAWS, INC. All Rights Reserved.
JIM DAVIS 12-21

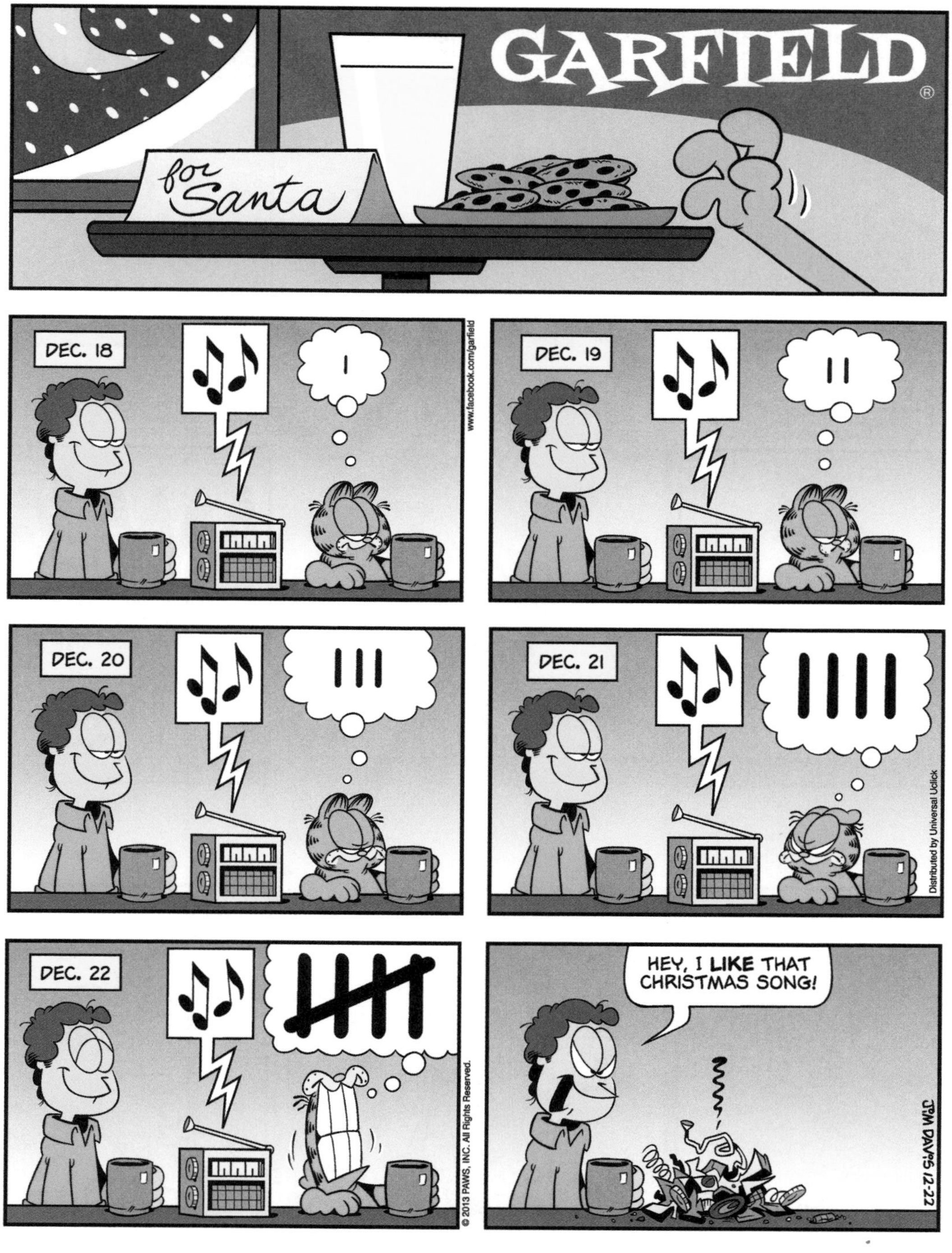
GARFIELD
for Santa
DEC. 18
www.facebook.com/garfield
DEC. 19
DEC. 20
DEC. 21
Distributed by Universal Uclick
DEC. 22
© 2013 PAWS, INC. All Rights Reserved.
HEY, I LIKE THAT CHRISTMAS SONG!
JIM DAVIS 12-22

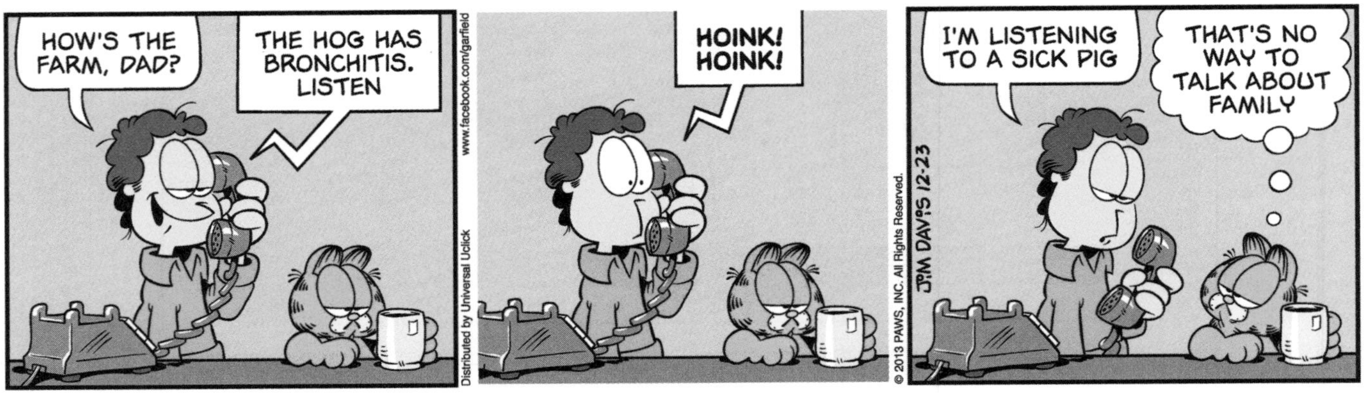
HOW'S THE FARM, DAD?
THE HOG HAS BRONCHITIS. LISTEN
www.facebook.com/garfield
Distributed by Universal Uclick
HOINK! HOINK!
© 2013 PAWS, INC. All Rights Reserved.
JIM DAVIS 12-23
I'M LISTENING TO A SICK PIG
THAT'S NO WAY TO TALK ABOUT FAMILY

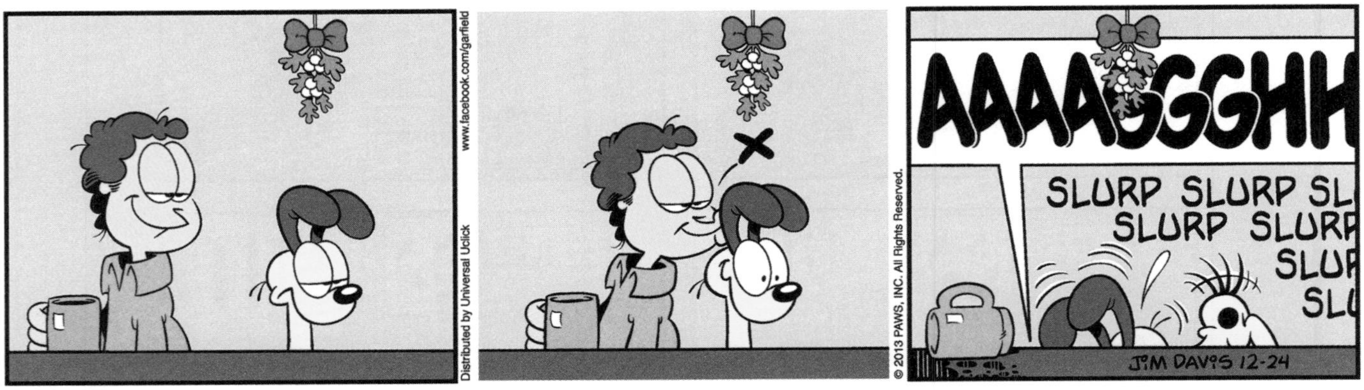
www.facebook.com/garfield
Distributed by Universal Uclick
© 2013 PAWS, INC. All Rights Reserved.
SLURP SLURP
SLURP
JIM DAVIS 12-24

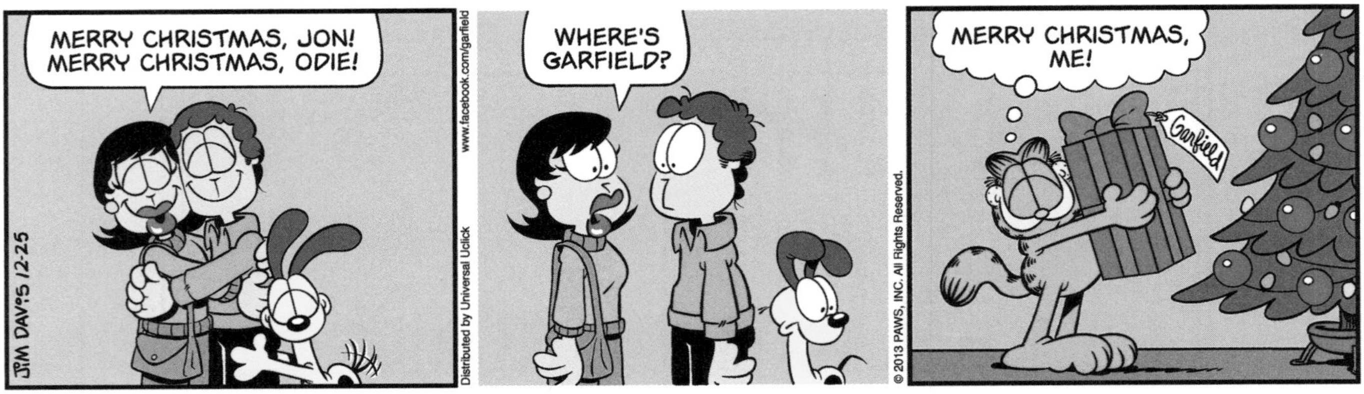
MERRY CHRISTMAS, JON! MERRY CHRISTMAS, ODIE!
JIM DAVIS 12-25
www.facebook.com/garfield
Distributed by Universal Uclick
WHERE'S GARFIELD?
© 2013 PAWS, INC. All Rights Reserved.
MERRY CHRISTMAS, ME!
Garfield

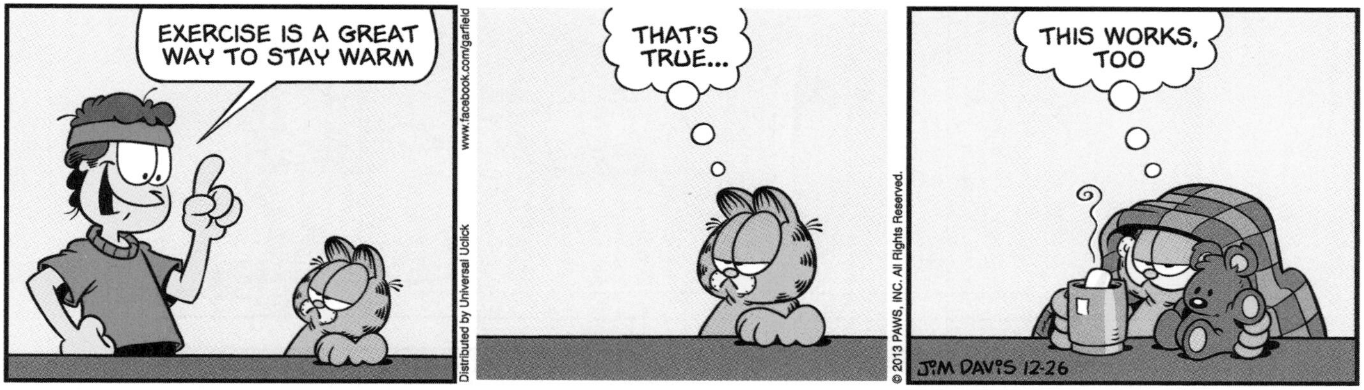
EXERCISE IS A GREAT WAY TO STAY WARM
THAT'S TRUE...
THIS WORKS, TOO
JIM DAVIS 12-26
Distributed by Universal Uclick www.facebook.com/garfield
© 2013 PAWS, INC. All Rights Reserved.

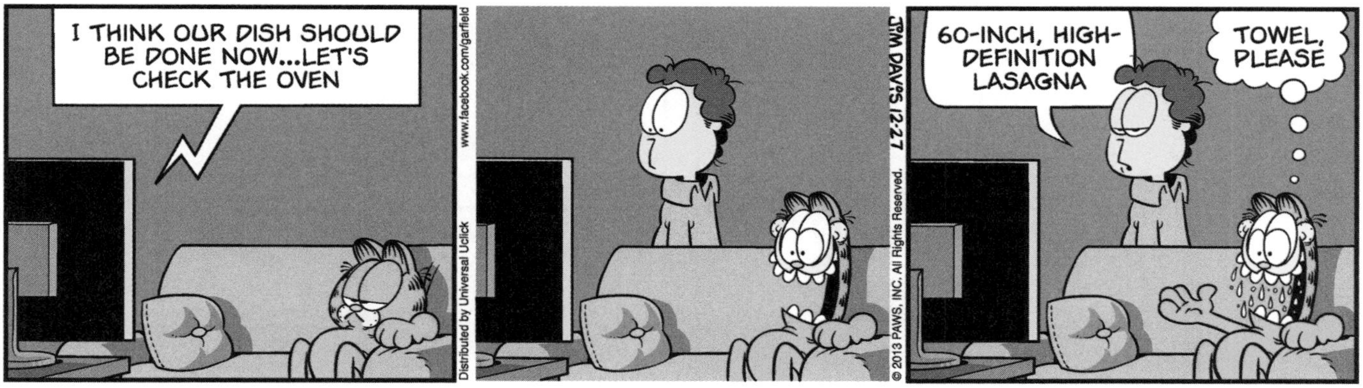
I THINK OUR DISH SHOULD BE DONE NOW...LET'S CHECK THE OVEN
JIM DAVIS 12-27
60-INCH, HIGH-DEFINITION LASAGNA
TOWEL, PLEASE
Distributed by Universal Uclick www.facebook.com/garfield
© 2013 PAWS, INC. All Rights Reserved.

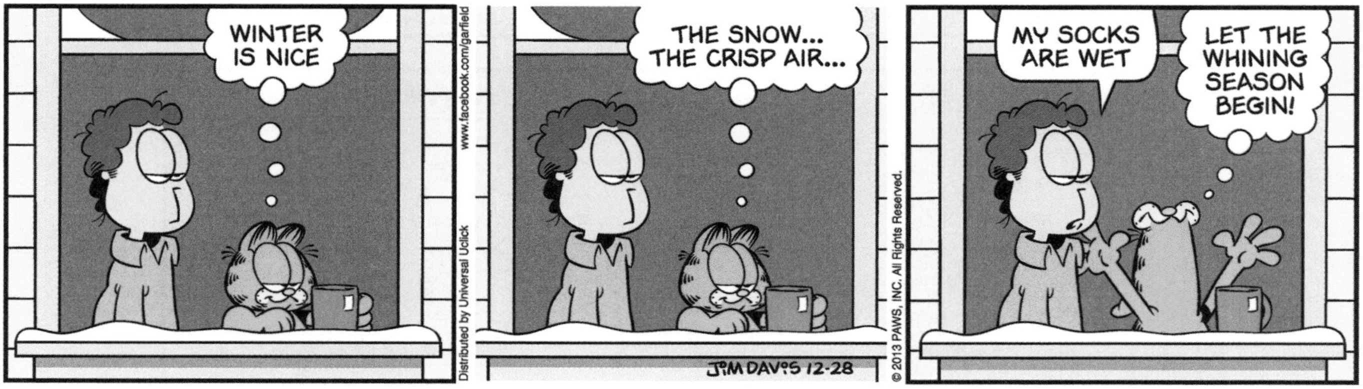
WINTER IS NICE
THE SNOW... THE CRISP AIR...
JIM DAVIS 12-28
MY SOCKS ARE WET
LET THE WHINING SEASON BEGIN!
Distributed by Universal Uclick www.facebook.com/garfield
© 2013 PAWS, INC. All Rights Reserved.

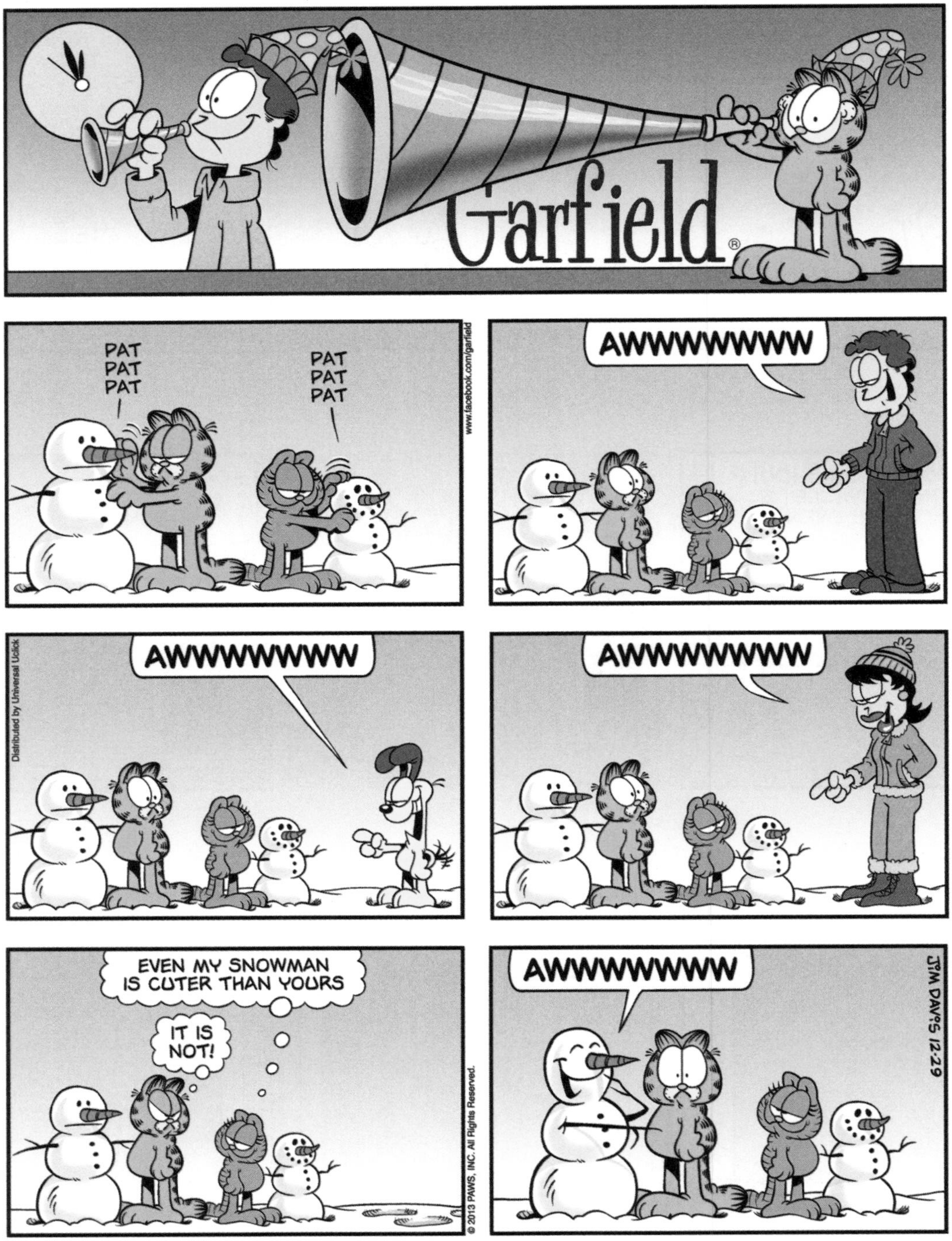

Garfield®
PAT PAT PAT
PAT PAT PAT
www.facebook.com/garfield
AWWWWWWWW
Distributed by Universal Uclick
AWWWWWWWW
AWWWWWWWW
EVEN MY SNOWMAN IS CUTER THAN YOURS
IT IS NOT!
© 2013 PAWS, INC. All Rights Reserved.
AWWWWWWWW
JIM DAVIS 12-29

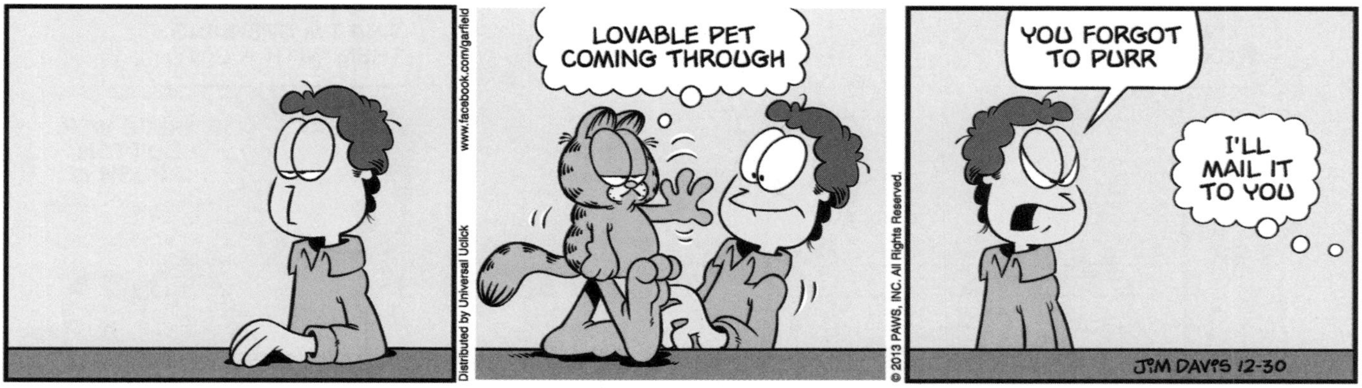
LOVABLE PET COMING THROUGH
YOU FORGOT TO PURR
I'LL MAIL IT TO YOU
JIM DAVIS 12-30
Distributed by Universal Uclick
www.facebook.com/garfield
© 2013 PAWS, INC. All Rights Reserved.

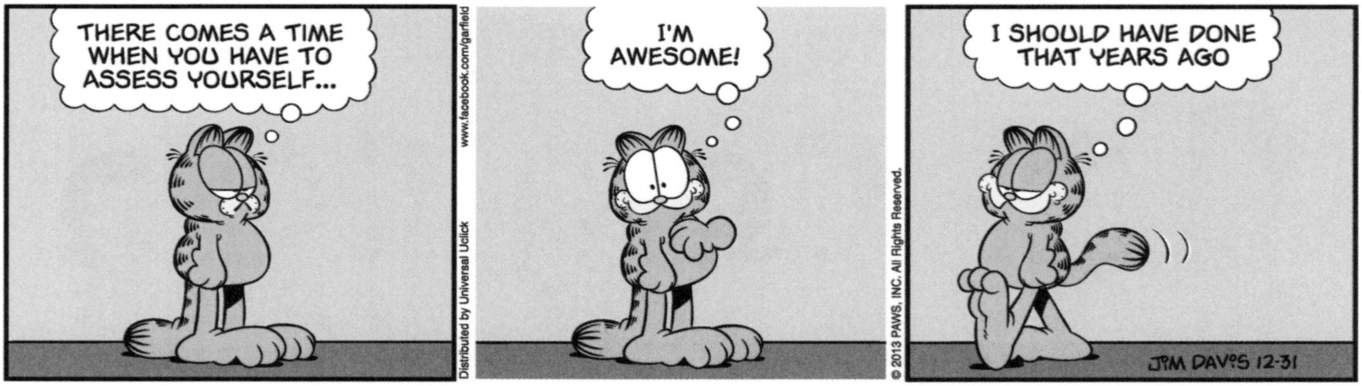
THERE COMES A TIME WHEN YOU HAVE TO ASSESS YOURSELF...
I'M AWESOME!
I SHOULD HAVE DONE THAT YEARS AGO
JIM DAVIS 12-31
Distributed by Universal Uclick
www.facebook.com/garfield
© 2013 PAWS, INC. All Rights Reserved.

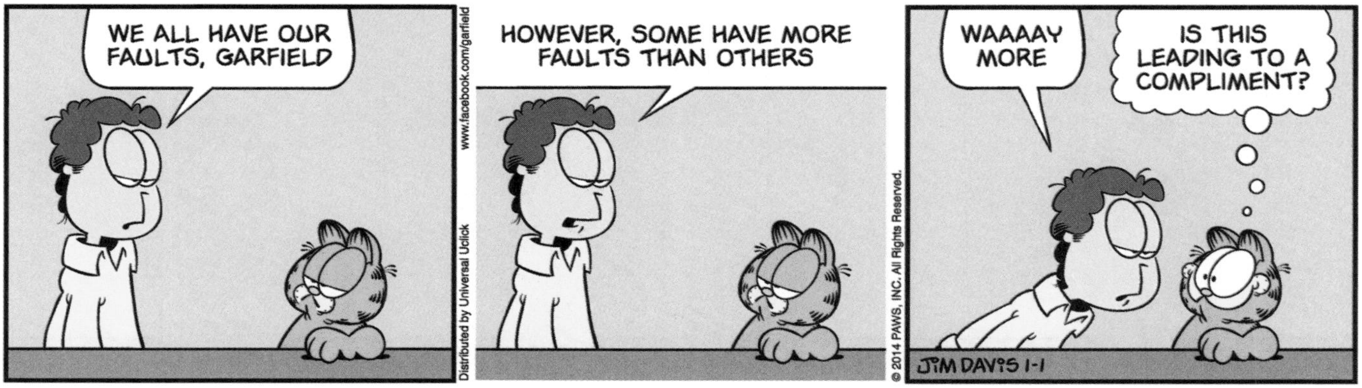
WE ALL HAVE OUR FAULTS, GARFIELD
HOWEVER, SOME HAVE MORE FAULTS THAN OTHERS
WAAAAY MORE
IS THIS LEADING TO A COMPLIMENT?
JIM DAVIS 1-1
Distributed by Universal Uclick
www.facebook.com/garfield
© 2014 PAWS, INC. All Rights Reserved.

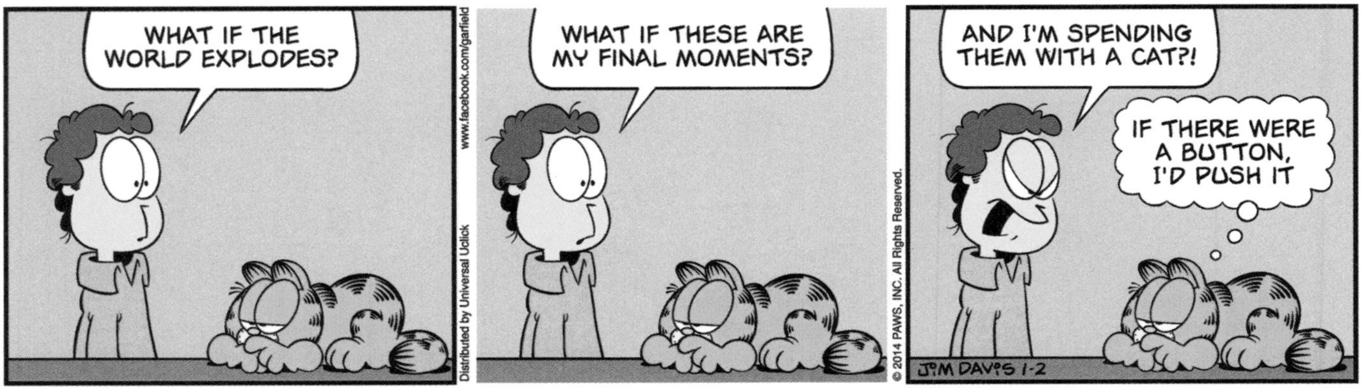
WHAT IF THE WORLD EXPLODES?
WHAT IF THESE ARE MY FINAL MOMENTS?
AND I'M SPENDING THEM WITH A CAT?!
IF THERE WERE A BUTTON, I'D PUSH IT
JIM DAVIS 1-2
www.facebook.com/garfield
Distributed by Universal Uclick
© 2014 PAWS, INC. All Rights Reserved.

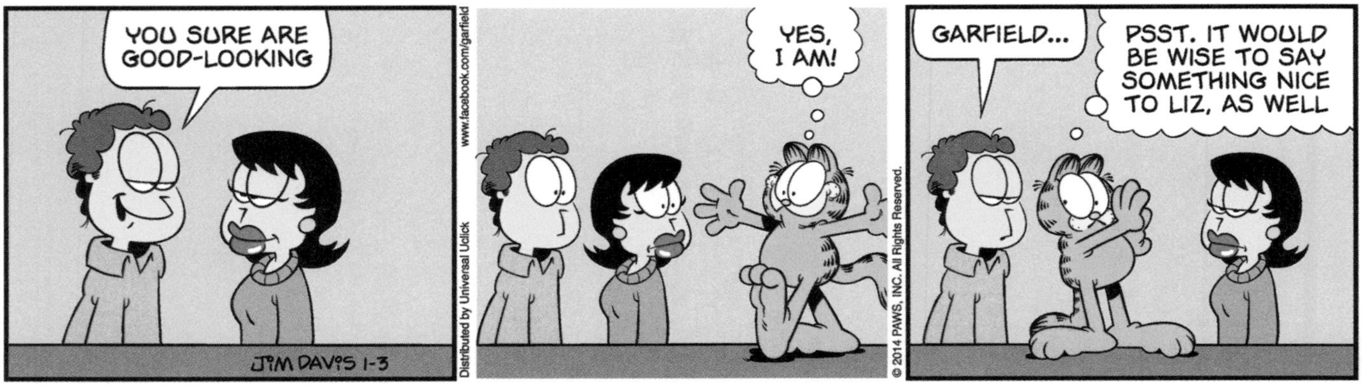
YOU SURE ARE GOOD-LOOKING
JIM DAVIS 1-3
YES, I AM!
GARFIELD...
PSST. IT WOULD BE WISE TO SAY SOMETHING NICE TO LIZ, AS WELL
www.facebook.com/garfield
Distributed by Universal Uclick
© 2014 PAWS, INC. All Rights Reserved.

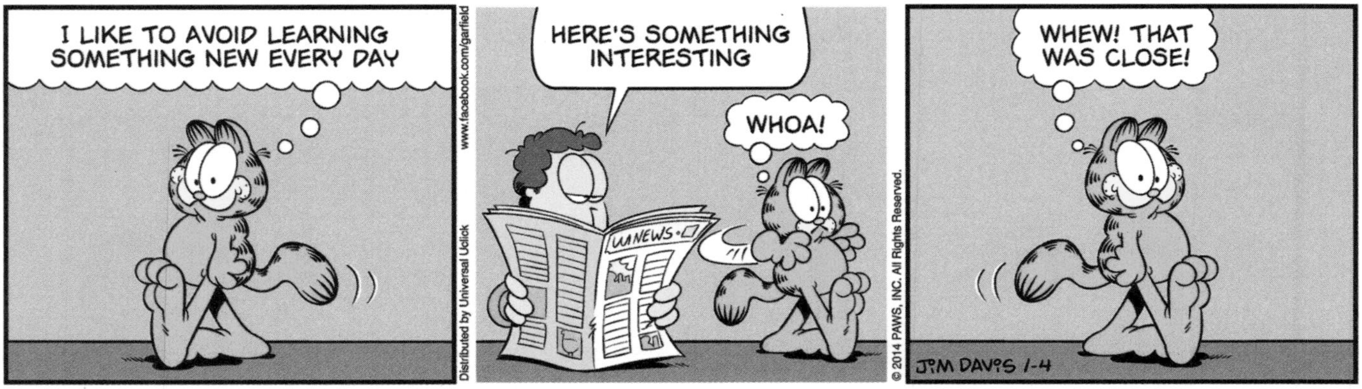
I LIKE TO AVOID LEARNING SOMETHING NEW EVERY DAY
HERE'S SOMETHING INTERESTING
NEWS
WHOA!
WHEW! THAT WAS CLOSE!
JIM DAVIS 1-4
www.facebook.com/garfield
Distributed by Universal Uclick
© 2014 PAWS, INC. All Rights Reserved.

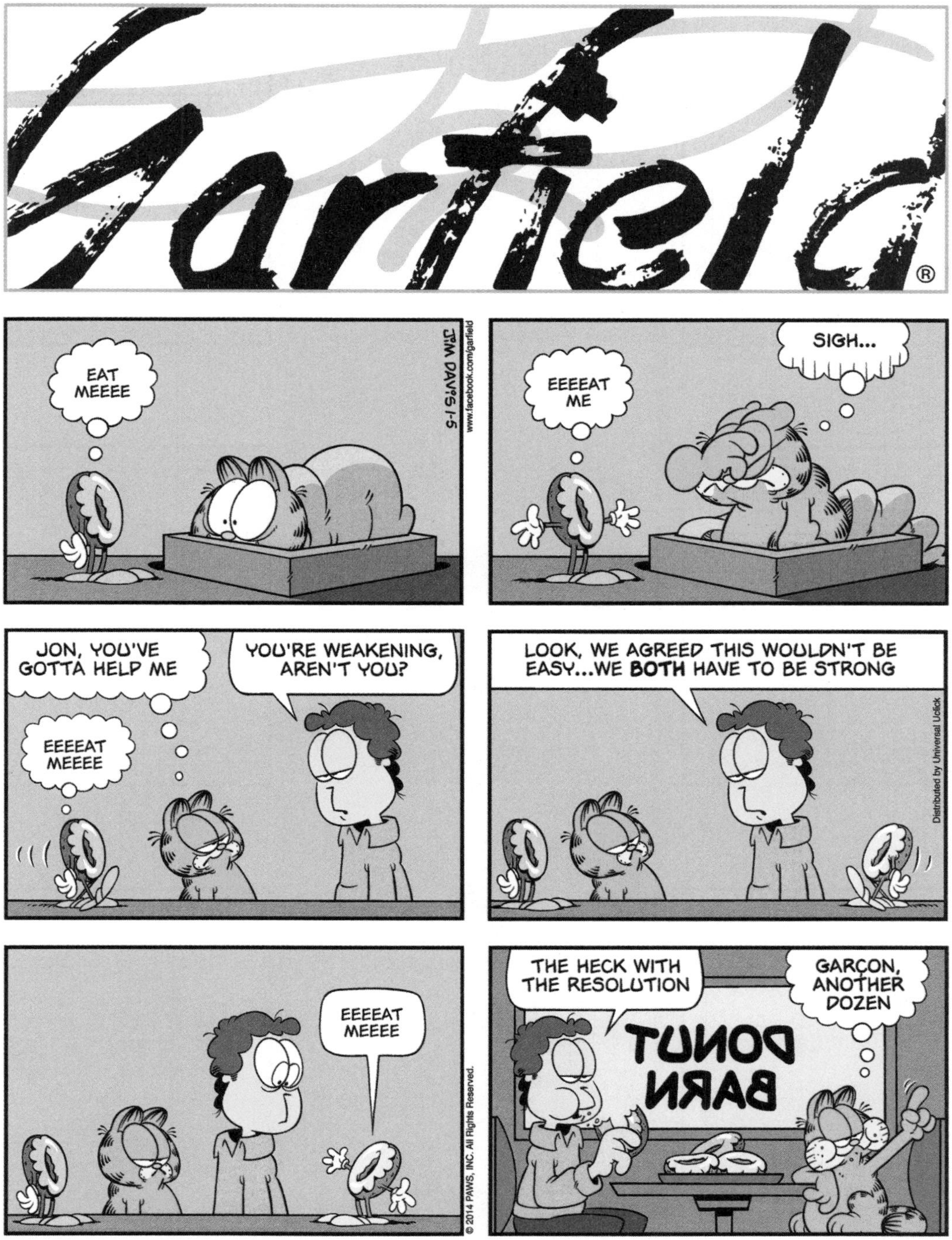
Garfield®
JIM DAVIS 1-5
www.facebook.com/garfield
EAT MEEEE
EEEEAT ME
SIGH...
JON, YOU'VE GOTTA HELP ME
YOU'RE WEAKENING, AREN'T YOU?
EEEEAT MEEEE
LOOK, WE AGREED THIS WOULDN'T BE EASY...WE **BOTH** HAVE TO BE STRONG
Distributed by Universal Uclick
EEEEAT MEEEE
© 2014 PAWS, INC. All Rights Reserved.
THE HECK WITH THE RESOLUTION
DONUT BARN
GARÇON, ANOTHER DOZEN

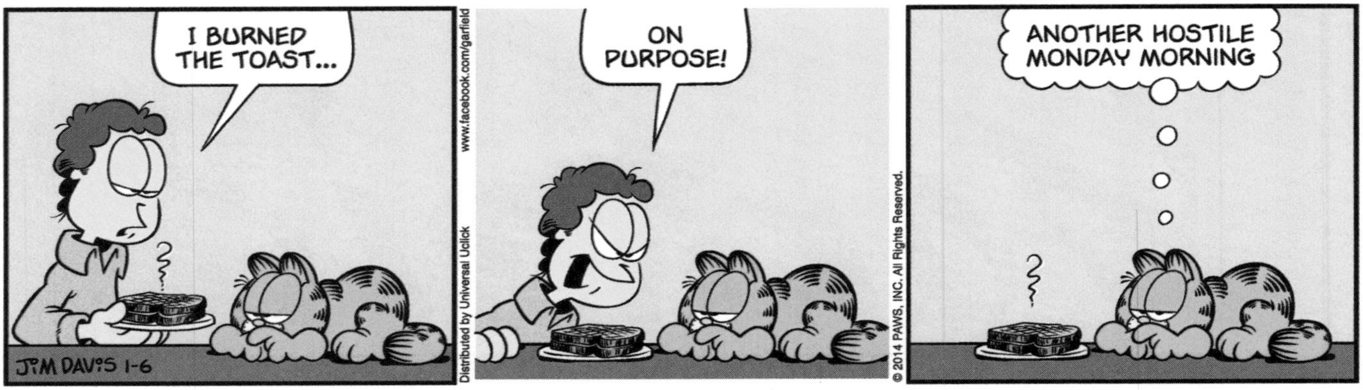
I BURNED THE TOAST...
JIM DAVIS 1-6
www.facebook.com/garfield
Distributed by Universal Uclick
ON PURPOSE!
© 2014 PAWS, INC. All Rights Reserved.
ANOTHER HOSTILE MONDAY MORNING

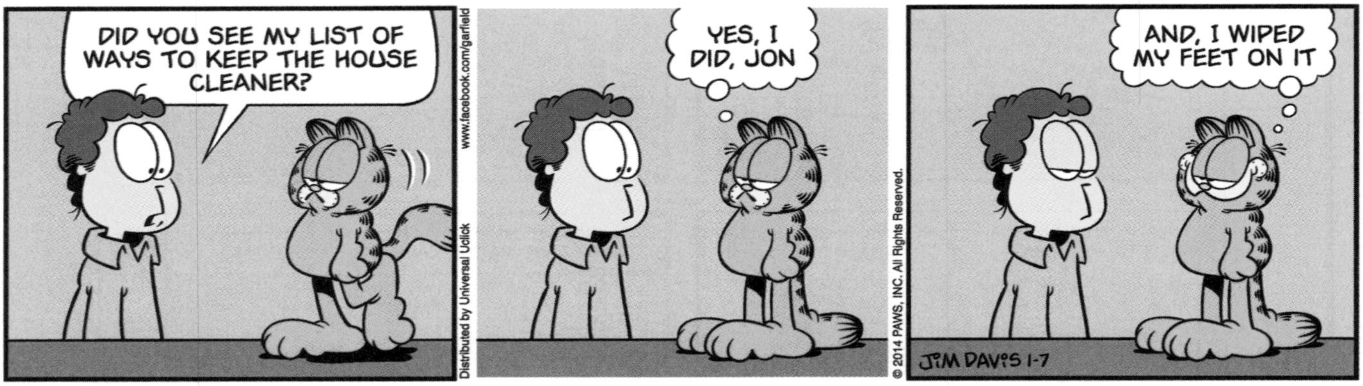
DID YOU SEE MY LIST OF WAYS TO KEEP THE HOUSE CLEANER?
www.facebook.com/garfield
Distributed by Universal Uclick
YES, I DID, JON
© 2014 PAWS, INC. All Rights Reserved.
AND, I WIPED MY FEET ON IT
JIM DAVIS 1-7

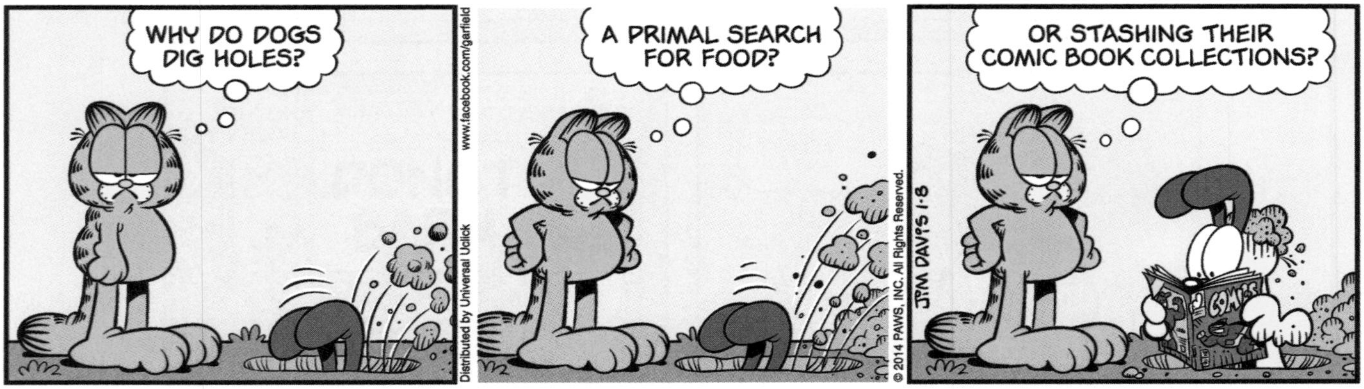
WHY DO DOGS DIG HOLES?
www.facebook.com/garfield
Distributed by Universal Uclick
A PRIMAL SEARCH FOR FOOD?
© 2014 PAWS, INC. All Rights Reserved.
JIM DAVIS 1-8
OR STASHING THEIR COMIC BOOK COLLECTIONS?
COMICS

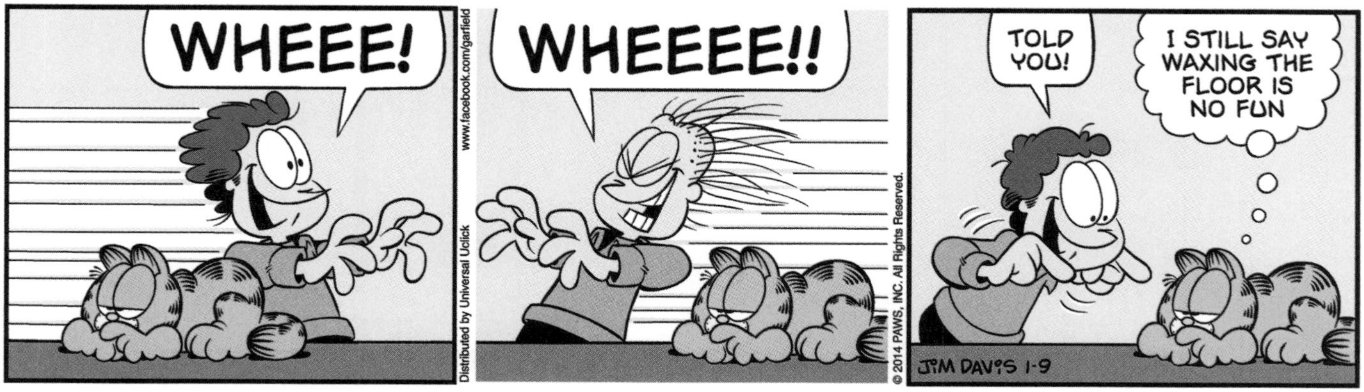
WHEEE!
www.facebook.com/garfield
Distributed by Universal Uclick
WHEEEE!!
© 2014 PAWS, INC. All Rights Reserved.
TOLD YOU!
I STILL SAY WAXING THE FLOOR IS NO FUN
JIM DAVIS 1-9

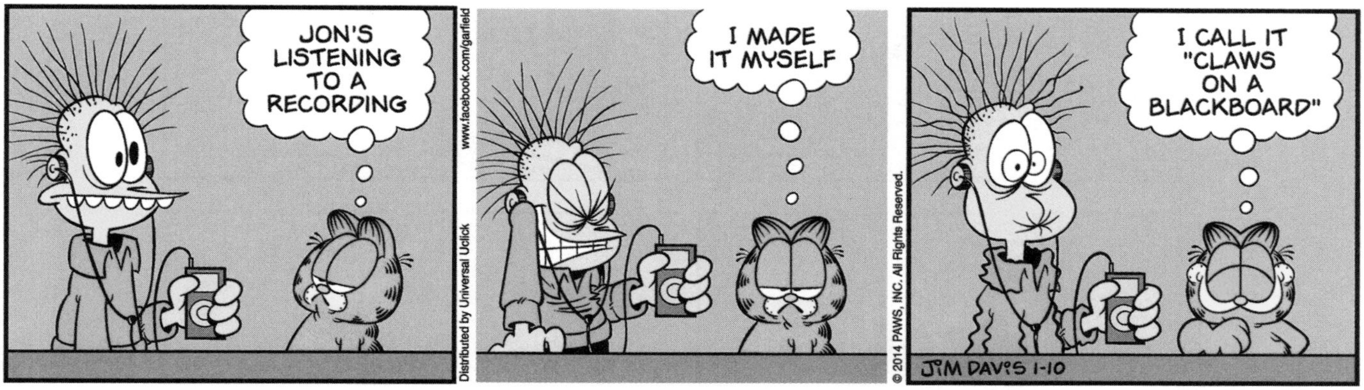
JON'S LISTENING TO A RECORDING
www.facebook.com/garfield
Distributed by Universal Uclick
I MADE IT MYSELF
© 2014 PAWS, INC. All Rights Reserved.
I CALL IT "CLAWS ON A BLACKBOARD"
JIM DAVIS 1-10

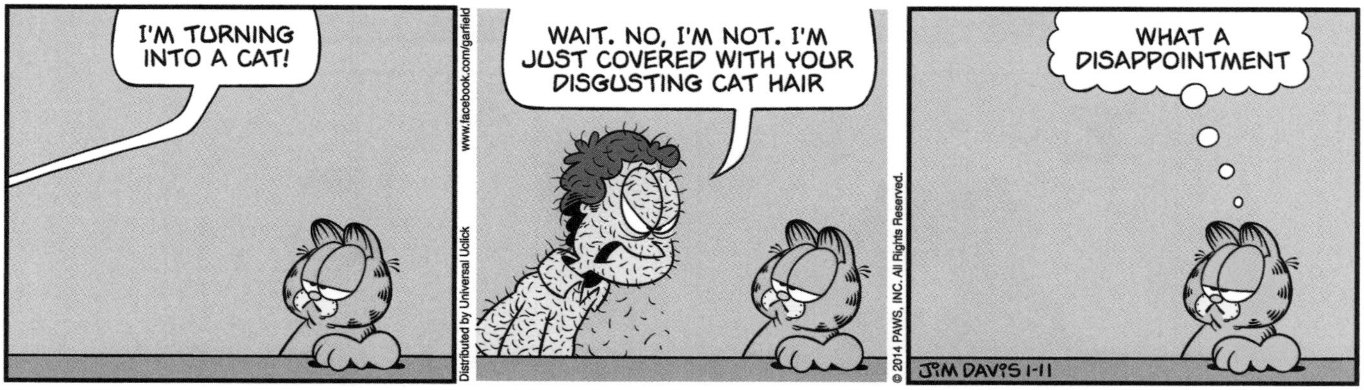
I'M TURNING INTO A CAT!
www.facebook.com/garfield
Distributed by Universal Uclick
WAIT. NO, I'M NOT. I'M JUST COVERED WITH YOUR DISGUSTING CAT HAIR
© 2014 PAWS, INC. All Rights Reserved.
WHAT A DISAPPOINTMENT
JIM DAVIS 1-11

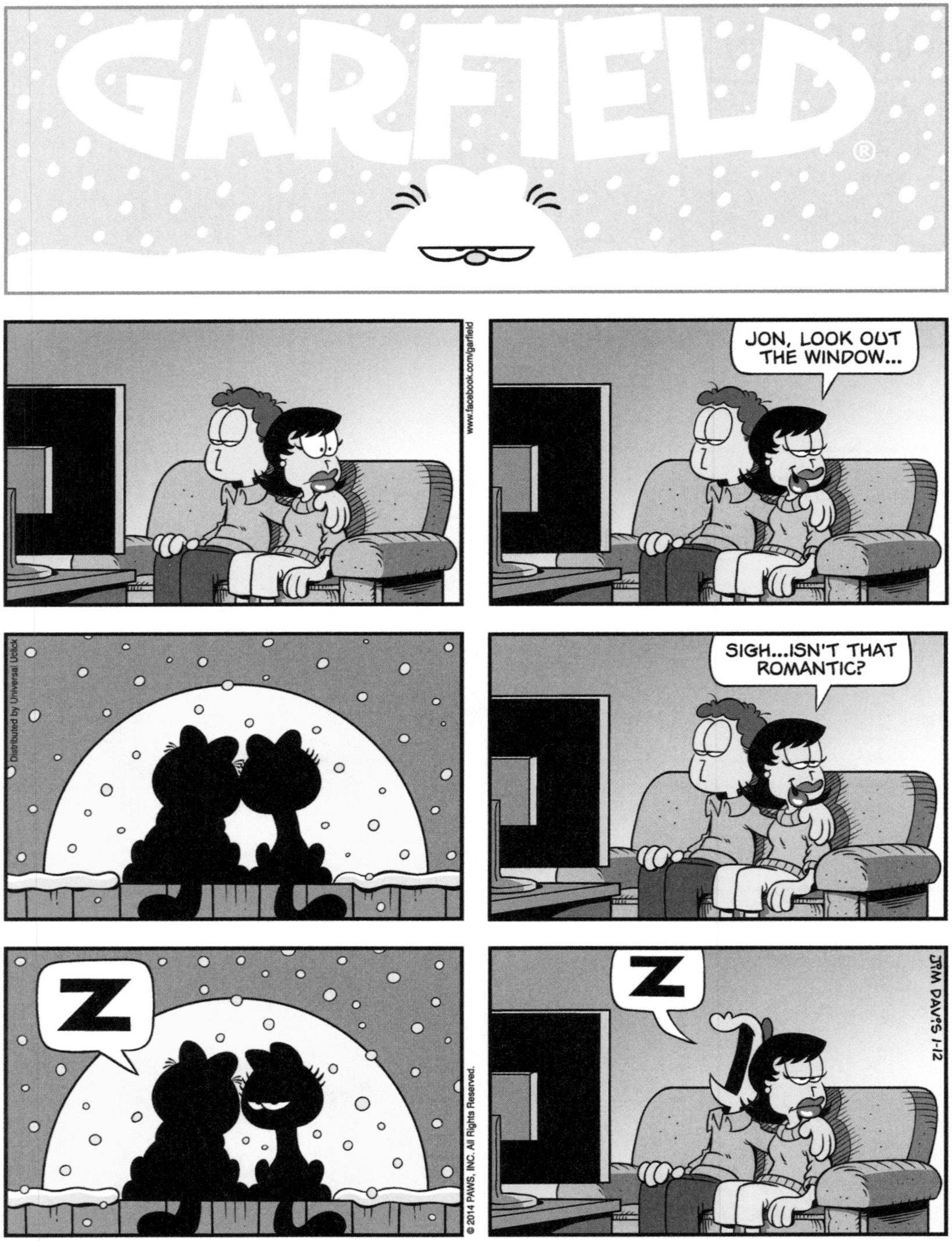
GARFIELD®
www.facebook.com/garfield
JON, LOOK OUT THE WINDOW...
Distributed by Universal Uclick
SIGH...ISN'T THAT ROMANTIC?
Z
© 2014 PAWS, INC. All Rights Reserved.
JIM DAVIS 1-12
Z

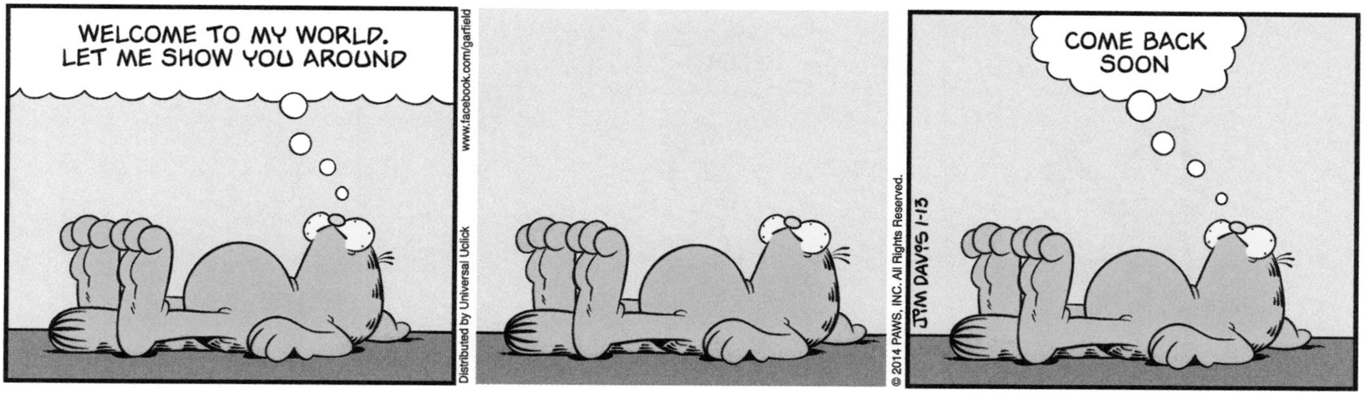
WELCOME TO MY WORLD. LET ME SHOW YOU AROUND
www.facebook.com/garfield
Distributed by Universal Uclick
© 2014 PAWS, INC. All Rights Reserved.
JIM DAVIS 1-13
COME BACK SOON

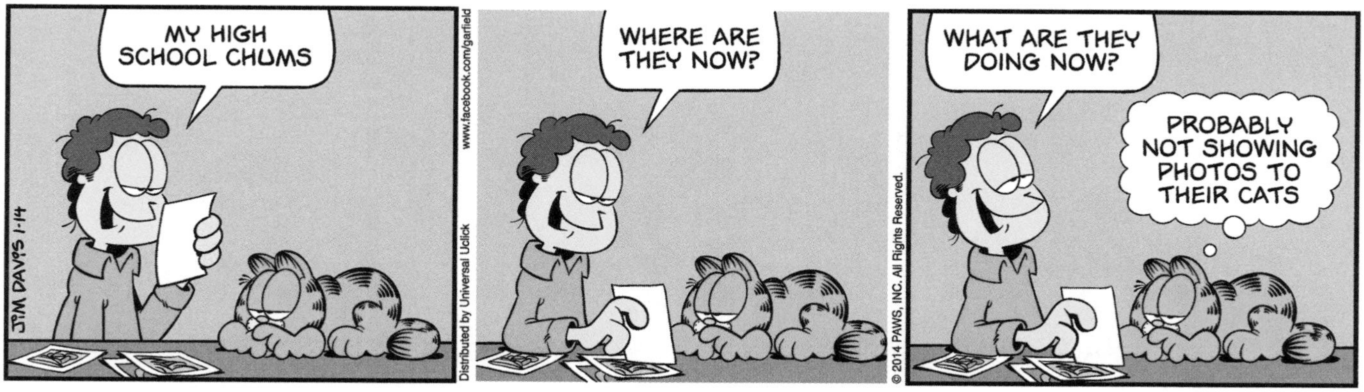
MY HIGH SCHOOL CHUMS
JIM DAVIS 1-14
www.facebook.com/garfield
Distributed by Universal Uclick
WHERE ARE THEY NOW?
© 2014 PAWS, INC. All Rights Reserved.
WHAT ARE THEY DOING NOW?
PROBABLY NOT SHOWING PHOTOS TO THEIR CATS

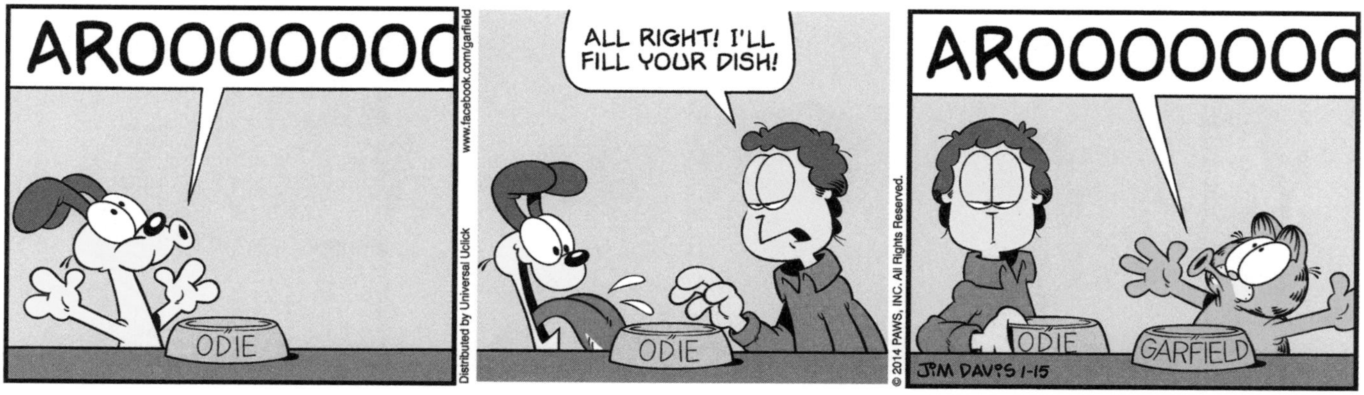
AROOOOOOO
ODIE
www.facebook.com/garfield
Distributed by Universal Uclick
ALL RIGHT! I'LL FILL YOUR DISH!
ODIE
© 2014 PAWS, INC. All Rights Reserved.
AROOOOOOO
ODIE
GARFIELD
JIM DAVIS 1-15

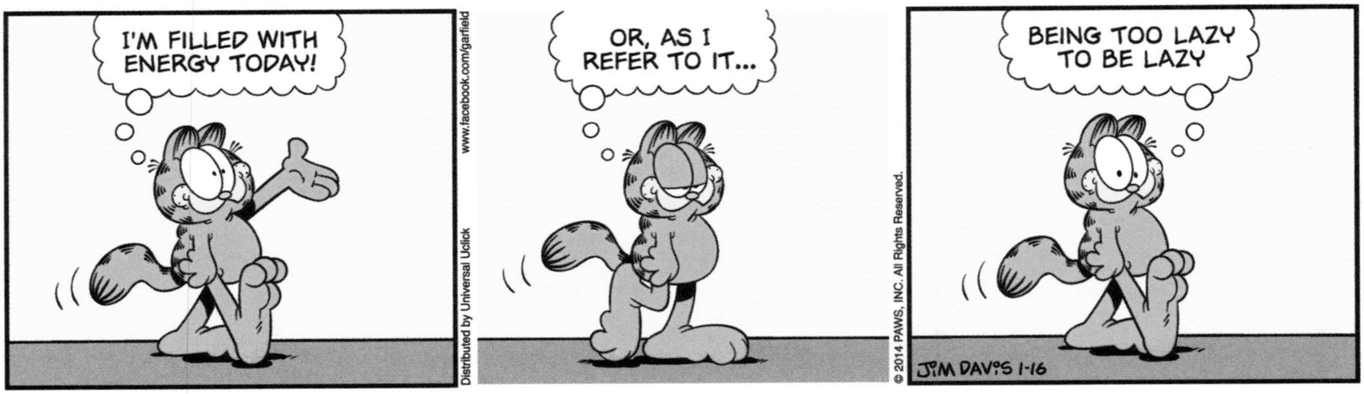
I'M FILLED WITH ENERGY TODAY!
OR, AS I REFER TO IT...
BEING TOO LAZY TO BE LAZY
Distributed by Universal Uclick
www.facebook.com/garfield
© 2014 PAWS, INC. All Rights Reserved.
JIM DAVIS 1-16

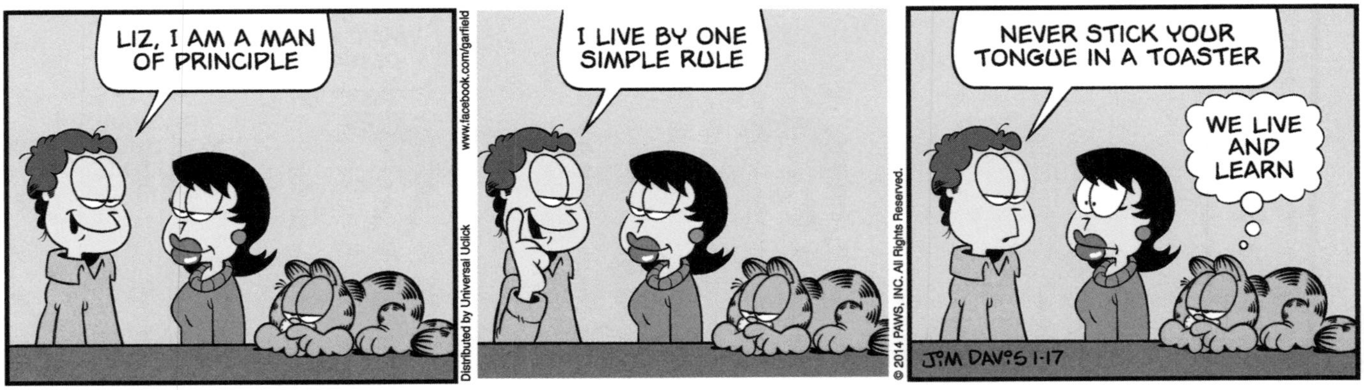
LIZ, I AM A MAN OF PRINCIPLE
I LIVE BY ONE SIMPLE RULE
NEVER STICK YOUR TONGUE IN A TOASTER
WE LIVE AND LEARN
Distributed by Universal Uclick
www.facebook.com/garfield
© 2014 PAWS, INC. All Rights Reserved.
JIM DAVIS 1-17

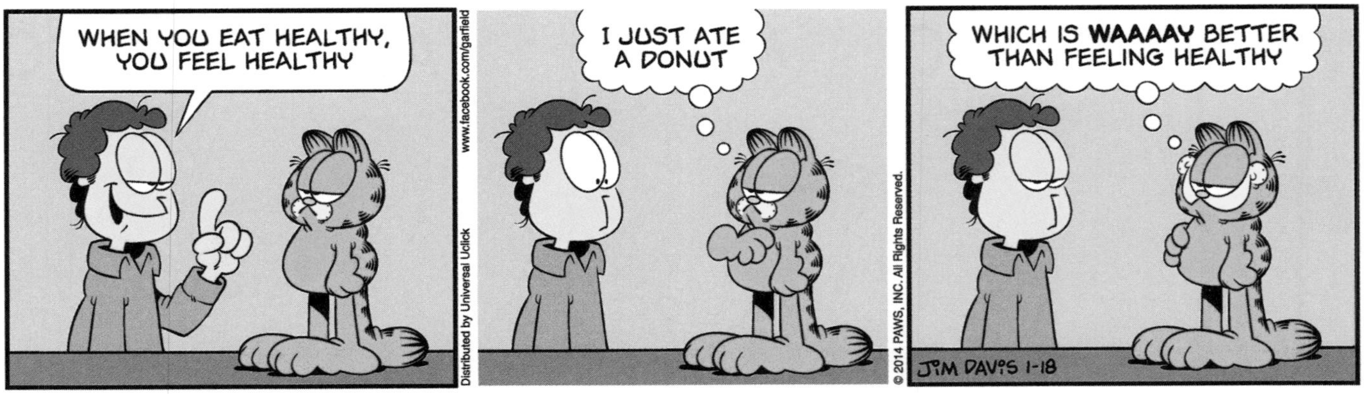
WHEN YOU EAT HEALTHY, YOU FEEL HEALTHY
I JUST ATE A DONUT
WHICH IS **WAAAAY** BETTER THAN FEELING HEALTHY
Distributed by Universal Uclick
www.facebook.com/garfield
© 2014 PAWS, INC. All Rights Reserved.
JIM DAVIS 1-18

HERE'S A CRAZY THEORY, GARFIELD
"CATS MAY BE INVADERS FROM ANOTHER PLANET"
I DON'T THINK SO
YOU'RE TOO LAZY TO MAKE THE TRIP
AND YOU'D NEVER ESCAPE GRAVITY
CERTAINLY NOT FROM THE PLANET FATSO
WHERE IS MY DISINTEGRATOR RAY GUN WHEN I NEED IT?
www.facebook.com/garfield
Distributed by Universal Uclick
© 2014 PAWS, INC. All Rights Reserved.
JIM DAVIS 1-19

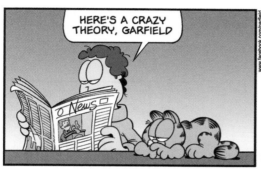

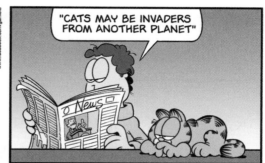

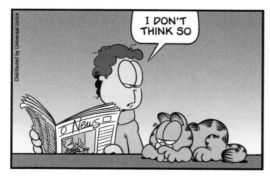

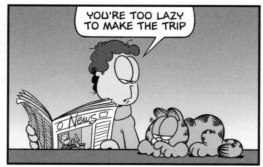

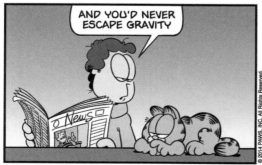

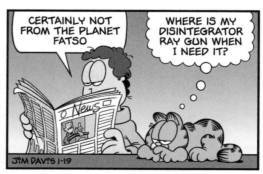

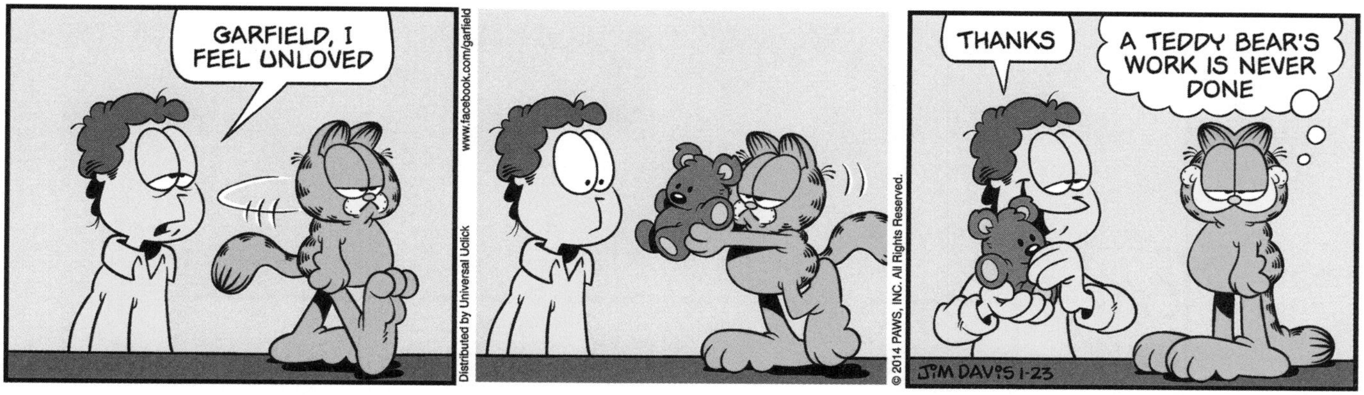
GARFIELD, I FEEL UNLOVED
Distributed by Universal Uclick www.facebook.com/garfield
THANKS
A TEDDY BEAR'S WORK IS NEVER DONE
© 2014 PAWS, INC. All Rights Reserved.
JIM DAVIS 1-23

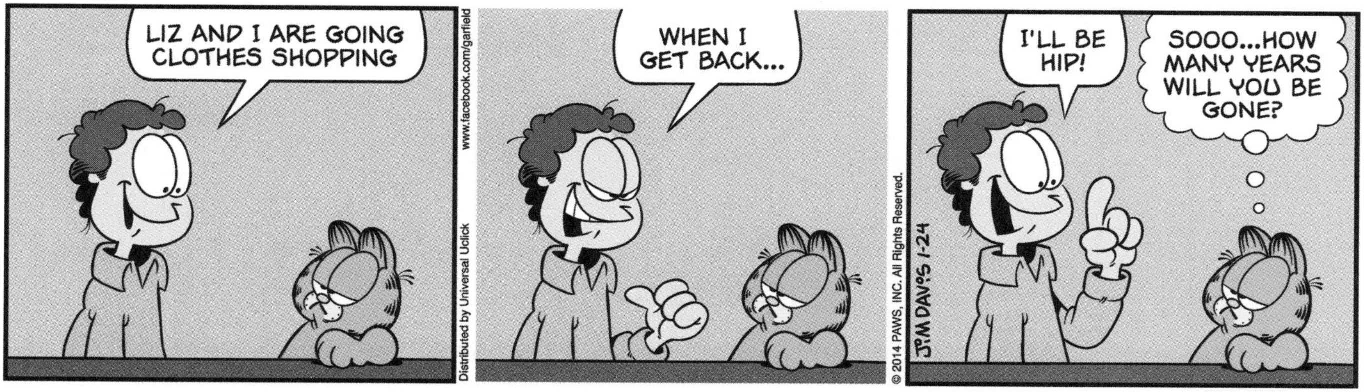
LIZ AND I ARE GOING CLOTHES SHOPPING
Distributed by Universal Uclick www.facebook.com/garfield
WHEN I GET BACK...
© 2014 PAWS, INC. All Rights Reserved.
JIM DAVIS 1-24
I'LL BE HIP!
SOOO...HOW MANY YEARS WILL YOU BE GONE?

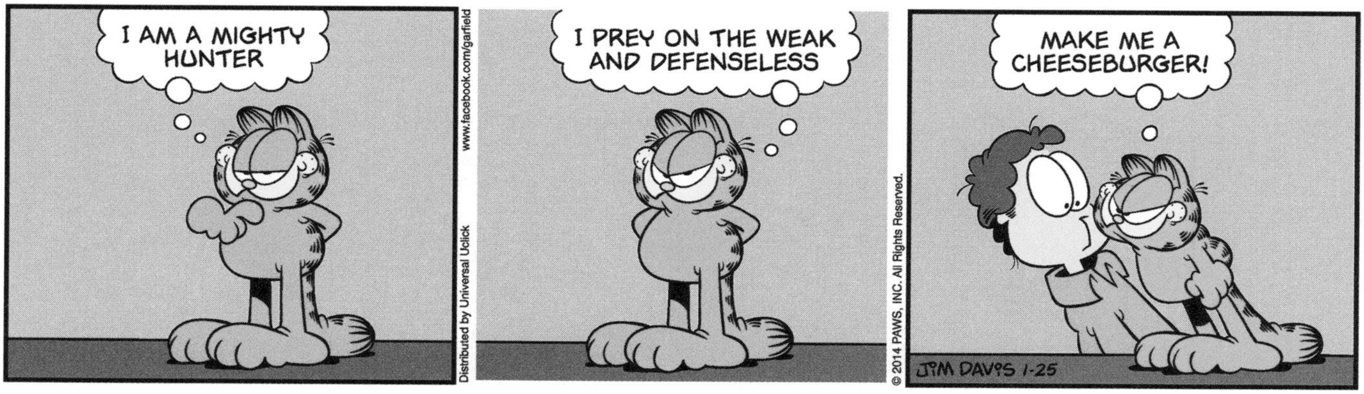
I AM A MIGHTY HUNTER
Distributed by Universal Uclick www.facebook.com/garfield
I PREY ON THE WEAK AND DEFENSELESS
© 2014 PAWS, INC. All Rights Reserved.
MAKE ME A CHEESEBURGER!
JIM DAVIS 1-25

More TRUTH about cats

Cats love milk...

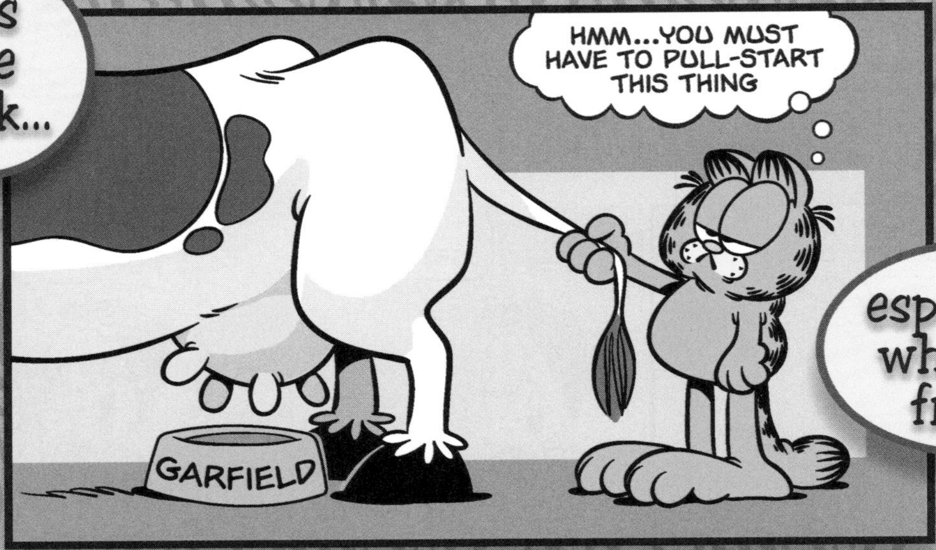
HMM...YOU MUST HAVE TO PULL-START THIS THING
GARFIELD

especially when it's fresh.

Curiosity doesn't always kill the cat...

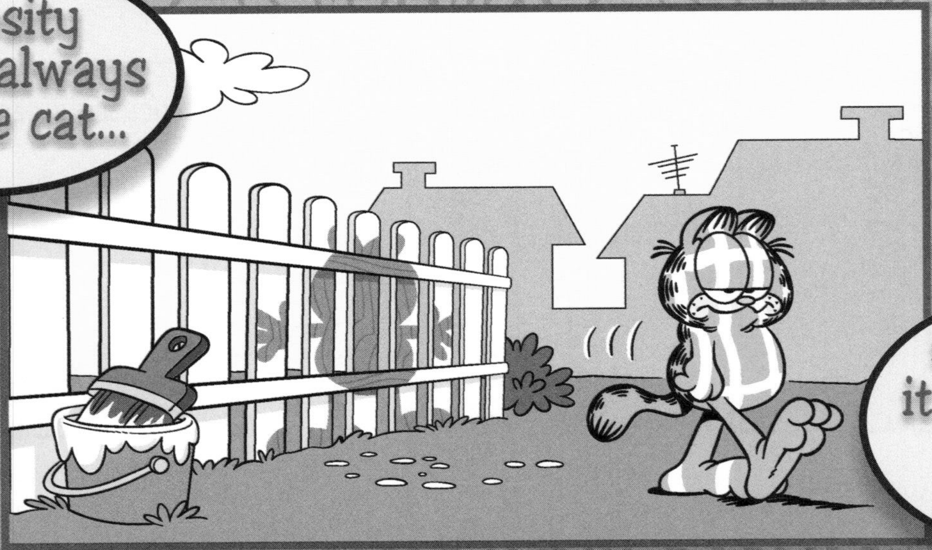

sometimes it just makes him look stupid.

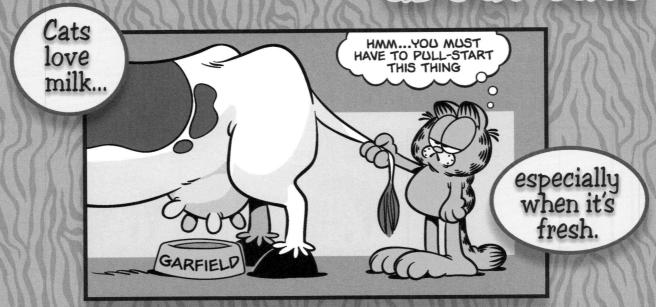

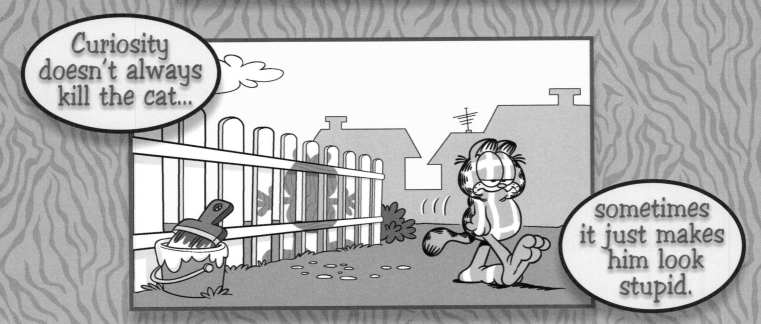

Watch. Read. Shop. Play.

DON'T FORGET THE SNACKS!

garfield.com

* ### *The Garfield Show*
  Catch Garfield and the rest of the gang on *The Garfield Show*, now airing on Cartoon Network and Boomerang!

* ### The Comic Strip
  Search & read thousands of GARFIELD® comic strips!

* ### Garfield on Facebook & Twitter
  Join millions of Garfield friends on Facebook. Get your daily dose of humor and connect with other fat cat fans!

* ### Shop all the Garfield stores!
  Original art & comic strips, books, apparel, personalized products, & more!

* ### Play FREE online Garfield games!
  Plus, check out all of the FREE Garfield apps available for your smartphone, tablet, and other mobile devices.

STRIPS, SPECIALS, OR BESTSELLING BOOKS . . .

GARFIELD'S ON EVERYONE'S MENU.

Don't miss even one episode in the Tubby Tabby's hilarious series!

New larger, full-color format!